Adobe Premiere Pro 2025 Handbook

The Comprehensive Guide to Practical Video Editing From Beginners to Experts

Tim Elvis

OVERVIEW

The goal of this Adobe Premiere Pro tutorial is to easily and clearly walk you through the basics of video editing. This video will assist you in navigating Premiere Pro's tools, capabilities, and workflow, regardless of your level of experience as an editor or a novice learning the ropes. I'll start by going over the program's structure, timeline, and media import procedure. To create a polished final video, you'll learn how to arrange and edit clips on the timeline, add smooth transitions, and make precise adjustments. We'll also look at color correction and grading, offering helpful advice on how to make your film look better, from subtle adjustments to well-chosen color effects. Additionally, this book will show you how to edit audio so that you may add effects and produce well-balanced sounds to your project. With advice and shortcuts for a quicker workflow, each part is made to help you comprehend the tools in an easy-to-understand manner. After reading this tutorial, you'll know how to use Adobe Premiere Pro to realize your artistic vision, whether you're making short films for social media or high-end projects. Jump right in and let's begin honing your Premiere Pro editing skills.

CHAPTER ONE
ADOBE PREMIERE PRO: GETTING STARTED

INTRODUCTION

The advanced video editing application Adobe Premiere Pro is widely used to produce material for a range of venues, such as professional filmmaking and social media. It comes with a full suite of tools for creatively and precisely turning unprocessed video into finished films. The timeline-based interface of Premiere Pro makes it simple to drag, drop, and organize clips to create your project. With this format, you may seamlessly blend media components and create intricate sequences by layering many audio and video files. With the software's precise editing features, you may chop segments, adjust speed, and apply transitions to make your video flow naturally. Color correction and grading are crucial components of Premiere Pro, which offers tools for adjusting brightness, contrast, and color balance to enhance the visual appeal of your film. By making minor or major adjustments to your project to fit your preferred style, you may give it a polished look with tools like the Lumetri Color panel. You can now effortlessly adjust sound quality, mix audio levels, and add effects for a clear, well-balanced audio experience using Adobe Premiere Pro's audio editing features. Adding animations, effects, and a polished, professional look to your work is made simple with Premiere Pro's plug-ins and integrations with other Adobe programs, including After Effects, Photoshop, and Audition. All things considered, Premiere Pro's adaptability, advanced features, and ease of integration make it a desirable choice for anyone looking to produce high-caliber video.

Adobe Premiere Pro 2025: An Overview

Numerous changes in Adobe Premiere Pro 2025 enhance editing effectiveness and user experience. Important updates consist of:

Premiere Pro's Properties panel

Premiere Pro is now easier for new users to learn and more efficient for seasoned professionals thanks to the new context-aware Properties panel, which automatically displays the most frequently used tools when you need them. A single panel now contains context-sensitive controls for text, graphics, audio, and video adjustments, along with Quick Actions and one-click access to more tool when required. Additionally, Premiere Pro allows you to change the properties of numerous clips at once for the first time.

 To enhance and create a unique design, pick the text, shape, or music and use the options on the Properties tab.

Modern, updated design

Premiere Pro looks brand-new, streamlined, and dependable. You may change the look and feel with two dark settings, a bright mode, and a high contrast accessible mode. By alternating between these modes, you may select the one that best fits your environment and tastes, whether you're looking for improved visibility or readability based on the lighting conditions at the moment. Cleaner fonts and typography are now available to you, making all Adobe Creative Cloud products easier to read and consistent. Instead of having to retrain how to use features in our numerous programs, you will have more time to create.

Dialog box for creating a new project

By offering choices for name, storage, template, project parameters, and a skip import mode, Premiere Pro's New Project Creation window streamlines the process of creating new projects.

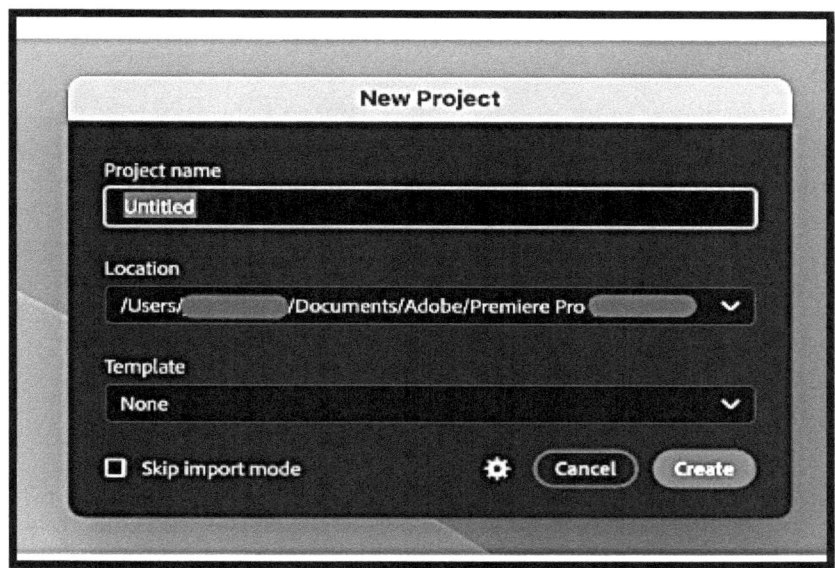

Increased support for Canon

Utilize Canon EOS C80 camera files directly. Open files and begin editing right away. Transcoding is not required.

System Installation and Requirements

In order for Adobe Premiere Pro 2025 to run at its best, your system must meet or surpass the following requirements:

Regarding Windows

- **Operating System:** Windows 11 or Windows 10 (64-bit) version 22H2 or later.
- **Processor:** AMD Ryzen™ 3000 Series/Threadripper 3000 Series or AMD 11th Gen or newer CPU with Quick Sync.
- Memory (RAM): 32 GB or more for 4K and higher resolutions; 16 GB for HD media.
- Graphics Card (GPU): For HD and 4K video, the GPU must have at least 4 GB of VRAM; for 4K and greater resolutions, it must have 6 GB or more.

4

- Storage: Fast internal SSD for caching and installing apps; extra fast SSDs for media.
- DisplayHDR 1000 for HDR workflows; 1920 x 1080 resolution or above.
- Sound Card: Microsoft Windows Driver Model or ASIO compliant.
- Network: 10 gigabit Ethernet is used for 4K shared network workflows, whereas 1 gigabit Ethernet is used for HD workflows.

Regarding macOS

- **System of operation:** macOS Monterey (version 12) or above.
- **Processor:** Apple's M1 Pro, M1 Max, M1 Ultra, or a more recent model.
- 16 GB of unified memory is the amount of memory (RAM).
- **Graphics:** unified memory of 16 GB.
- **Storage:** Fast internal SSD for caching and installing apps; extra fast SSDs for media.
- **Display:** HDR 1000 for HDR processes; resolution of 1920 x 1080 or higher.
- **Network:** 10 gigabit Ethernet is used for 4K shared network workflows, whereas 1 gigabit Ethernet is used for HD workflows.

Visit Adobe's official system requirements page for further details.

Steps for Installation

- Adobe Creative Cloud Account Verify that you are currently a member of Adobe Creative Cloud.
- **Get the Creative Cloud Desktop App:** Go to the official Adobe Creative Cloud website to get the desktop application.
- **Install the Creative Cloud Desktop App:** To complete the installation, launch the installer and adhere to the on-screen directions.
- **Sign In:** Enter your Adobe ID to log in to the Creative Cloud desktop application.
- **Get Premiere Pro installed:**
  - ➤ In the Creative Cloud app, choose the Apps tab.
  - ➤ After choosing Premiere Pro, click Install.
  - ➤ The application will install and download on its own.
- **Launch Premiere Pro:** To install Premiere Pro, select Open in the Creative Cloud application or locate it in the applications folder on your computer.

Improving the performance

Try these tactics to enhance Adobe Premiere Pro's functionality:
- **Make GPU acceleration available**
  - ➤ Rendering and playback can be significantly enhanced by using your system's GPU.
  - ➤ Select General under File > Project Settings.

➢ Choose Mercury Playback Engine GPU Acceleration from the Video Rendering and Playback menu.

♣ Modify the Resolution of Playback
➢ Real-time editing responsiveness can be improved by lowering the playback resolution.
➢ Adjust the playback resolution to 1/2 or 1/4 in the Program Monitor.

♣ Empty the Media Cache
➢ Performance can be slowed by accumulated cache files.
➢ Select Edit > Preferences > Media Cache from the menu.
➢ Click Delete to remove unnecessary media cache files.

♣ Make Memory Allocation Better
➢ Slowdowns can be lessened by giving Premiere Pro ample RAM.
➢ Select Edit > Memory under Preferences.
➢ Modify the RAM allotted for other apps to make sure Premiere Pro has the right amount of memory.

♣ Employ Workflow Proxy
➢ Performance can be enhanced by editing with lower-resolution proxies, especially when using high-resolution video.
➢ Right-click your media in the Project window, then choose Proxy > Create Proxies. Observe the instructions.

♣ Produce Intricate Effects
➢ Adding intricate effects to rendered parts might enhance playback.
➢ Establish the required sections in and out points.
➢ To see the specified area, press Enter.

♣ Turn Off Superfluous Clips and Effects
➢ You may conserve system resources by turning off unnecessary clips and effects.
➢ You can right-click on a clip and choose "Disable" to temporarily deactivate it.By putting these strategies into practice, editing in Adobe Premiere Pro can become more fluid and effective.

CHAPTER TWO
THE BASICS OF PREMIERE PRO
Concerning the User Interface of Premiere Pro

Since there are so many options available, the Premiere Pro UI initially seems overwhelming, making it hard to concentrate on anything in particular. Yes, there are many resources available; all you need to do is concentrate on the most crucial subjects. There are nine menu headers at the top of the screen, so start there.

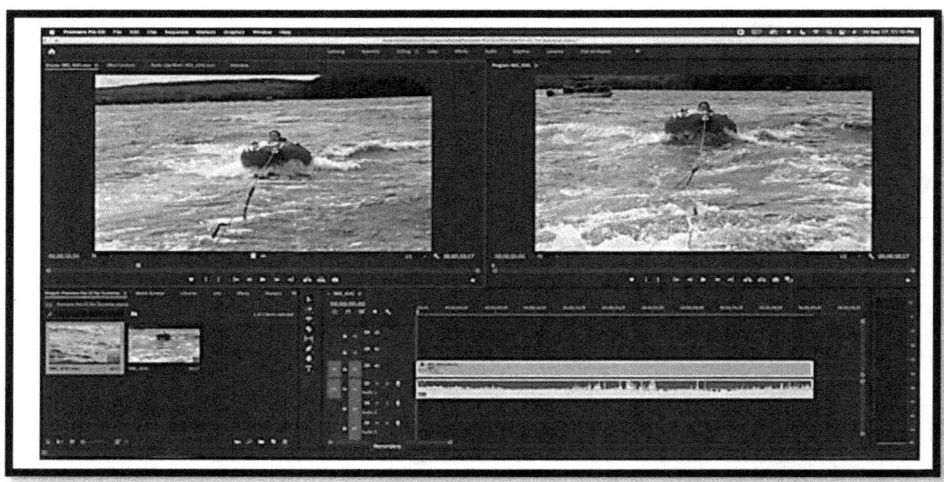

The workplace is rather sensible, despite its apparent complexity. You simply need to think of it as a group of discrete elements that, when combined, become a single entity. The timeline (located lower right in the picture) shows a modified clip, while the Project panel (located lower left in the picture) shows the ingested movie files. While the Program Monitor panel is in charge of playing the clips on the timeline from top to bottom, the Source Monitor panel shows the content of the clips.

About Editing and Ingesting

The process of importing your video clip from the camera or card device into Premiere Pro is known as "ingesting." The process of organizing the consumed content into a coherent whole is called editing. When the workplace is separated into several areas, called panels, each of which has a distinct function, staring at the screen becomes far less frightening. Although each panel serves a distinct purpose, they are all connected and cooperate. For instance, you can save your sequences and assets in the Projects section. After that, you can view them in the Program Monitor window and drag them onto the timeline. Then, by selecting an option in the Effects panel and adjusting it in the Effect Controls panel, you may decide whether or not to color-correct the video.

Comprehending the Panels

Premiere Pro's panels are not just visually appealing but also practical and simple to use once you get the hang of it. Clicking on one panel will allow you to interact with another panel. This allows you to choose a clip in the Projects panel, configure its In and Out points, and then drag it into the timeline without any problems. Now that you're there, you can click on the clip, turn on the Audio Meters, and make adjustments to the sound. Despite being regarded as separate entities, each panel collaborates to produce your video. It is not necessary to comprehend every panel in order to generate exceptional work. Studying the operation of a few panels will get you started quickly, but the more you learn, the more you may achieve. But it's easy to get started. To indicate that a zone is active, a blue barrier appears when you click inside a certain panel. When you click inside the panel, this happens. This gives you the ability to perform any task the panel gives you. For instance, you can move clips, alter their length, or remove them when you select the Timeline panel.

Navigating the Work Area

You may alter the location of several elements in the Premiere Pro interface, unlike many other programs (like Office 365). Think about the workspace and how it is set up, as well as the interface you see on the screen. Although the saying "timeline on the bottom monitors on top" is becoming more and more popular, the opposite is equally true. A deep timeline allows users to monitor multiple audio and video channels simultaneously, and some users tuck the history to enhance their view of the Project panel. Others choose to keep it small in order to make the most of their available display space. The most important factor is freedom of choice, which Premiere Pro emulates by giving you the ability to choose what you want on your plate and how much of it you want on it. Although there are several pre-made workspaces available in the Windows Workspaces option in Premiere Pro, the choice ultimately comes down to personal taste. Anytime you wish to carry out particular duties, you can switch between several layouts. Depending on the panel you want to highlight, each panel operates independently. You can navigate to a particular panel by simply clicking on it; a blue border shows that the panel is now active. The pull-down menus are a helpful addition to the workflow because they give you an extra way to achieve an action or consequence or because they give you more possibilities. When you use Premiere Pro, a significant portion of your work will be completed in three panels: There are three panels: the Program and Source Monitor panels, which show the playing; the Timeline panel, which contains the clips; and the Project panel, which houses your video. As you are getting to know Premiere Pro, you should be aware of the video editing features that each panel offers. You need to know the layout of the house you're moving into. Before you can find the restroom, you might have to unlock a couple closet doors. I'll walk you through these important Premiere Pro panels in the upcoming parts.

Understanding the Project Panel

Consider Premiere Pro as an office building, with the Project panel serving as a sizable office space connected to a few rooms off of it. This panel, which is seen in the image below, contains all of the sequences you have created. You may locate your media assets, like music files, still photos, and movie clips, there as well. You can decide how panel information is shown at the bottom of the palette, and the accessible functions will be presented in the bottom-left corner of the panel. The palette's elements can be viewed as different-sized icons or you can use the list view to explore each element with its own data.

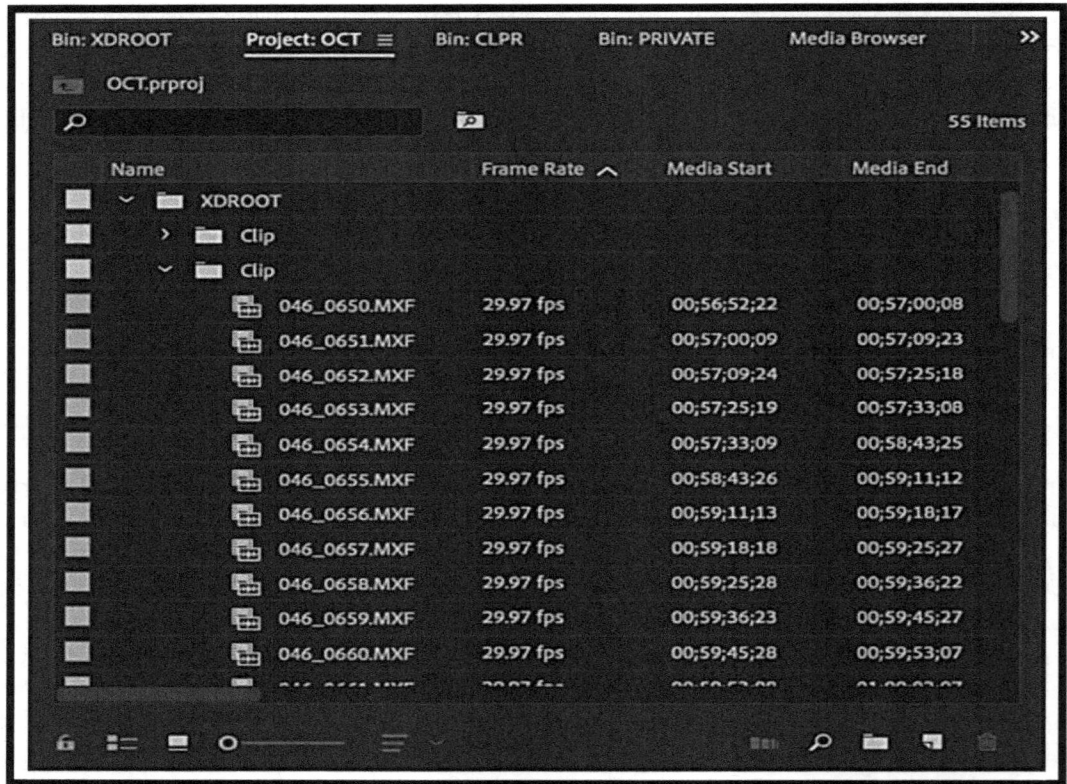

Here is a comparison of the perspectives:
+ **List View:** This mode shows key data including frame rate, clip length, and in/out points in the Video and Audio Info panel. The audio's duration, compression, and format are shown in the Audio Info window. The slider at the bottom of the panel makes it simple to adjust your viewpoint.

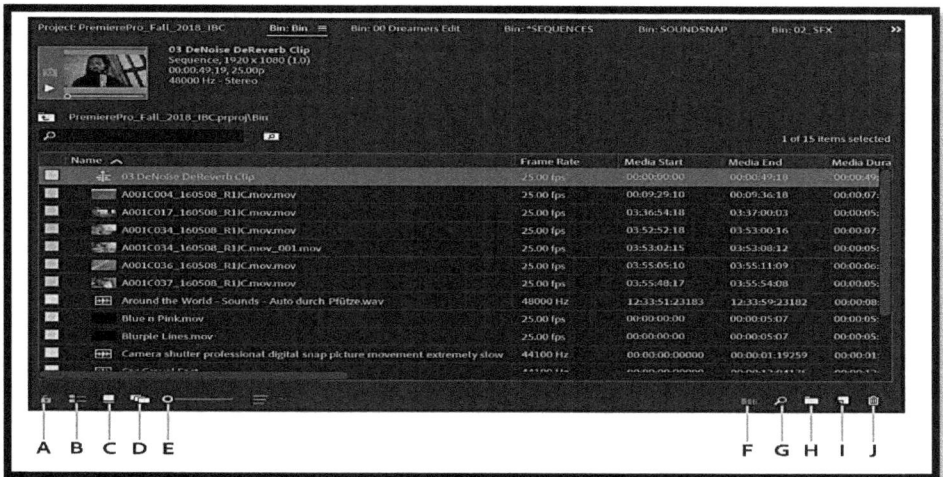

A. Lock **B.** List view **C.** Icon view **D.** Freeform view **E.** Zoom slider **F.** Automate to sequence **G.** Find **H.** New Bin **I.** New item **J.** Clear

⁜ The Icon view shows thumbnails of the content of a clip, making it easy to locate it in a congested folder.

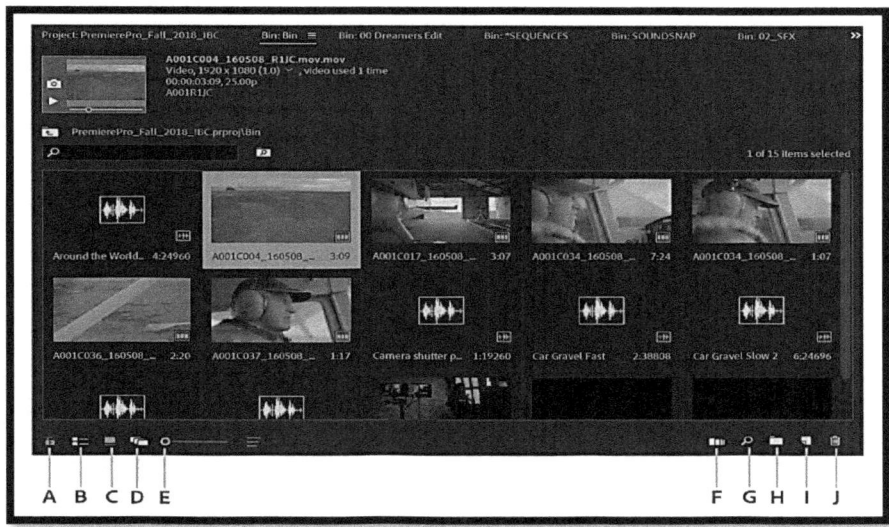

A. Lock **B.** List view **C.** Icon view **D.** Freeform view **E.** Zoom slider **F.** Automate to sequence **G.** Find **H.** New Bin **I.** New item **J.** Clear

Either select View > List or View > Icon from the Project panel's menu, or click the List View or Icon View buttons at the bottom of the panel to transition between views.

- You can arrange videos in the freeform view in a more aesthetically pleasing manner, using thumbnails to make it easier to discover what you're looking for. You may preview thumbnails, choose In and Out points, and arrange your clips in the Project window. This view lets you drag and arrange clips in a different way than the Icon and List views. When you are working on a video, you will notice that the Project panel has a few more useful features.
- The Search section at the top of the panel might assist you in locating particular clips while working with a big number of them.
- By enabling you to create a bin, give it a name, and drag files into it, the New Bin feature clears the Project panel of clutter. There are two ways to build a bin: either click on the panel and choose New Bin, or choose New Bin from the File menu.

You can utilize anything in this Panel and the bins that follow it at any time and in any order.

The Panel for Timelines

In order to build the ideal sequence for your film, you must first drag, probe, and poke clips in the Timeline panel. Here's where the magic happens. The content that will be shown on the screen is queued up in this panel. While you wait, you can edit, reorganize, or enlarge the clips to make sure they are in the right order and alter their sequence. You can adjust the content being played back by turning on and off audio and video tracks here. As you can see in the screenshot below, you may adjust the audio levels from within the timeline. The sequences are the separate updates that are included in the timeline, even though the timeline is the panel where you make your modifications.

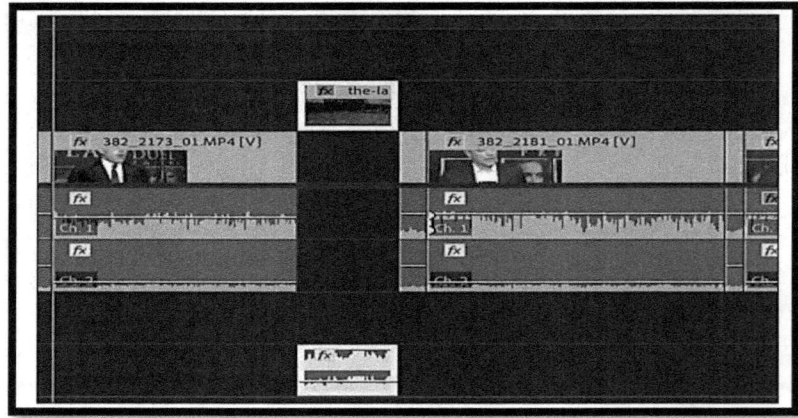

Here are some things to think about:
- Your audio and video content will play in chronological order on the Timeline panel, which serves as a staging place for transitions.

- Additional audio and video tracks can be created by users for layout, mixing, and effects.
- Tracks that will focus on a specific clip within the sequence can be enabled or disabled; audio and video clips can be edited directly in the Timeline pane.

Getting the Most Out of Program and Source Monitors

Keep in mind that you can see what you're doing by combining the dynamic Source Monitor and Program Monitor. It's nearly as though your Premiere Pro office had two TVs. They all serve the same purpose, with the exception that each panel is in charge of a different task. In the Project panel, you can examine your clips using the Source Monitor. After that, you can choose whether or not to include them in the timeline. Then, before you drag the clips into the timeline, you may set the In and Out points, which indicate the section of a lengthier clip that you want to include. You can watch the replay of your clips in the Program Monitor once you've added them to the timeline. The replay plays the information in the exact order that it was originally captured. You can notice how comparable each panel's displays are in the picture below.

Double-clicking the icon or, if you'd rather, the filename in the Project panel will allow you to preview clips in the Source Monitor. This will enable preview access to the clips. Both screens will play and then stop when you hit the spacebar. A number of buttons at the bottom of each screen seem to be standard playback controls. Playback is indicated by the triangle pointing to the right on these buttons. These buttons are capable of more than just playing a video clip, though.

They let you do a number of things, like scrub the video (take a fast glance at it), review it frame-by-frame to make fine modifications, insert, add marks, and more.

Understanding the panels for Effects and Effect Controls

Like Batman and Robin, the Effects and Effect Controls panels are two separate but connected panels. The image below shows the six folders that are part of the Effects panel. These folders contain effects, audio and video presets, and transitions. Among these skills are a few repair tools. These include problems with scaling, color correction, audio levels, and a host of other challenges.

Once you've made your choice, the Effect Controls panel shows the appropriate options to adjust the effect rather than stacking a bunch of superfluous effects. This enables you to modify the impact to suit your tastes. The procedure of changing settings is made easier by the fact that you have distinct controls for each affect.

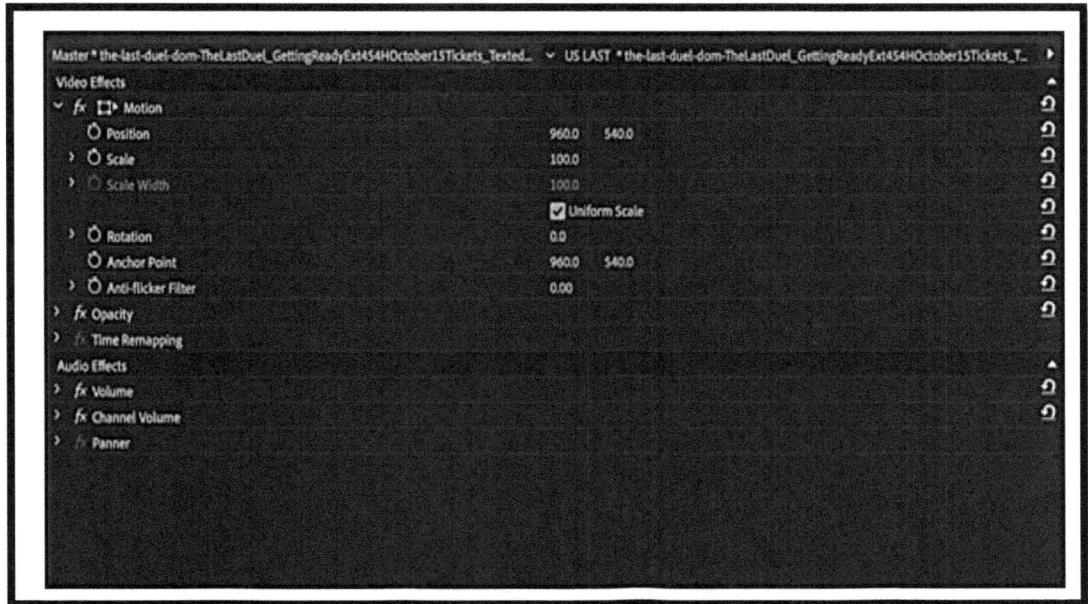

The folders in the Effects panel and some of the subfolders that have specific effects nested within them are listed in the presets section. Changed effects like Bevel, Mosaics, and Lens Distortion Removal are stored in the Presets folder and can be found in the Effects bins for later use.

Lumetri Presets: Keep your film's color correcting presets in this folder. After applying the preset, you can use it to create a new clip that is identical to the one you just applied.

Audio Effects: To improve the audio quality of your video recordings, there are numerous settings available in the Audio Effects folder. This folder contains the controls.

Audio Transitions: A range of crossfade settings guarantee seamless changes between audio snippets.

Video Effects: Color correction, blurring, and borders are just a few of the potent video effects that Premiere Pro provides.

Video Transitions: This group includes video transitions like Wipe, Zoom, Slide, and Dissolve. While Dissolve is the most often used, the other three were popular favorites in the Star Wars series.

Investigating the Other Panels

The aforementioned panels would be in the starting lineup if Premiere Pro were a baseball club. Don't undervalue the players who came off the bench later, though. those who are used to carrying out roles with more distinct boundaries. This panel is similar to the other Premiere Pro panels.

A brief synopsis of the remaining panels is provided below:
+ **Panel for Audio Mixing:** You can manipulate each track in the timeline separately and make significant audio adjustments with the virtual studio mixer. Because every sequence has a different mixer that only impact that sequence, you must choose the appropriate mixer for each sequence. Simple tasks like adjusting audio levels, adding effects, combining songs, and immediately recording audio can be completed with this panel, which is seen in the image below.

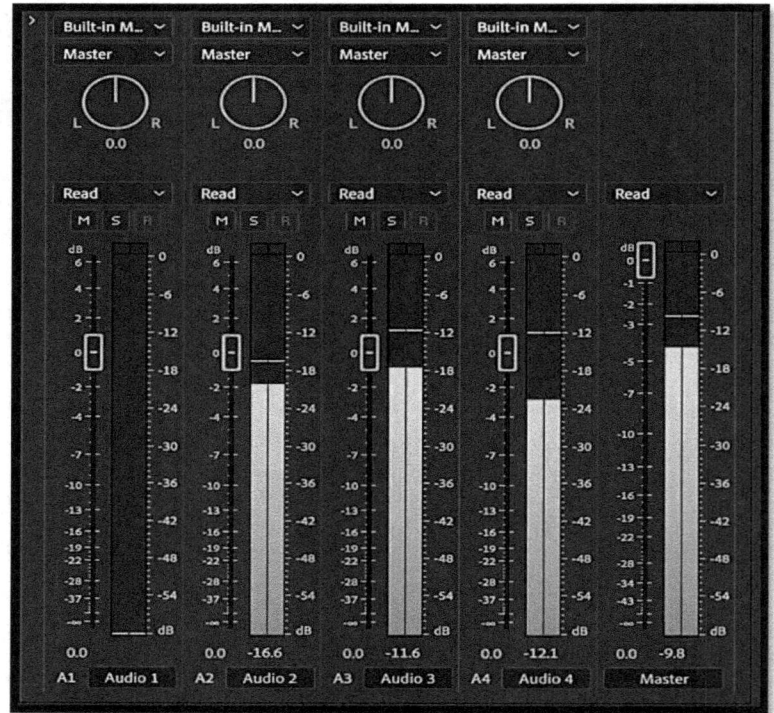

+ **Audio Meters Panel:** A crucial component of your setup. The audio level of the clips on the timeline is displayed by this VU (Volume Unit) meter.
+ **History Panel:** This panel serves as a visual representation of the Edit > Undo function. Since the project's inception, every action that has taken place on it is listed in this panel. This could be a reference to all of your actions since you reopened it during the last session. This is useful if you have altered your sequence in a way that you are not happy with and would like to go back to a previous state while working on the current task. Every time you close and reopen a project, it automatically resets itself, much like the Undo feature.
+ **Info Panel:** Located inside the Project panel, the Info panel is a tab. It gives details about the specific item that is currently selected in the timeline or Project panel. The arrangement and duration of the track are contained in this data.

+ **Marker Panel:** Helpful for identifying specific video clip chunks. Whether it's the most memorable take, a sentimental feeling, or an awkward circumstance, simply press the M key to mark them. This useful panel allows you to analyze the markers in an active clip or sequence, modify the color coding, and add clarifying notes.
+ **Graphics Template Panel:** This panel arranges the program's titles and motion graphics. Additionally, it gives you access to Adobe Stock, where you may get additional visuals and titles.
+ **Media Browser Panel:** It lets you see and examine files on any drive that's attached to your server or workstation. It allows you to quickly access all of the resources while editing.
+ **Metadata Panel:** This is where the properties of every clip are stored. These attributes consist of the clip's runtime, date of production, file size, and format. This panel can be used to enter additional crucial data, such as the scene details, location, or anything else you want to include for best organization.

Organizing Your Work Area

Premiere Pro will extend a warm welcome to you when you launch it. As you can see below, this welcoming environment provides you with a range of options, which facilitates your initial steps. Work on an existing project, start a new one, or go back to your most recent endeavor. Tutorials and other useful options are also available. If you are currently working on a project, you won't see this screen.

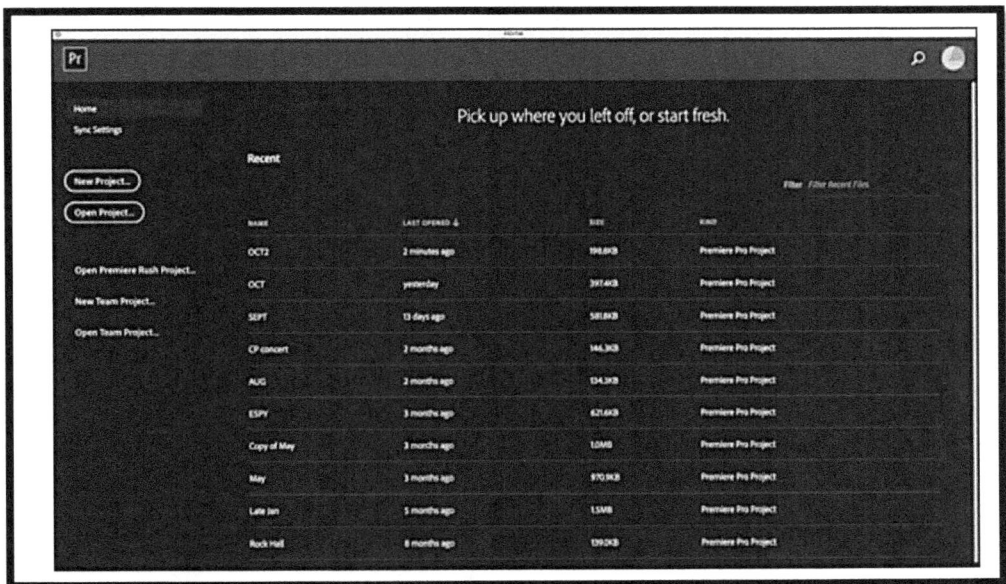

Using Presets for Workspace

A list of predefined workspaces will appear at the top of the program window. These work areas are made to accommodate specific editing tasks. You can choose a preset that is specific to a particular task or project in addition to the standard editing workspace. To modify a preset, navigate to Windows > Workspaces and review the available settings. These options are also visible at the very top of the program window, where the one that is presently selected is indicated in blue. **An outline of every workstation can be found here.**

- **Assembly:** Having a workspace like this could assist launch your project. Because of its simple format, it's great for organizing and analyzing footage, especially when you're watching them for the first time. Make a lot of sequences for your movie that include scenes, interviews, and B-roll, or supplemental video. The project's latter phases may draw inspiration from these scenes. To put it simply, you may examine all of your files and arrange bins and sequences using the Project panel, which is situated on one side of the screen. You can navigate between the Source Monitor and Program Monitor panels using the little timeline that shows beneath the top right panel.

- **Editing:** In editing, you will present your work and tell your tale. It serves as the de facto design. The Project and Timeline panels are arranged at the bottom, while the Source and Program Monitor panels are at the top.

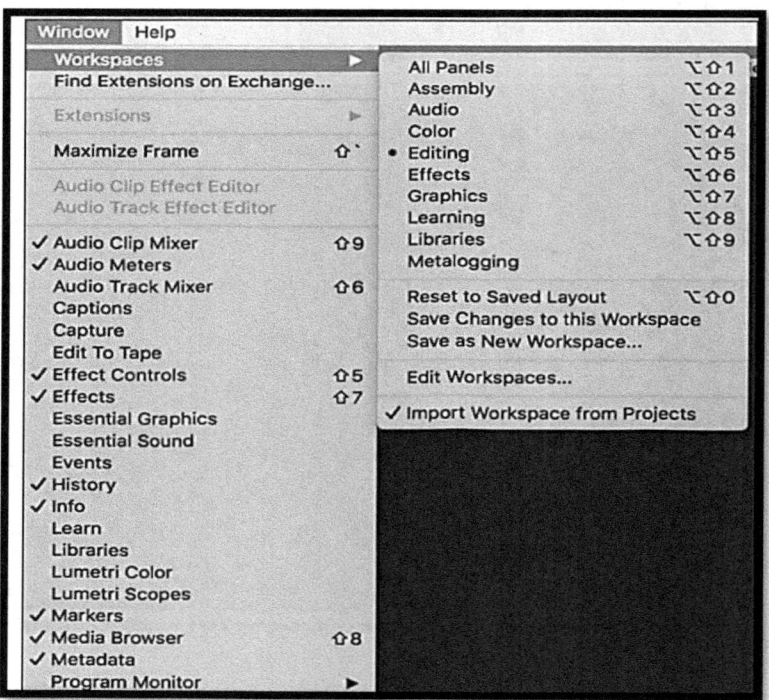

- **Color:** You will use this workspace to ensure that the tone of your film is acceptable. This preset workspace gives you access to all of the effects and parameters that affect color, brightness, contrast, RGB curves, saturation, and stylistic effects, saving you the trouble of manually loading them. The robust Lumetri Color panel, which includes correction choices, is another tool at your disposal. In the Color workspace, which is quite similar to the Editing workspace, these panels are reduced in size. The workspace's left side now has the correcting effects as well.
- **Effects:** The Effects panel provides more options than only color adjustment, much as the Color workspace. Additionally, you may add text-based effects like animated text, movie-style credits, lower-third graphics, and a variety of other options using the Properties tab.
- **Audio:** As the name suggests, the Audio workspace maximizes capabilities for audio enhancement and tuning. It contains the Audio Clip and Audio Mixer panels in addition to the Essential Sound panel. Sending and receiving audio samples is possible with Adobe's Audition audio editing application, which you can use to enhance recordings.
- **Learning:** The Learning workspace is similar to the Editing workspace; however it is superfluous because it does not have panel tabs. This workspace will display some educational resources when you initially activate it. When you first begin using Premiere Pro, these will be helpful. For people who are new to the program and want to get a feel for what it's all about, this workspace is perfect.
- **Graphics:** The Graphics panel provides access to Adobe stock and graphic templates and is the same as the Effects panel. Some require payment, while others allow additions without charge. By selecting the check box in the panel, you can look at either or both of the groups.
- **Libraries:** Encourage a culture of teamwork in the workplace. In addition to Adobe Stock and other libraries, it lets you access and share data from the library you are currently using. This workspace shows the Libraries and Project panels prominently and allows you to swap content both inside and outside the program.
- **Metalogging:** Though editing is not advised, this workspace provides more options for categorizing and organizing your content, much like Assembly. This is quite helpful when you have a lot of material that needs precise explanations because it makes it easier to find the stuff once you begin editing. You have total control over the entire clip when working on a big project, including the resolution, frame rate, and any other settings you choose. To access this workspace from the Program Window, you must click the chevron on the far right. This is due to the Overflow Menu being the workspace's default setup. To access the various options, you can still use the pulldown menu.

Modify the Workspace Order

You don't need to click the chevron icon to access some preconfigured workspaces. Instead, you can adjust the order of the Program Window by selecting Window, then Workspaces, and finally Edit Workspaces. In addition, you can select an item from the pulldown menu by clicking on the chevron.

Including a Description for the Clip

Whether you're editing a film or working on a joint project, it's vital to maintain track of shot metadata. Premiere Pro simplifies the process. The Project panel contains property information for your film, such as frame rate, video information, and audio information. When choosing clips from a packed bin, this knowledge is helpful because it allows you to find exactly what you need. The scope of this information extends beyond the actual properties; you are free to include your own features and descriptions. Your type of workplace is the same as everyone else's. Even if adding comments to the clip description seems like a time-consuming task, it will be beneficial, particularly in a project panel with a lot of activity. You may quickly locate a clip by entering its name into the UI's search box once you've entered the necessary information. This is how comments can be added to a clip's description. You can change the Tape Name, Description, Log Notes, or Scene box by scrolling over the List view and clicking on it. This will make the field editable, allowing you to begin entering data immediately.

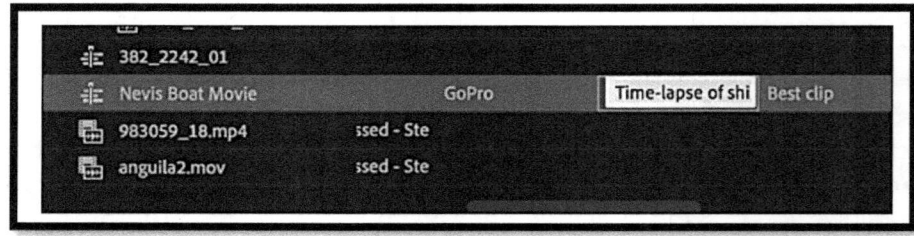

Personalizing and Preserving Your Work Area

Regardless of the options and choices Premiere Pro offers, you will surely go through the process of making little adjustments. Choose the best process for you and take control of your workflow, becoming its interior decorator. When it comes to home improvements, you have the option of doing the job yourself or opting for the convenience of hiring bonded professionals. It is all entirely up to you.

How to Personalize Panels

With Premiere Pro's easy-to-use editing panel customization interface, users may customize their workspace for maximum productivity.

A comprehensive guide to changing panels in the software may be found here.

+ **Including an Extra Panel:** Select the missing panel from the dropdown option in the Window bar to add a new panel. It will naturally show up in your place of employment. After that, you can click and drag the panel to the correct spot in the interface.
+ **Panel Rearranging:** All you have to do is drag an existing panel to a new spot. Panels can be positioned in the middle of another panel, at the top, bottom, left, or right. If moved to the middle, it will nest in a grouping zone underneath the existing panel. The panel occupies the entire width of the window when it is moved to its farthest edges.
+ **Undocking a Panel:** Click the three bars to the right of a panel's title, then pick the option you want to use. As a result, the panel becomes smaller and more movable. This feature helps you keep an eye on multiple film folders or shooting days at once and makes it simple to move panels to a second monitor for a larger workspace.

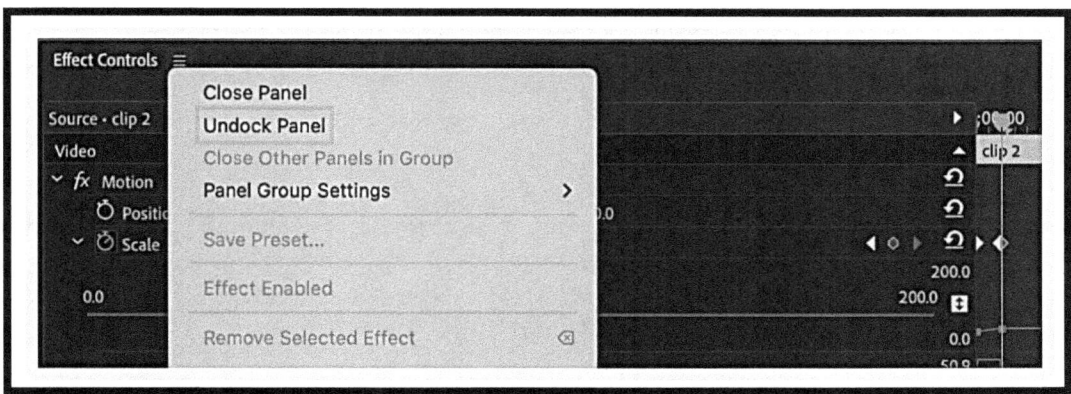

+ **Redocking a Panel:** Drag the panel back to the interface drop zone to redock it.
+ **Panel resizing:** Panels can be easily resized by clicking and dragging their edges to the appropriate size.

Utilizing Adobe Premiere Pro Workspace Presets

One of Adobe Premiere Pro's best features as an editing application is how adaptable it is to your editing requirements. A couple Workspace options will appear when you move up to Window. They are also located in the editing screen's top panel. You may easily adapt your workspace's entire configuration to suit a variety of commonly used video editing tasks, including color correction, audio editing, graphics special effects, and more, with these helpful preset options. You can also save the settings you've selected. Presume you've finished the fundamental editing of your video and are prepared to concentrate on color-correcting your segments. You may get a clearer look at all of the color-specific parameters that you'll probably need by swiftly switching to the color correction preset window. Then you could concentrate only on the sound. You will be sent to a quick and simple layout made especially for audio correction when you click on the preset audio panel.

Preserving your workspace

Productivity and efficiency can be raised by setting up your Premiere Pro workspace to suit your unique needs. But it's just half the fight to get it just the way you want it. Save it with that name if you like the work you've done and want to experiment with different settings before going back to your favorite. If not, the region in question will be affected by the changes you make. In addition to the pre-made workspaces like Assembly and Metalogging, you may also make name alliterations like Aubrey's Audio or Ed's Editing.
Here's how to do that:
- To save a workspace, choose Window > Workspaces > Save as a New Workspace.
- To modify an existing workspace, choose Window > Workspaces > Save Changes to this Workspace.
- By selecting Window>Workspaces>Reset to Saved Layout, you can return a workspace to its initial configuration.

Workspace Presets Hiding

A panel can be filled with specific workspaces. The chevron, sometimes called the double arrow sign, indicates that you may have too many options. To get rid of a panel, just click on it, or close it if it seems cluttered. To remove a custom workspace, choose it from the Edit Workspaces menu, press the Delete button in the lower left corner, and then confirm the removal.

Configure Preferences

From the brightness of the user interface to the default transition duration, Premiere Pro's look and feel can be altered. Until you change them, the majority of these preferences will stay in place. Nevertheless, your projects are saved with the scratch disk settings you choose. **The scratch disks you chose when you started the project will be used by default when you launch it.**
- To open the Preferences dialog box, select the category of preferences you want to change by clicking Edit > Preferences (Windows) or Premiere Pro > Settings (macOS).
- To return to the default settings when the application is starting up, hold Alt (Windows) or Option (macOS). You can use the Alt or Option keys once the splash screen appears.
- Holding Shift-Alt (Windows) or Shift-Option (macOS) while the application launches will concurrently restore the plug-in cache and default preferences. Press and hold the Shift-Alt or Shift-Option keys until the splash screen appears.

The following address is where preferences are stored:

> - **For Windows:** <drive>\Users\<user name>\Documents\Adobe\Premiere Pro\ <version>\.Profile-<User Name>
> - **For macOS:** <drive>/Users/<user name>/Documents/Adobe Premiere Pro/<version>/Profile-<user name>

Configure General Preferences

Transition time and tool hints are among the many parameters that can be changed in the Preferences dialog box's General section.

> - At Startup
> - When Opening a Project
> - Bins
> - Projects
> - Show Event Indicator
> - Show Tool Tips
> - Enable Display Color Management

Establish Preferences for Appearance

The Appearance part of the Preferences dialog box contains the three themes and the high and low contrast settings.
- Select Premiere Pro > Appearance > Settings.
- Choose between Light, Dark, and Darkest.
- To improve visibility and focus on information, a new toggle lets you alternate between high-contrast and low-contrast settings.
- Click OK after choosing the parameters that work best for you.

Configure Your Audio Hardware Preferences

You may set up your computer's audio equipment under the Audio Hardware tab of the Preferences dialog box (Edit > Preferences > Audio Hardware). Additionally, you can choose among the audio playback and recording options that Premiere Pro uses, including CoreAudio (available only on macOS) or ASIO and MME (available only on Windows). The default input, default output, master clock, latency, and sample rate are among the hardware settings for that device type that are shown in this dialog box when you connect an audio hardware device.

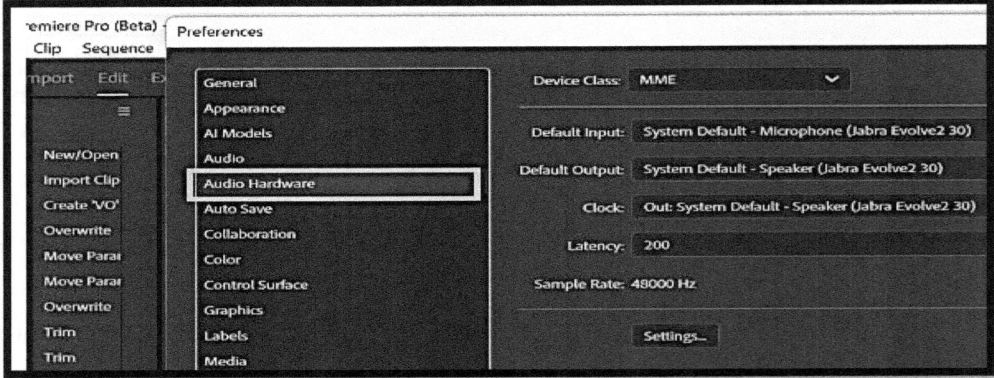

Set up the audio outputs and inputs

The following sound card drivers are compatible with Adobe Premiere Pro when you configure inputs and outputs for recording and playback:

 ⊥ While MME drivers typically support basic cards, ASIO drivers in Windows support professional cards.
 ⊥ Professional and regular GPUs are supported by CoreAudio drivers for macOS.
 ⊥ ASIO and CoreAudio drivers are utilized because of their better performance and lower latency.
 ⊥ Additionally, you may hear changes to the volume, pan, and impact while the audio is being recorded and monitored when it is being played back.
   ➢ Choose Edit > Preferences > MacOS Audio Hardware or Edit > Preferences > Windows Audio Hardware.
   ➢ From the Device Class menu, pick the relevant sound card driver.
   ➢ Choose the card's default input and output.
   ➢ To guarantee correct sample alignment, choose the input or output to which other digital audio devices should be synchronized (MME/CoreAudio).
   ➢ To prevent audio dropouts, set the minimum I/O buffer size (ASIO and CoreAudio) or delay (MME). The speed of your system determines the best choice, therefore some trial and error is necessary.
   ➢ Choose the audio hardware's sampling rate.
   ➢ Click Settings to maximize the performance of the ASIO and CoreAudio cards. Consult the sound card manual (Optional) for further information.
   ➢ Under Output Mapping, you can specify the target speaker for each compatible audio channel in your computer's sound system.

Establish Playback Preferences

You can select your chosen audio or video player and set up pre-roll and post-roll settings in the Preferences dialog box's Playback tab. The device parameters for third-party capture cards can also be changed. **The player is used by Premiere Pro to play media from clips and sequences for the following purposes:**

- Source Monitor
- Program Monitor
- The preview area at the top of the Project panel
- Trim mode
- Trim Monitor
- Multi-Camera Monitor
- The video transition preview is in the Effect Controls panel
- You can use the default player on your computer or a third-party plug-in player for Premiere Pro. Some third-party players come pre-installed with capture cards.

+ **Pre-roll:** The amount of time that passes before an edit point while footage is being played back for various editing uses.

+ **Post-roll:** The amount of time that passes after an edit point while video is being played back for various editing purposes.

+ **Move forward or backward Many:** Determines how many frames are moved when you use the Shift+Left or Right arrow keyboard shortcuts. Ten frames are the default.

+ **Pause Media Encoder queue during playback:** This setting allows you to pause the encoding queue of Adobe Media Encoder while you are using Premiere Pro to play back a project or sequence.

+ **Sound Equipment:** From the Audio Device option, pick an audio device.

+ **Video Equipment:** Click on Settings to configure DV and external devices for output. Click the Settings button to bring up the Mercury Transmit dialog box, which contains video and pixel formats, if you have a third-party capture device installed. There is a checkbox to turn off video output while it is running in the background.

Changing the Project Panel

Clips can be imported into the project by either going to File -> Import or right-clicking on the panel or choosing Import. After being imported, clips are placed to the panel as assets. To organize your assets in the spirit of decluttering, go to File-> New-> Bin and create one or more bins. You have the option to display your assets in the List or Icon perspectives. The List view displays clip metadata, but the Icon view looks like a collection of thumbnails. You can quickly navigate through the video by hovering over it. You can manually scroll through the Source monitor, set In and Out points, and drag the video onto the timeline by clicking on it. The movie also shows some important information in this mode. The clip has already been added to the timeline if the filmstrip indication is colored. You can see how many times it has been used by moving your cursor over it. This is particularly helpful when using a longer tape that has multiple scenes.

CHAPTER THREE
SETTING UP THE PROJECT

Beginning a New Project

To begin a new project, take the following actions:
⊥ Choose New Project from the home screen.

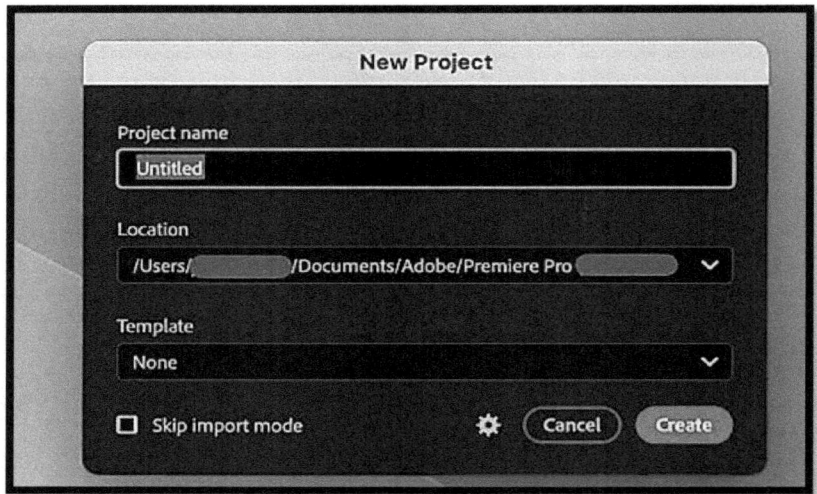

Make sure your new project has a name and a location. You can select a project template here if you're using one.

⊥ Indicate the template; file location, and project name. Another option is to use a project template that is stored on your computer.

⊥ To add content directly from the Project panel, bypass the import mode. Unless it is eliminated, it will remain selected for further projects (Optional).

⊥ To access Project Settings, including General, Color, Scratch Disks, and Ingest Settings, click the Settings icon.

⊥ Choose media assets and video clips for your project. The assets show up in the Selection Tray at the bottom of the window as you choose your media. You can right-click an object to remove it from the tray, or you can empty the tray if you need to.

Advice

➢ Hover and scrub over individual clips to examine them.
➢ To view more media content, switch to list view.

- By selecting the star icon next to frequently visited storage websites, you can add them to your favorites.
- **Select the following choices from Import Settings on the Import desktop to organize your files:**
  - Media organization: Before you start editing, use this to arrange the media for your project. The material will be shown rather than moved to the new location, so make a new bin and give it a name.
  - Toggle to copy media files from a temporary location, like a removable drive or a camera card. While Premiere Pro replicates the content in the background, you may begin editing. To ensure that no files are corrupted after copying, use MD5 checksum checking.
  - Make a new sequence: Make a new sequence called Toggle in order to reduce clicks. The initial object chosen by Premiere Pro determines the sequence settings, including resolution and frame rate.
  - If you choose Create New Sequence, the new media is added to your project as a new sequence.
  - If Create New Sequence is toggled off, the new media is added to the Project panel.
- To import your content into a sequence in Premiere Pro, select Create.

The outcome

A brand-new project is made.

Add Media to an Already-Started Project

To start selecting your materials for an existing project, select Import from the upper left corner of the newly added header bar. Your chosen media is added to the ongoing project.
- Activate Create New Sequence to add new content to your project.
- By turning off "Create new sequence," new content is added to the Project panel.

Additional Import Choices

For specific processes, Premiere Pro provides a few other import methods:
- From the navigation bar, select File > Import.
- To add new media from various locations on your system, use the Media Browser in Edit mode.
- Double-clicking the Project panel will launch the Windows or macOS Finder window.
- To drag files or media to the Project panel in Windows or macOS, open the Finder window.

View Team Project Versions and Autosaves

View Team Project Versions

Team Project generates and saves a new version of the project each time a collaborator submits a change. You can quickly review or go back to a previously published version. Versions are a simple and permanent way to maintain the documented history of Team Project current. There are multiple methods to view and access your team project.

- Select the Team Project name from the header bar in Premiere Pro. Next, from the drop-down menu, choose Version History.

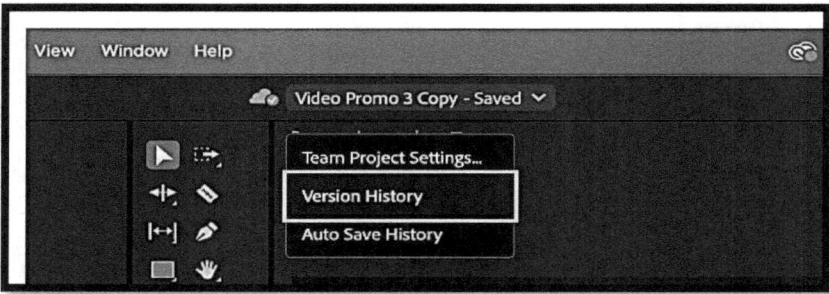

- Open the Media Browser and choose Edit > Team Project > Browse Versions to obtain the most recent version of the project.

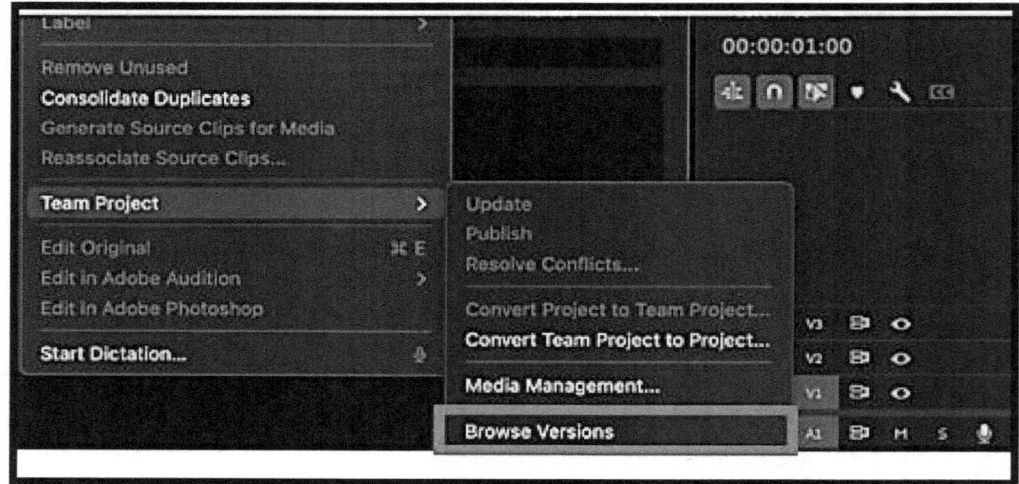

- Select Team Project from the Media Browser window, and then perform a right-click. Next, select Team Project Versions to see a dialog box with a list of all versions and related information, such as comments that have already been shared.

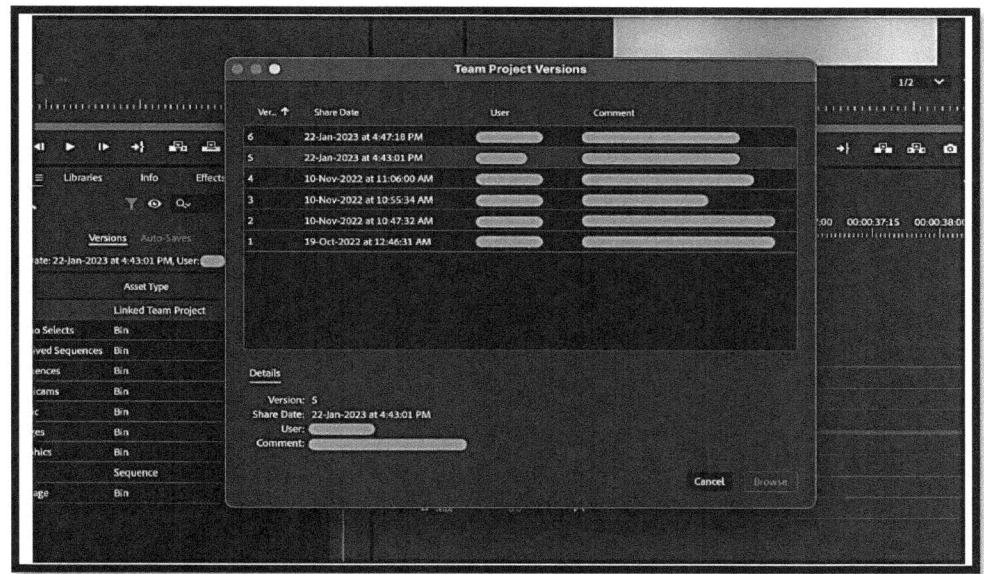

+ Select the Team Project after opening the Media Browser window. Use the vertical slider under the Versions tab to visually switch between versions.

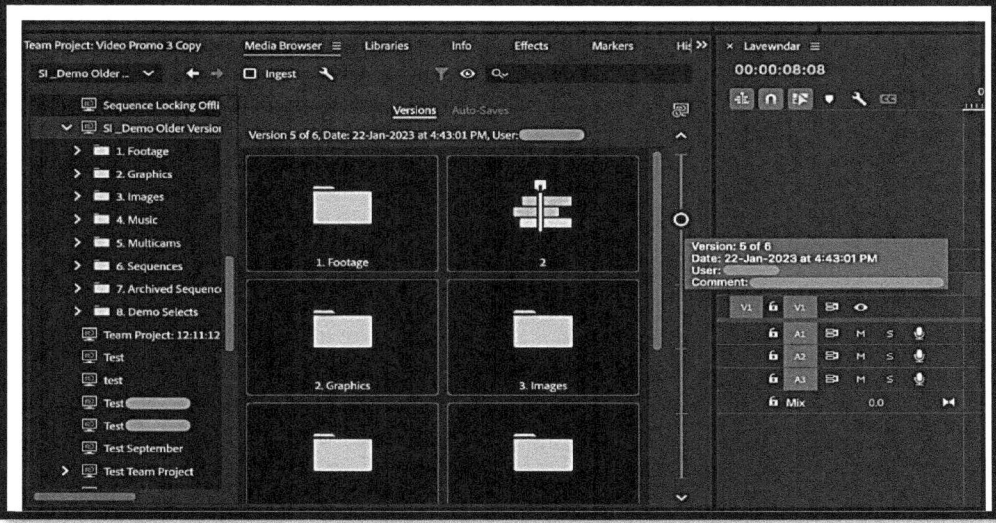

Generating a new team project from a version

To view the versions in the Media Browser window, follow any of the previously mentioned methods.

+ Navigate through all project versions in the Media Browser using the version vertical slider until you get to the most recent version.

- In the Media Browser panel, right-click the Team Project under Creative Cloud and choose New Team Project From Version to create a new Team Project from an already shared version. **The following choices are displayed in a dialog window that opens:**
  - ➢ Copy and enter the name of the existing Team Project.
  - ➢ The list of collaborators from the original Team Project should be used.
- Select OK to create a Team Project.

Indicate the location of the auto-save cache

While working on a shared project, any change you make is instantly stored locally. Additionally, it immediately synchronizes with Adobe Cloud. The option allows you to save the Team Project Auto Save cache to a specific location on your local system. As you work and make modifications, Team Project will automatically save to this location in the background.

Take note: The Automatically Save Every option in Preferences indicates that local projects are saved at regular intervals, while Team Projects are saved with every change. You don't have to worry about your changes being lost because you don't have to manually save your Team Project after every edit.

- From the menu bar, choose Premiere Pro. Next, select Settings (for macOS) or Preferences (for Windows) > Auto Save.
- Select the system location you want to use by clicking Browse on the Team Projects tab.

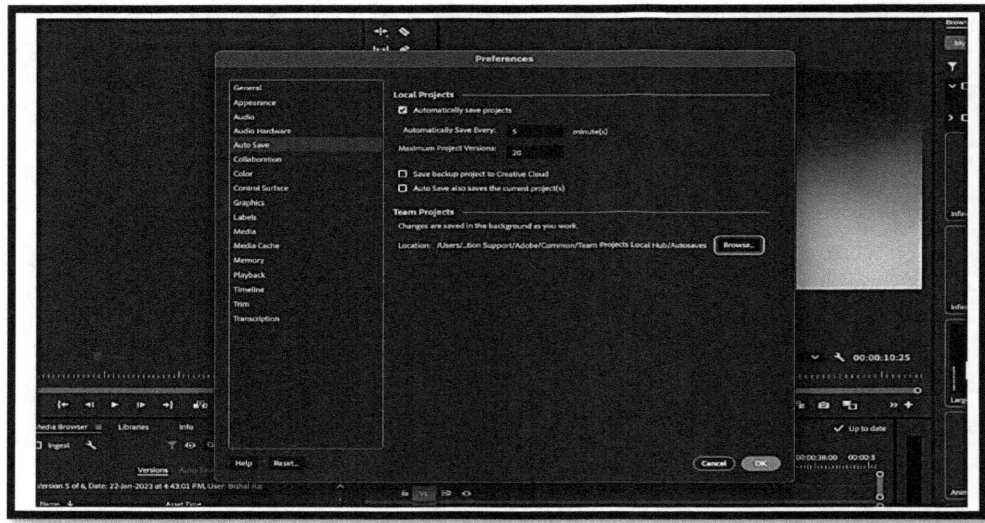

- Following your completion, the modifications you outline will be applied to the subsequent Team Project you initiate.

Auto-Saves Viewing

You may view all of your auto-saves, see when your changes were auto-saved, go back to a prior **auto-save, and even start a group project from an auto-saved modification by using the Auto Saves tool.**

- Choose Edit >Team Project > Browse Auto-Saves to see your auto-saves for the active Team Project.
  - After choosing the Team Project name in the Premiere Pro header bar, you can also choose Version History from the dropdown menu.

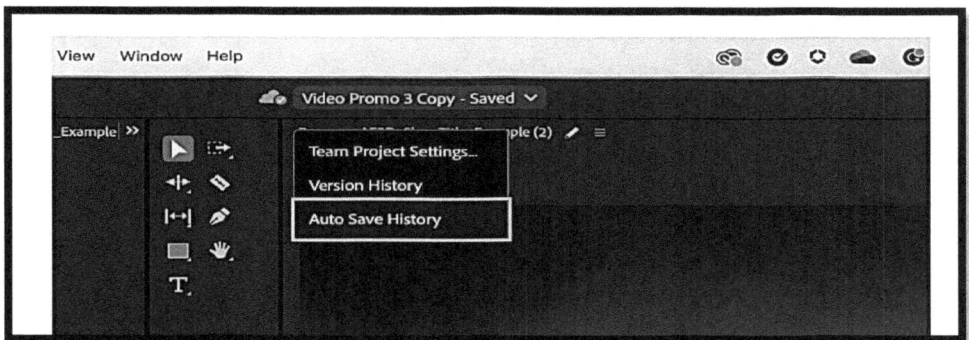

- Alternatively, you may right-click Team Project in Creative Cloud and select Team Project Auto-Saves... from the menu to see a list of all your Team Project auto-saves. In Team Project, you can also navigate through auto saves using the vertical slider.

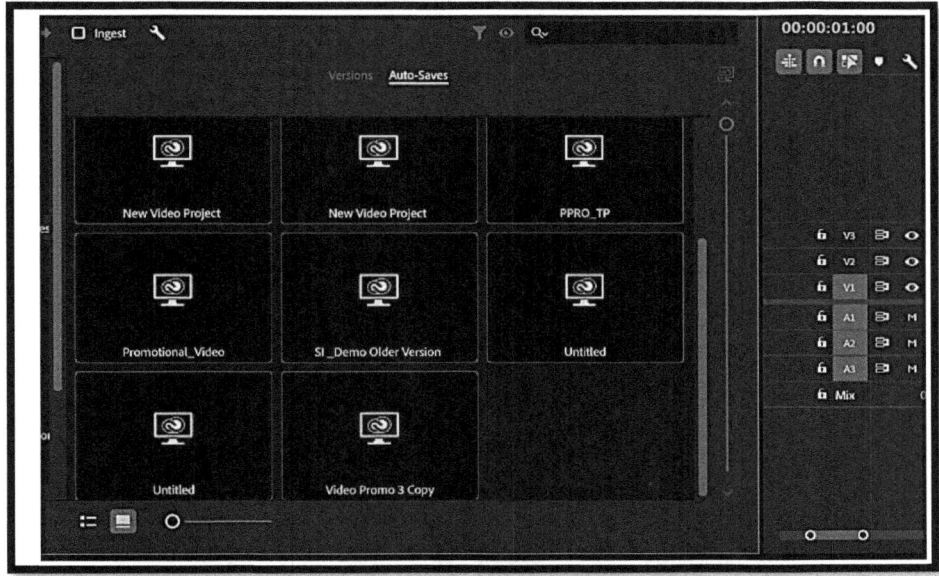

- Choose Make Auto-Save the Latest to reverse a recent update and make a previous auto-save the current one.
- To start a new Team Project from Auto-Save, right-click on the Team Project in Creative Cloud, choose New Team Project from Auto-Save, and then click OK. **A dialog box appears, showing:**
  - ➢ Fills in the current Team Project's name automatically.
  - ➢ Adds a copy that is automatically saved.
  - ➢ Recruits the same group of partners as the initial Team Project.

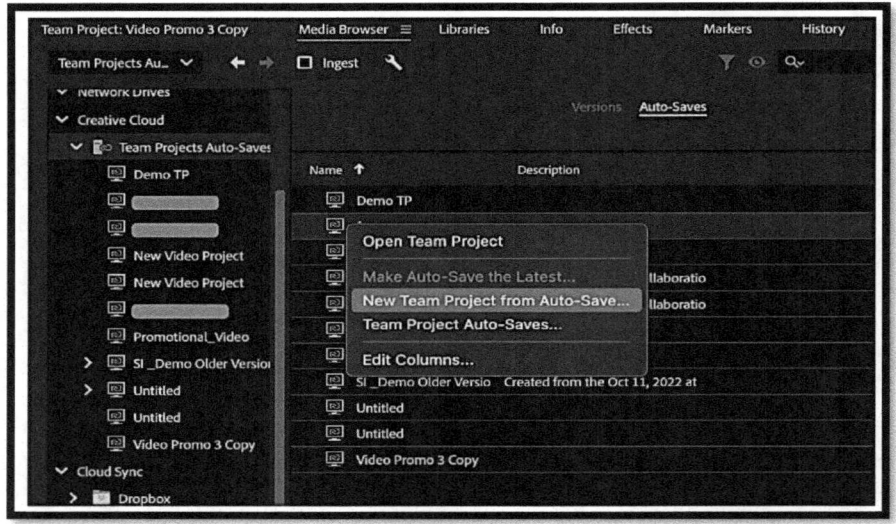

Configure Your Trim Preferences

Big Trim Offset

Go to Premiere Pro > Preferences > Trim on a Mac. Select Edit > Preferences > Trim on a PC. Set to 10 frames for the Large Trim Offset. You can see the revised numbers in Trim Mode after adjusting the offset.

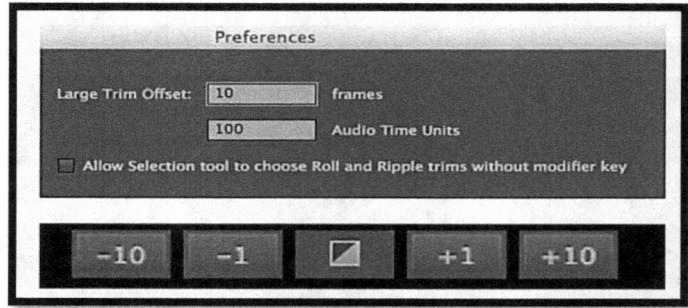

➢ Give the selection tool the ability to select roll and ripple trims without the need for a modifier key. This feature enables you to modify rolling and ripple without the need for a modifier key.

➢ Turn on this feature to move any overlapping track objects during a ripple wipe, including clips that overlap the trim point during ripple trimming.

➢ To keep both sides of the trim in sync, ripple trim adds edits: If you wish to modify clips that overlap with trim, turn on this parameter. These additional edit points will then be clipped alongside the edit points you've chosen to trim in order to prevent clips from moving out of alignment on either side of the edit.

➢ Trim monitor loop playback is determined by the position of the playhead: Use this option to loop playback around the playhead location instead of the entire edit point selection.

Configure Transcription Settings

The settings and configurations for transcription of audio clips in Premiere Pro are referred to as transcription preferences.

+ **Automatically transcribe clips:** Select this option to have clips automatically transcribed.

+ **Preferences for transcription:** Select if all imported clips should be automatically transcribed or just certain clips in order.

+ **Labeling of speakers:** If you would like distinct labels for every speaker, select Yes. Select "no." Don't divide speakers without assigning each one a unique name.

+ **Turn on language auto-detection:** Select this option to turn on language auto-detection when transcribing clips.

+ **Default language:** This lets you choose the language to use while transcribing clips.

Methods for Transcription of Source Media

The steps listed below should be followed if you want to transcribe your full source media:

+ Open Premiere Pro and start a new project.

+ From the load Settings menu, choose automatic transcription when your content loads.

+ For the selected import media, you can choose the language, speaker labeling options, and transcription parameters.

+ Examine your source transcripts using the Text-Based Editing workspace after your transcripts are complete.

Methods for Transcription of Specific Source Files

Videos with spoken dialogue are the only ones that need to be transcribed. You can import your source material and then transcribe specific files if you don't need to transcribe everything.

- Go to the text-based editing workspace. In the Project box, double-click the clips you want to transcribe.
- In the Text field, pick the blue Transcribe option.
- In Premiere Pro, choose your language and if you want speakers to be divided.
- When the transcription is finished, the chat will show up in the Transcript box.

Techniques for Transcript Editing

Use the built-in spell checker or search and replace function when spelling unusual words or names. Select Speakers to add the speakers' names to the transcript when a source file has many voices.

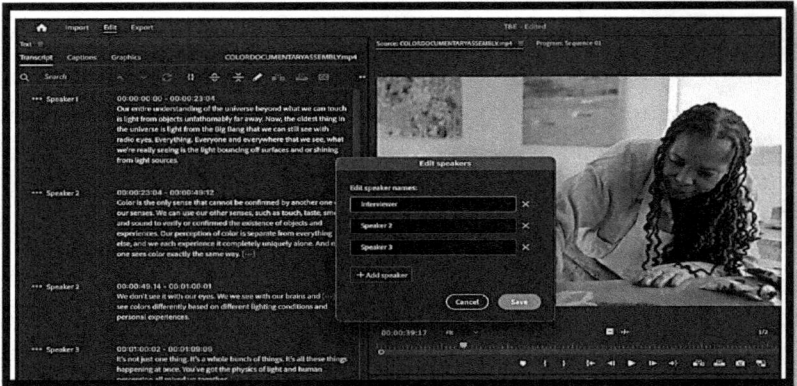

How to Include Videos in the Timeline

Three-point edits can be used to create a timeline sequence in Text-Based Editing.
- To find the information you require, either browse the text in the Transcript window or utilize the search function.
- Highlight the text in the transcript and click the Insert button to add it to the sequence.
- Add clips from the original content to the timeline after you have everything you want to use.

Editing a Sequence: A Guide

Premiere Pro will automatically create a new sequence transcript whenever you add clips to the Timeline. **You can make changes to your rough cut using this new document.**
- To obtain the sequence transcript and continue editing, choose the Timeline panel.
- To move clips, copy and paste the words you've chosen from the sequence transcript. As you edit the text, the Timeline is instantly updated.
- Clips from a series can be removed by trimming or erasing text. The sequence is automatically given a ripple edit ◀▮▶ by Premiere Pro.

➕ To improve audio, add titles and graphics, pace, color grade, and review your first cut, use a video editing program.

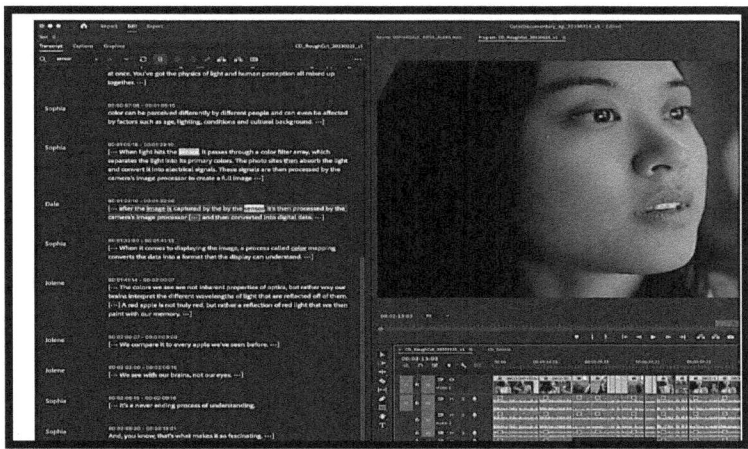

Locating and Eliminating Filler Words in Large Quantities

You can find and remove uh and hmmm filler words from transcripts in large quantities using text-based editing.

➕ Select the ▼ icon after opening the Transcript panel.
➕ Choose whether passages, pauses, or filler words to remove all at once.
➕ After that, you have the option to remove specific instances or the entire searched text, pauses, and filler all at once.

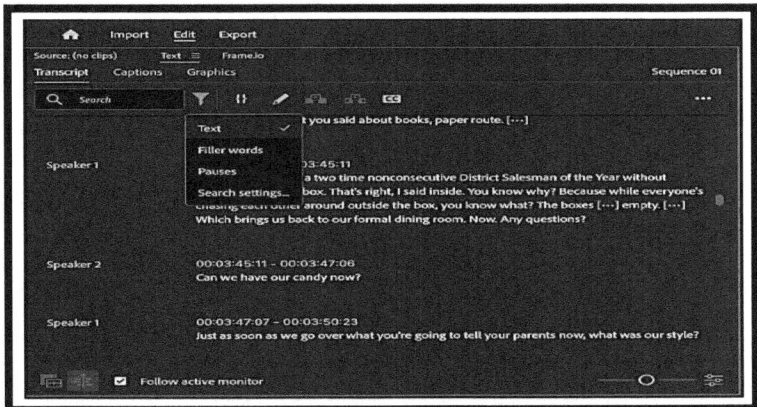

Click the three dots in the top-right corner of the text panel, and then select Transcript View Options to change the minimum number of pauses Premiere Pro will detect.

CHAPTER FOUR
SETTING UP MEDIA

Editors have a lot of video to sort through in a short amount of time. The foundation starts to crumble when you add the pressure of meeting strict delivery deadlines. Being organized and maintaining it is the most important success factor. By honing this skill, you will be able to locate film both now and in the future. Returning to a project that was completed six months (or six years) ago and not knowing what it all means or who completed it is the worst thing in the world. The fact that you did it is acknowledged. Here, I'll demonstrate how to use the Project panel to minimize pain and how to view and identify movies in the most efficient manner.

Making Use of the Project Panel

The Project panel gives you access to the media assets for your projects, including still photos, graphics, audio files, video clips, and sequences. You can utilize bins in the Project panel to arrange your assets. All of your sequences, synthetics (such titles), and material (captures and imports) are kept in the Project panel. It keeps track of every clip that is utilized in your project, making it its beating heart.

The Project panel can be easily navigated in a number of ways. To select an element (clip, sequence, or bin), simply click on its icon. Adobe Premiere Pro knows you want to change the name when you click on it. Click the List View or Icon View buttons at the bottom of the Project panel to easily transition between icon and list views. You can use Shift+[to make your thumbnail icons smaller or Shift+] to make them larger. The slider at the bottom of the Project window can also be used to manually change the project's size. The Project panel can be navigated with the keyboard. The Project panel can be navigated with the up and down arrow keys. To open and close bins in list view, use the left and right arrow keys. There are numerous columns of data visible when working in list view. The fields in each column include important details about your clips. Duration and Pixel Aspect Ratio are among the pre-filled settings. You can also fill out other areas (like Description and Log Note) to record important information. Press Tab or Shift+Tab to advance or Shift+Tab to go back to switch fields with ease.

Just click the column header to sort by a property (like Name or Duration). Click it twice to change and reverse the sorting order. Drag columns from left to right to rearrange them. Click a clip in the Source Monitor, Timeline, or Project panel, then choose File > Acquire Properties For > Selection to get more details about it. You can alternatively click Shift+Command+H (Shift+Ctrl+H) to obtain this information. The Project panel's bottom row contains a number of icons, most of which are shortcuts for operations like finding and creating new bins, sequences, or synthetics. Most Adobe Premiere Pro panels have a panel menu in the top-right corner that includes shortcuts and other important options in addition to commands that let you modify the panel. By altering the Project panel's layout and positioning, you can expedite your process.

Make the Project Panel Look Different

The asset's name appears in the Project panel when you receive it. All of the assets in your project are listed in detail in the Project panel. **The following views are available for viewing and sorting assets in the Project panel:**

```
•   List view
•   Icon view
•   Freeform view
```

+ **List View:** This view offers more details about every item. The data it shows can be altered to suit the requirements of your project.
+ **Icon View:** The clip in the Project panel can be seen with the Icon view (hover scrub). The video will play either forward or backward when you move your cursor over an icon.
+ **Freeform View:** You may use the freeform view to organize your things in an artistic way and utilize them to make storyboards.

Click the List View or Icon View button at the bottom of the panel to switch between views. As an alternative, choose View > List or View > Icon from the Project panel menu.

Making Use of the List View

Select List View to view all of your media files. To locate or categorize your files, you can employ a number of different criteria.

+ In List View, choose the required column headers to arrange objects. Items sort from the top level of the Project panel hierarchy down when bins are increased. To change the sorting order, click the column heading once again.
+ Use the View > Preview Area option in the Project panel to reveal or conceal the thumbnail viewer and clip metadata.
+ Choose Thumbnails from the Project panel menu to reveal or conceal thumbnails. To change the thumbnails' size, drag the Zoom slider.
+ A tooltip displays details about clips when you hover over them.
+ A tooltip with details about a column appears when you hover over it.

Utilizing the Icon View

You can view your media files as a grid of thumbnails by using Icon See. Clips can be previewed in this window.

The following features are included in Premiere Pro's Icon View:

- Use the Zoom slider to change the icons' sizes. To make your media's content easier to see, you can magnify the icons.
- **Use one of the following to go through the contents of a clip:**
  - ➤ You only need to move the pointer over the thumbnail (without clicking) to view the video clip. This pastime is called Hover Scrub. Before editing a clip into a sequence, it's useful to rapidly examine its contents using hover scrubbing. You may view the entire length of a clip by hovering over thumbnails and scrolling from left to right. The Media Start point and Media Endpoint of a clip are located to the left and right of the thumbnail, respectively. The thumbnail returns to the poster frame if you move the mouse pointer outside the clip's borders or if you turn your attention away from the Project panel. When hover cleaning, no sound is played.
- Press Shift + H or navigate to the Project panel menu to turn off hover scrub.
- Holding down the Shift key after turning off Hover Scrub will temporarily reactivate it.
- To define the clips in and out positions during hover scrubbing, use the keyboard shortcuts I and O.
- Double-click the symbol when hovering over a segment to load a clip into the Source Monitor. This method makes it possible to quickly add or remove timeline changes.
  - ➤ Click the symbol to select it. Slide the playhead across the slider to clean the film.
  - ➤ A clip playhead appears when you click the thumbnail's slider. You can do the following:
- To view the video or hear the audio, drag the playhead.
- Use the keyboard keys J-K-L to move around the clip.
- Use the keyboard keys I and O to indicate the in and out locations of the clip when you stop or shuttle. A yellow bar indicates the location of the In and Out points after the clips with these points have been designated.
- Press Shift+P (Windows) or Command+P (Mac OS) after dragging the playhead or shuttle to the desired frame to create an icon poster frame. Use Option+P (MacOS) or Ctrl+Shift+P (Windows) to remove the poster frame.
- Hover your cursor over the filmstrip icon and see the tooltip to see if a clip has been used in a sequence. It also shows the number of times the clip occurs in the sequence.
- Use the context menu's Sequence and Sequence Location (timecode) option when you right-click on the filmstrip icon to find a clip inside a sequence. In the proper order, the playhead advances to the following clip.
- To rearrange items in the Icon view, drag them to a different grid area. A vertical bar that indicates the object's placement displays as you move it. An object enters the bin when you drag it to a container.

Utilizing the Freeform View

There are no grid or sort order restrictions when using the freeform view, so you can freely arrange clips into a unique arrangement. Stacking or grouping media assets, structuring clips as storyboards and assembly cuts, and thinking spatially are all made easier with the help of the Freeform view. Additionally, you can save and swap between layouts for a single project. There are certain things you can do in the freeform view. You can zoom in and out of clips. **Use one of the following options to zoom in and out of clips.**

+ As you move the mouse wheel, hold down the Opt/Alt modifier.
+ To use pinch zoom, use a trackpad.
+ To move across the screen, use the + and - keyboard shortcuts.
+ Use the zoom slider; double-clicking will return it to its default zoom.

Using the Bins

Bins resemble folders on your hard drive in both appearance and functionality. They make it easier for you to organize and store your clips. Similar to a hard drive, you can have several bins inside of other bins to create a folder structure as extensive as your project calls for. One significant distinction between bins and folders on your hard drive is that bins are exclusive to your Adobe Premiere Pro project file. You won't see individual project containers on your hard drive.

Generating Bins

+ Choose the New Bin button folder located at the bottom of the Project panel.
+ You can change the name of the new bin that Adobe Premiere Pro creates. When you first build your bins, it's a good idea to start naming them.
+ Let's get rid of the movie snippets. Theft Unexpected is the name of the bin.
+ The File menu allows you to create a bin. From the File menu, select File > New > Bin.
+ Give the PSD files names.
+ You can quickly build a new bin by choosing New Bin from the Project panel's right-click menu. Give it a try right now.
+ Give it the name Illustrator Files.
+ Simply drag and drop existing clips into the New Bin button located at the bottom of the Project panel to create a new bin for them.

Footnote: It could be challenging to locate an empty spot to click if the Project panel is crowded with clips. Try clicking to the left of the icons inside the panel.

+ In the New Bin, drag and drop the Seattle Skyline.mov clip.
+ Give it the name City Views.
+ Use the keyboard shortcut Control+/ (Windows) or Command+/ (Mac OS) to create a new bin.
+ Give it the name Sequences.

⊹ The Project panel's list view shows bins among clips in name order.

Bin Opening

There are multiple options available to you when you open a container. It can be opened instantly in place, as a distinct tab in the Project panel, or in a new window.
- ⊹ **Launch in a fresh tab:** Double-clicking a bin will open it in a new window. You can dock or drag this stand-alone window to any location on the screen.
- ⊹ **Launch a fresh tab:** Holding down the Option (Alt) key while double-clicking opens the bin in a new tab within the Project panel.
- ⊹ **Open in place:** Holding down the Command (Ctrl) key while double-clicking will open the bin in that location. This obscures the remainder of the project while navigating the view inside the bin. By selecting the project name or folder at the top of the pane, you can close the bin.

Personalizing Clip Views and Bin Views

You must be able to view your media dynamically once you have arranged it into bins. Studying your material is made easier when each shot is represented by a symbol. Accessing a photo's metadata is frequently helpful, for example, when attempting to identify the camera that captured the image. You can occasionally include extras like a synopsis of the content. To discover what you can achieve, let's begin by altering your point of view.

Altering Views

A bin can be viewed as either an icon or a list. List view is used by most editors since it lets them view multiple clips at once. On the other hand, the icon view offers a number of benefits, such as a storyboard view, hover scrub, and fast visual sorting. Click the buttons in the lower left corner of the Project panel to switch between list and icon views. Press

Command + Page Up (Ctrl + Page Up) or Command + Page Down (Ctrl + Page Down) to transition between list and icon views.

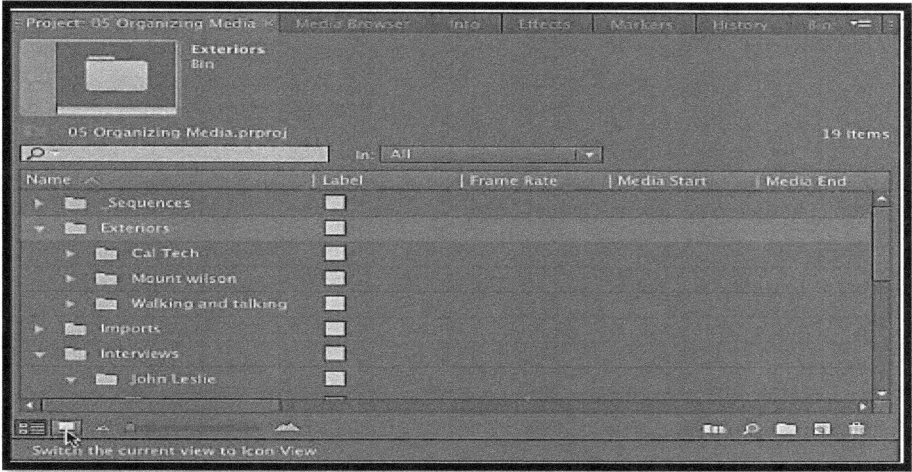

List View

Most editors sleep, eat, and breathe in the list view while working on a project. The most crucial element, the name of the clip, appears on the left of this simple list. The amount of content that can be displayed and the sorting options make this view the most helpful. Thumbnails of the photos appear when browsing a list. Go to the Project panel menu and change the icon's size and appearance. From the Project panel menu, select Thumbnails. The same keys, Shift+[and Shift+], can be used to shrink and increase thumbnails in icon view.

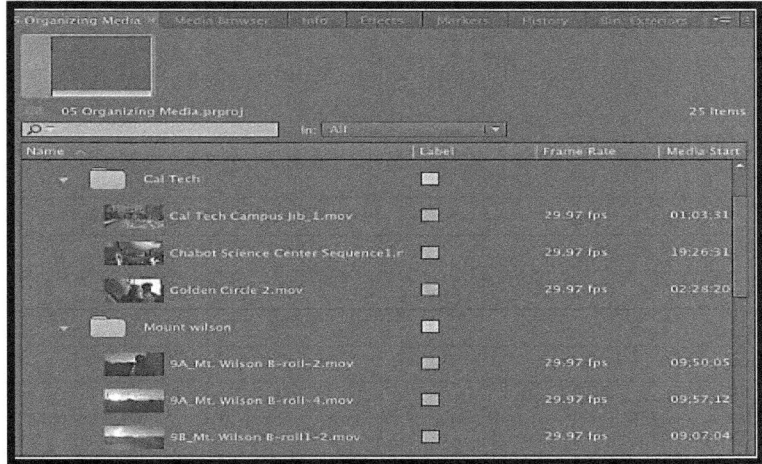

View of Icons

Adobe Premiere Pro CS6 has a new function called "hover scrub," which lets you move your mouse pointer over a clip and scrub over it to view the movie interactively. We've come to love this technique for rapidly cleaning your video, especially when the thumbnails are big. It makes getting to know the movie lot easier, especially if you have the bin full-screen, but it does not take the place of the Source Monitor. **Icon view has the following benefits:**

- ♣ Without loading the clips into the Source Monitor, you can view them by icon.
- ♣ By dragging the mouse pointer over a clip, you can swiftly scan its contents with hover scrub.
- ♣ This is a fantastic method for getting acquainted with fresh footage.
- ♣ Many file-based cameras (still or video) use a series of digits as the clip title. Icon view is a great method to see what the clips are without altering the labels that the camera has applied.

Examining the Video

Premiere Pro has to know the frame rate, pixel aspect ratio (pixel shape), and, if the clip is interlaced, the order in which the fields appear in order to play the video correctly. You can circumvent Premiere Pro's normal ability to extract this information from the file's metadata. **To begin, take these actions:**

- ♣ Go to the Media Browser panel in order to import a video.
- ♣ Double-clicking will open the clip in the Source Monitor. It is broader than the standard 16:9 because it is in full anamorphic widescreen. To attain this higher aspect ratio, bigger pixels are needed.
- ♣ Right-click the video and choose Modify > Interpret Footage from the Project window.
- ♣ Since this clip lacks audio, switching audio channels is not possible.
- ♣ The anamorphic 2:1 pixel aspect ratio of the file is now used in the clip. The pixels are therefore twice as long as they are wide.
- ♣ Select OK, Square Pixels (1.0), and conform to in the Pixel Aspect Ratio section.
- ♣ Examine the clip in the Source Monitor. It looks like the clip is almost square!
- ♣ Try out different aspect ratios. In the Project window, right-click the clip and choose Modify > Interpret Footage.
- ♣ DVCPRO HD (1.5) should be chosen. To examine the video, click OK and then go back to the Source Monitor.

The pixels in the clip will now be viewed by Premiere Pro as being 1.5 times wider than tall. By doing this, the image gets resized to the common widescreen 16:9 ratio. Changing the pixel aspect ratio is rarely a feasible option when making artistic choices because it compresses or expands the image's horizontal space—for instance, all circles will become ovals. On the other side, the pixel aspect ratio interpretation might need to be changed for technical reasons if all squares appear to be rectangles and all circles look to be ovals.

Premiere Pro's Freeform View

The Freeform View tool in Premiere Pro lets you arrange data in creative ways. Similar to Icon View, Freeform View lets you reorder your clips, set in and out points, and preview thumbnails. Clips in Freeform View are not fixed to a grid, so you can arrange them anyway you like. To construct any desired visual pattern, you can manipulate individual clips or stack clips on top of one another. Lastly, this will provide you more flexibility in how you envisage your project. In the spring of 2019, Premiere Pro version 13.1 introduced Freeform View. Make sure you are always using the latest version of Adobe Creative Cloud in order to take use of this new feature!

How to Utilize Premiere Pro's Freeform View

Use these detailed instructions to get started with Freeform View. Once you understand all of the choices, you can start personalizing the panel to suit your needs.

How to Begin Using Freeform View

- Select the Assembly workspace in the Project panel, then select the Freeform View button.
- To adjust the zoom level in your workplace, use a trackpad or slider.
- To start organizing, drag & drop clips into the panel. There are no restrictions; you may even stack clips on top of each other!
- To enlarge a single clip or a collection of clips, select them, right-click, and then pick Clip Size.

Customization of Freeform View

Personalized Metadata Display

Choose Freeform View Options from the panel menu to modify the data that appears beneath each thumbnail. Each clip may have up to two metadata descriptions shown.

Poster Frame Placement

The tiny graphic that displays your clip in the Project panel is called a poster frame. By using a poster frame that appropriately displays the clip, you can quickly determine which is which. After selecting a frame by hovering the scrub over the clip, hit Command + P (or Shift + P on a PC).

Assign Labels

Right-click and choose Label from the drop-down menu to give clips color labels. These color descriptors will also be displayed on the timeline.

Layouts can be saved in Freeform View

You can refine your strategy by trying out various storyboards once you've made one layout in Freeform View.

- Right-click in the Project window, then choose Save as New Layout.
- Name the arrangement.
- In the future, try out different combinations and flows.
- Right-click and choose Restore Layout to restore previously stored layouts.
- To begin anew, choose Reset to Grid from the menu when you right-click the project panel. Any information from this page can be used to sort.

Editing Freeform Views

You may handle footage and start doing a simple edit in Freeform View.

- Hover over each clip and scrub over it to change the in and out points. Press I to make an in point and O to make an out point.
- Press the spacebar or J-K-L to play and pause clips while editing in Freeform View.
- Sequentially arrange your clips in the Project panel.
- You can select and drag edited clips to your timeline.

Innovative Applications for the Freeform View

Although you have a lot of creative freedom when utilizing Freeform View, there are basically two methods to approach your footage:

- Sort the items by type
- Arrange in a logical order

- **Sorting Clips by Type in Freeform View:** One of the best ways to begin editing is to group clips. List View Bins can be used for this kind of arrangement, but Freeform View gives you a far clearer view of what you're dealing with. **The following categories could be used to arrange the footage:**
  - ➤ **Shot:** Does the same shot exist in multiple variations? Start by stacking them, then go back and select what you want.
  - ➤ **Angle:** For establishing shots and close-ups, keep your angles constant.
  - ➤ **Character:** It could be helpful to keep all of the same character's shots together while editing dialogue.
  - ➤ **B-Roll:** Get cutaway pictures ready for placement.
  - ➤ **Action-Items:** Are there any clips that need extra work, like titles, effects, or color correction? Sort them into action item groupings.

Clips can be arranged in a variety of visually appealing ways in Freeform View. Your working style and the quantity and kind of footage you have will determine your method. For instance, you may stack the clips on top of each other or arrange them in a row.

✦ **Using Freeform View for Storyboarding:** Given that video editing is a visual activity, it makes logical to create a sequence graphically. When storyboarding, think about stacking or overlapping clips in Freeform View to represent cuts in your final edit. Preserving layouts is another helpful aspect for storyboarding. Try out various cuts and save the outcomes as layouts. Take layouts into account while producing numerous versions of the same movie for various devices. For instance, you might keep one layout for IGTV and another for YouTube videos. A simple yet effective way to go over and put your footage in perspective is to organize them. Making preparations in advance could save you time throughout the editing process and allow you to view your product in fresh perspectives. Fresh video can be seen visually with Adobe Premiere Pro's Freeform View. Look around and share your experiences using the Freeform View in various ways!

Changing Clips

The In and Out points of a clip designate a certain segment of the clip or sequence. The process of identifying the in and out places of a clip is called marking. The first frame in a series that you wish to include is called the "in point." The outpoint is the last frame of a sequence. In a standard workflow, a clip's In and Out positions are specified using the Source Monitor. The process of altering a clip's in and out positions after it has been edited into a sequence is called trimming. Clips that have been trimmed usually change how they replay in a sequence. For instance, you might wish to cut to the incoming clip a bit earlier than planned when marking clips while you watch the edit. Use Premiere Pro's trimming tools to cut the clip in order to fix the problem. Editing clips is possible in the Program Monitor, Source Monitor, and timeline. You can trim the clip by sliding its edge. The edge of a clip, sometimes referred to as its edit point, is its in or out point. You can edit more than one clip at once. Using specialized tools to trim an edit point is simple and precise, minimizing the number of steps while preserving sequence integrity.

Choosing an Audio Channel

There are sophisticated audio control tools in Premiere Pro. You can target specific output audio channels and make complex sound mixes using real clip audio. You can manage mono, stereo, 5.1, Ambisonics, and even 32-channel sequences and clips with fine-grained control over audio channel routing. To create sequences that are mastered in stereo, you should often use mono or stereo source clips if you're just getting started. The default settings will most likely be adequate in this situation. It is common practice to record one microphone on one audio channel and another microphone on another when using a professional camera to capture audio. Now, completely different sounds are played on the same audio channels that are typically utilized for stereo audio.

Keep the following in mind while interpreting audio clip channels: All of the available audio channels will be shown in the Modify Clip dialog box. Any channels in your source audio that you don't require can be unchecked, and your clip sequence won't contain those empty channels. When adding the clip to a sequence, you could require a different kind of audio track if you override the audio channel interpretation (mono, stereo, etc.) of the original file. The number of audio clips that will be added to a sequence once it has been edited in is shown by the list of clips on the left, which could be as small as one. Use the checkboxes to choose which source audio channels to include when modifying the clip into a sequence. This suggests that, depending on your project's requirements, you can split up or combine multiple audio channel sources into a single sequence clip. Clip instances that have already been edited into a sequence will not be affected by changes to the channel interpretation of audio clips. The next time you add a new clip to a sequence, the new interpretation will be applied. This implies that two copies of the same clip with distinct audio channels can be used in a sequence.

Using the Source Monitor to Work with Audio Clips

You can work with audio clips and audio from audio and video files in the Source Monitor. It is possible to view, clean, and zoom in and out on audio waveforms.

Listen to Waveforms in Audio

Audio waveforms are automatically displayed in the Source Monitor when an audio clip is selected. You can see the audio waveforms in the Source Monitor when you open a clip with multiple audio channels. Click Timeline Display Settings, the wrench tool in the timeline panel, to change the style of an audio track. To show audio as waveforms on the timeline, select Show Audio Waveform.

Clean the Waveform of the Audio

Moving the playhead across a section of an audio waveform is known as "scrubbing." It is a quick method for recording audio. A clip in the timeline panel can be opened in the Source Monitor by double-clicking on it. When you click an audio clip, the playhead appears. Click forward or backward across the video to progress or scrub it. To turn off scrubbing, go to Edit > Preferences > Audio and uncheck the box next to "Play audio while scrubbing."

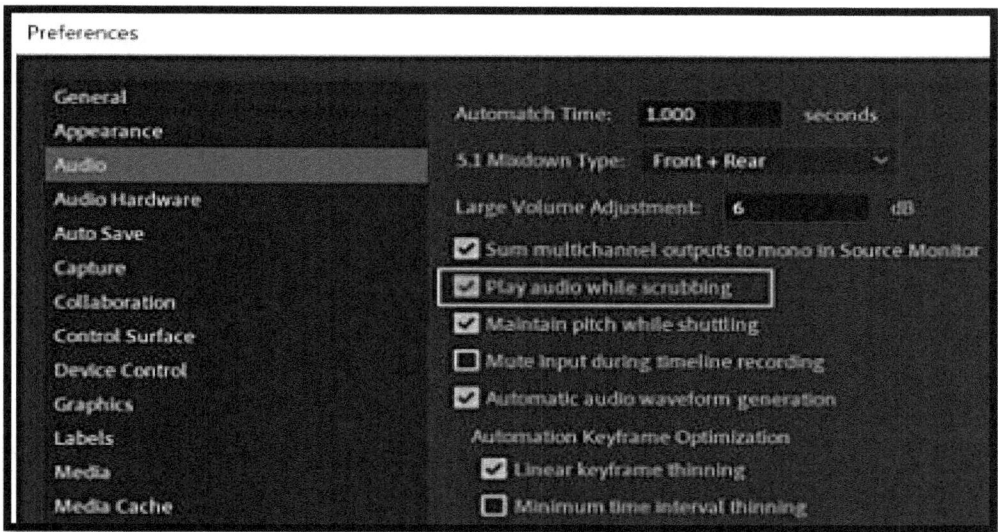

Zoom in or out of the Source Monitor's audio waveform

In the Source Monitor, you can zoom in on an audio waveform to better see markers and in/out points. An audio clip can be opened in the Source Monitor by double-clicking on it in the Project or Timeline panels. Drag either end of the zoom scrolling bar beneath the Source Monitor's time bar to zoom in horizontally. All channels' waveforms, as well as the time bar, extend or shrink horizontally.

The following actions can be taken to zoom in vertically:

Drag either end of the vertical zoom bar to enlarge a single channel. The decibel ruler is located at the right side of the Source Monitor. You can shift-drag either end of the vertical zoom bar to enlarge any channel. The waveforms of one or more channels and the decibel ruler both grow or shrink vertically.

CHAPTER FIVE
HOW TO USE THE PROPERTIES PANEL

When working in Adobe Premiere Pro, you can access frequently used features through the Properties window. Premiere Pro versions 25.0 and later no longer include the Essential Graphics panel. While the Graphics Templates panel allows you to experiment with Motion Graphics and Stock Audio, the new Properties panel facilitates the editing of titles, subtitles, audio, video, and graphics.

What does the Properties Panel allow me to do?

The most frequently used properties and tools for the selected text, images, audio, or video are shown in the Properties panel. It lets you change the audio volume and change the subtitles and videos (transform, position, scale, rotate, and change clip opacity).
In what ways does the Properties panel improve upon earlier workflows?
   + Edit many clips at once. You can choose and modify the attributes of multiple clips simultaneously using the attributes window.
   + You can quickly and contextually change a clip's morph, speed, and cut.
   + A wide range of functions and panels, such as Stock Audio, Motion Graphics, Effect Controls, Transitions, and Lumetri Color, are easily accessible.

Use the Properties Panel to Edit Text

Create a project, add media, and set up a chronological order before you start.
   + First, choose the Type tool.
   + The text track will appear on the Timeline above the footage once you type your words.
   + **To enhance and produce a unique appearance, select the text and utilize the Properties panel's tools:**
      ➢ **Text:** To access the Text panel, advanced Effect Controls, or Graphics Templates, select the three-dot icon.
      ➢ **Appearance:**
         ▪ **Fill:** Use any color you choose to fill in your text.
         ▪ **Stroke:** You can add numerous strokes or outside, inner, or center strokes to text.
         ▪ Shadow: To produce a variety of intriguing effects, apply one or more shadows to a form.
         ▪ **Mask with Text:** Make a text layer that serves as a mask, allowing only the text's shape to reveal underlying visuals or video.
         ▪ **Align and Transform:** Use the top, bottom, left, vertical, or right edges to align and change text.
         ▪ **Linked Style:** To preserve font choices and look inside a specific style, use linked styles for titles and track styles for captions.

- **Responsive Design:** Position: Make visuals that adapt to variations in the aspect ratio of a video frame or the scale or position of another layer.

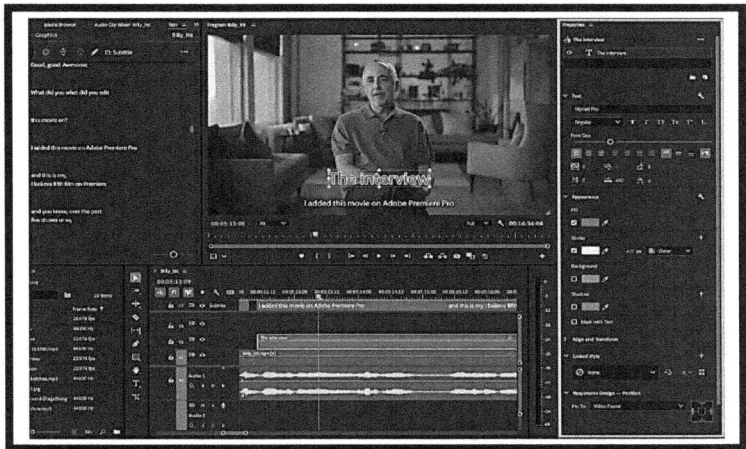

Use the Properties Panel to Modify Shapes

To access the Ellipse and Polygon shape tools, choose and hold the Rectangle tool. Choose a shape tool and drag it onto your image to create a form.

- Use the Selection Tool (V) to move or modify your form's width, height, rotation, or anchor point.
- **To create a unique appearance, adjust the Properties panel's settings:**
  - ➢ Appearance
  - ➢ **Fill:** Add any color you choose to your shape.
  - ➢ **Stroke:** Apply many strokes or outside, inner, or center strokes to form a shape.
  - ➢ **Shadow:** To produce a variety of intriguing effects, apply one or more shadows to a form.
  - ➢ **Mask with form:** Make a layer of form that serves as a mask, exposing underlying images or video only inside the shape.
  - ➢ Use the top edges, bottom edges, left edges, horizontal centers, or right edges to align and transform objects.
  - ➢ **Position-Based Responsive Design:** Create visuals that automatically adjust to changes in the aspect ratio of a video frame or in the scale or position of another graphic layer.

Utilize the Properties Panel to Modify Audio

- From the timeline, pick one or more audio clips.
- Select Window > Properties if the Properties window is not displayed.

The contextual audio parameters available for the clip are shown in the parameters section.

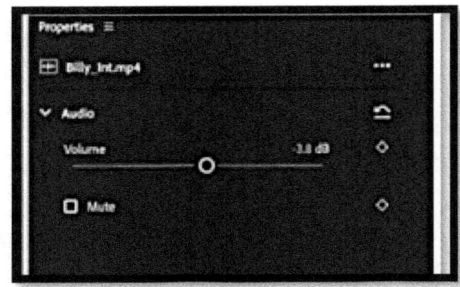

+ To adjust the volume, move the Volume slider.
+ Choose Mute and turn off the clip's audio.
+ The Pan slider allows you to adjust the sound output between the left and right speakers when editing a mono clip.
+ Decide whether to include keyframes in the timeline audio clip.
+ To make more intricate changes, go to the three-dot menu and select Browse Adobe Stock audio or Open additional audio controls to find music and sound effects.

Hint: By choosing multiple graphics in your timeline, you can change the properties of many clips simultaneously.

The control will show that value if every value in the highlighted clips is the same throughout the selection. Each clip that is selected will change if that value is overwritten. The control will show a dash if any of the values don't match throughout the selection. The value of each track item can be changed by dragging the dash. Apply the same absolute value to every clip in the selection after selecting the dash.

Use the Properties Panel to Edit Video

+ From the timeline, pick the clip.
+ Use Position, Scale, Anchor Point, Rotation, and Opacity to switch up your clips; Fill frame and Fit are used for quick operations.
  > **Change:** To automatically adjust the video's size, choose Fill Frame or Fit to Frame. If the picture's aspect ratio is different than the frames, Fill Frame may crop portions of the image in order to fill the frame completely. Contrarily, "fit to frame" means modifying the content so that it completely fits inside the frame while maintaining its original aspect ratio; if the aspect ratios are not the same, this could lead to letterboxing.
  > **Crop:** To eliminate pixels from the top, bottom, left, and right corners of a video, use percentages.
  > **Modify speed:** To quickly speed up or slow down your movie, use the Clip speed/duration option.

CHAPTER SIX
THE ESSENTIAL VIDEO EDITING

Essential Editing Features and Tools

An editing station with an illuminated viewer, adhesive, a splicer, and lint-free gloves were among the many tools needed to edit 8mm film in the past. A little panel next to the timeline now houses several of these tools. **The following features are present in the toolbar as seen in the image below.**

- **Selection Tool:** The main tool for rearranging clips throughout the timeline is this one. It enables you to easily grab and reposition clips. Additionally, you can adjust the duration of clips by hovering over their borders and expanding or compressing them. You can use the shortcut key 'V' or click on the tool's designated icon to activate it.

- **Track Select Forward/Backward Tool:** This tool selects all clips to the right or left of the current clip, in contrast to the Selection Tool. It selects clips to the left (or nearer the start) of the selected clip in backward mode, and clips to the right (or finish) of the selected clip in forward mode. Clicking the icon will activate the forward tool; holding the icon will activate the backward tool. The shortcut buttons 'A' and 'Shift-A' allow you to swiftly switch between various tools.

- **Ripple Edit Tool:** With this tool, you can change the boundaries of clips to show more or less of the clip while keeping the changes made to other clips. When a clip is trimmed, a ripple effect is created that modifies the subsequent clips accordingly.

- **Rolling Edit Tool:** This feature, which is integrated into the Ripple Edit tool, lets you modify the first clips out point while simultaneously modifying the second clip's in point. The ability to edit two clips simultaneously increases editing efficiency overall. 'N' is the keyboard shortcut.

- **Rate Stretch Tool:** Tucked away in the Ripple Edit tool, the Rate Stretch Tool lets users alter a clip's tempo without changing it's In and Out points. Using the shortcut key 'R', it offers a straightforward method of changing the clip speed.

- **Razor Tool:** This clip-breaking tool is distinguished by its vintage razor image. Users simply move the razor over the relevant section of a clip and click to divide it. The Select tool can then be used to control the divided clip, including relocating, copying, pasting, and deleting. 'B' is the keyboard shortcut.

- **Slip Tool:** By adjusting a clip's In and Out locations inside the timeline, the Slip tool offers more control than the Razor tool and enables precise cutting. For making frame-by-frame changes while maintaining a constant clip length, this tool is quite helpful.

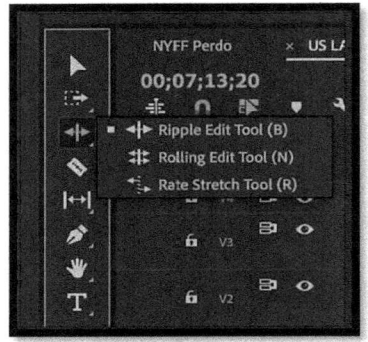

- **Slide Tool:** Located inside the Slip tool, the Slide tool has a different purpose but works similarly to the Slip tool. When used, it automatically fills in any gaps in the timeline and modifies the content of a clip. Making seamless changes without leaving any gaps is made much easier with this. The keyboard shortcut U can be used to open this program.
- **Pen Tool:** This practical audio editing tool looks like the nib of a fountain pen. By adding key points to an audio file, users can precisely modify the audio level at specific points during the footage. Users can effectively change the audio volumes in specific areas by raising or lowering these points. This tool's shorthand is 'P'.
- **Hand Tool:** By enabling users to scroll up and down, the Hand tool facilitates timeline navigation. Its main purpose is to navigate the timeline so that different project areas can be quickly accessed. This utility can be rapidly activated by pressing the 'H' hotkey.
- **Zoom Tool:** The Zoom tool functions as a chronological magnifying glass and is housed within the Hand tool. Users can make more precise modifications by clicking on it to enlarge the clip inside the timeline. All you have to do is type 'Z' to access this utility.
- **Type and Vertical Type Tools:** With choices for both horizontal and vertical orientations, these tools facilitate the addition of text to the video screen. Customers can provide their chosen content in the content layer that displays after clicking on the video. Although there isn't a specific shortcut for the Vertical Type tool, it may be accessed by hitting and holding the 'T' key on the Toolbar. This shortcut key makes it simple to use the Type tool.

Establishing a Sequence

Here's where the magic happens. The actions you take to link your audio, video, and other timeline elements create your movie. Since not every sequence is made in the same way, the crucial phrase is created here. Every sequence is made to work with a specific resolution and frame rate. You can generate multiple sequences within the same project, but it is preferable to work with a single master sequence to create your video.

Configuring Every Sequence

To get started, select File > New > Sequence to launch the New Sequence window. Verify the information before becoming overly excited and clicking OK. There are several options for resolution and frame rate on the panel's left side. Details about a preset appear on the panel's right side when you select it. You can choose the best one based on your demands. Most likely, you're working with HD material. If so, there are many of options, so you can stick with the codec you selected for your initial production. Selecting a setting that corresponds with your camera and the type of recording—such as 4K or HD—never hurts. By selecting one of the common HD formats and clicking the down arrow next to DVCPROHD, you may get the two options for 1080i and 1080p. High-definition versions of the i50 and i60 are essentially the two analog color TV systems used in Europe and the Americas, PAL and NTSC. Choose DVCPROHD 1080i60, which is interlaced—that is, it has lines of resolution that are similar to what we used to see on our television screens—and conforms to US standards. The standard is established by the National Television System Committee. Choose PAL if DVCPROHD 1080i50 is your preferred standard. Click OK once your sequence has been named.

Creating a Unique Environment

Making your own preset and even name it after yourself is an option if you're not the cookie-cutter type or have particular requirements. Do the following:
- Choose File > New > Sequence to open the sequence panel.
- From the menu on the left, pick any choice. Any decision you make won't matter since you'll alter and preserve it. You will test the top option using the down arrows in this example, and when you get to 1080, you will select it.
- Select the tab for Settings. At the top of the Settings panel are a number of settings. Go to the top and choose Custom, as shown in the picture below.

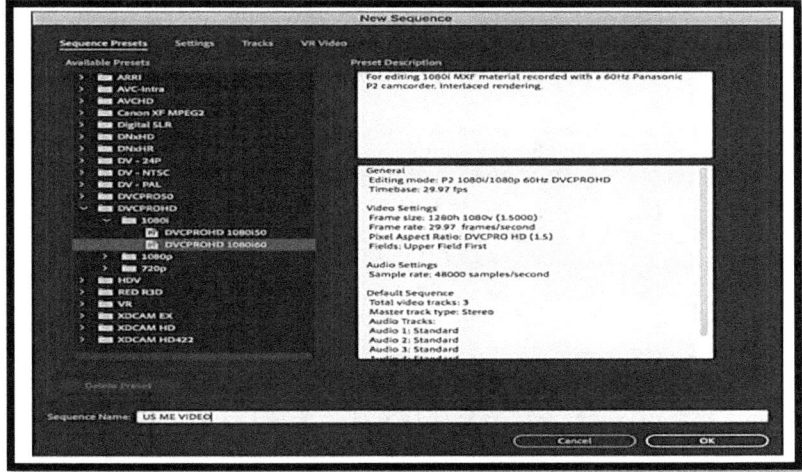

- **Select a Timebase:** The second pulldown menu under the Settings tab, called simply "frame rate," is crucial because it lets you choose whether your film will look like a video at 29.97 frames per second (fps) or more dramatically at 24 fps, which is the standard cinematic frame rate. Keep in mind that this number cannot be altered once editing has begun.
- The Settings page's Video section allows you to change the frame size. Most likely, the HD resolution will be 1920 x 1080. But, if it's different for any reason, you can enter that size. Select one option from the list below.

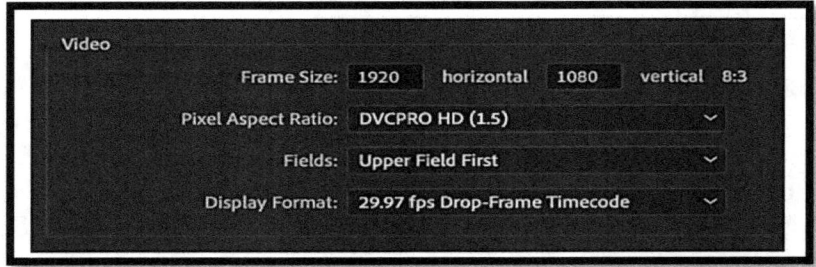

- ➢ Select square pixels for the Pixel Aspect Ratio.
- ➢ **Fields:** Select None.
- ➢ **Display Format:** Set it to match the Timebase configuration.
- Apply the default settings for the audio presets.
- Make the following adjustments to the Video Preview. (This is required to prevent playback from being slowed down.)
  - ➢ Select the first choice: MPEG with only the I-frame.
  - ➢ Adjust the resolution to the frame size of the sequence, such as 1920 x 1080. None of the boxes here need to be checked.
- Select "Save Preset." A dialog window will appear.
- Give a name to the preset. A dialog box will show up when you click the Save Preset button; name it and click OK. Now, you can choose when you need to.
- At the final step, the sequence might be renamed. Are you content? Click OK.

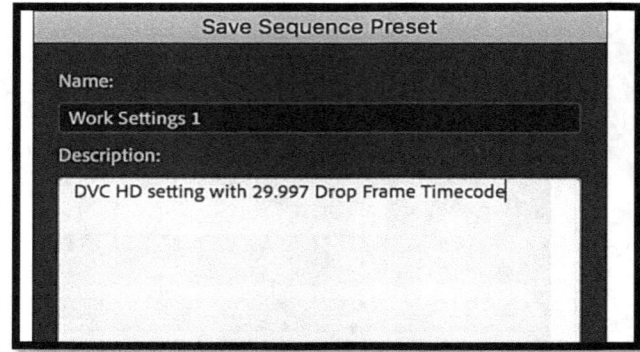

Modifying the Timeline

In its default configuration, the timeline provides enough information to get you going. But may minor adjustments be enough? No. All of the information entered into the timeline is included in the clips. Sometimes, these clips may be too long or too short. Zoom in on the frame to make it longer so you have enough room to trim any extra frames that need to be cut. It's incredibly helpful when watching a long-form video because you can see all of the cuts in one glance. **This can be accomplished in a number of ways.**

   + **Utilize the slider:** The slider can be found on the timeline's lower left side. On both ends are circular grips. The period is increased by moving a slider inward. Sliding the sliders out shortens the timeframe.
   + **Make advantage of the menu:** Click the wrench icon on the left side of the timeline to expand all tracks. Then a menu will show up.
   + **Put it in:** Use the (+) or (-) keys to change the timeline's size.
   + **Scroll to change timeline size:** If your mouse has a scroll wheel, you can move it up or down while holding down the Alt (Windows) or Command (Mac) keys to change the track length.

Clips for Trimming and Cutting

Clips for trimming

   + **Select Clip:** Find the clip you want to take out of your sequence on the timeline.
   + **Hover and Trim:** Drag the mouse pointer over the edge of the clip until the trim icon—a shape that resembles a bracket—appeals.

➤ **Drag to Adjust Length:** Click and drag the clip's edge inward or outward to adjust its length. By changing the clip's start or end point, this will change how long it lasts.

Splitting Clips

➕ **Position Playhead:** Place the playhead inside the clip at the frame you wish to cut.
➕ **The shortcut method**
　➤ To use Ctrl + K on Windows.
　➤ To access macOS, hit Command + K.
　➤ The keyboard shortcut will create two separate clips from the original by splitting the clip at the current position of the playhead.

As an alternative:
➕ **Choose Add Edit:**
　➤ Place the playhead in the sequence at the proper split point.
　➤ Choose Sequence from the top menu to begin the sequence.
　➤ Click Add Edit.
　➤ At the play head position, the action will split all of the sequence's clips, with the exception of those on locked tracks.

Raising the Audio and Video Tracks' Altitude

The audio and video tracks are by default small; the video track lacks waveforms and a thumbnail, and the clips appear as thick, multicolored lines. Thankfully, Premiere Pro may be used to enhance the vision. By now, it should be obvious that Premiere Pro provides multiple methods to achieve the same objective, and track height is no different. **Here's how to change a video or audio track clip's height:**

➕ **Using sliders:** Use the sliders on the right and bottom of the timeline (see image below) to change its height and zoom in. When the slider is pushed in, the bottom video track gets taller; when it is taken out to its original size, it gets much smaller. Track height can be adjusted with the side slider; pushing down deepens the track, while pushing up deepens it.

- **Using keyboard shortcuts to change a track's size:** To change a track's height, hit the plus (+) or negative (-) keys while holding down the Control (Windows) or Command (Mac) key.
- **Shrinking audio and video tracks concurrently:** This feature allows you to save one second of editing time by shrinking audio and video tracks simultaneously. While holding down the Shift key, you can use the (+) and (-) keys to make audio and video tracks larger.

Put a Panel on the Screen

When more is more, it becomes vital to work with a single panel. For instance, you can enter data into the Project panel or view your video filling the screen using the Program Monitor. To make a single panel larger, click Window > Maximize Frame. To get back to the grouped panels, click Window > Restore Frame Size. By pressing the accent key, you may also select the panel and change between isolated and grouped panel sizes.

Techniques for Editing Storyboards

The first stage in bringing a story to the screen is creating storyboards, which are visual representations of a script. They are used in pre-visualization for everything from live-action movies to Disney cartoons. Storyboards are a tool that lets the director communicate their ideas to a hundred other people on location, according to Mellon. A storyboard is a collection of drawings that depict the anticipated camera placements and action of a movie. Although storyboards resemble comic strips, they usually contain more technical components like sound effects, lines of dialog, and planned camera movements. Storyboard pictures can be created from clip thumbnails in a bin. By choosing the in and out points of a few clips in a bin, putting the clips in the proper order, and then constructing a sequence based on those points, a storyboard edit is a rapid way to put together a sequence. The first elements of a scene can be quickly assembled with a storyboard edit. First, let's make a storyboard edit. Sort the clips you'll need for each scene into distinct bins or folders in order to generate a storyboard edit. To give yourself plenty of workspace, double-click the bin to open it in its window and then expand it. If you remember from Final Cut Pro 7, you could drag icons around in windows and they would just 'float around freely.' While Premiere's more structured interface, which locks the positioning of clips into neat rows, makes storyboard changes a bit more visually responsive, you can still accomplish the same things with Premiere's more structured interface. Select User Order from the sort icons drop-down box, adjust the icon size to your preference, then activate the Thumbnail view in the newly opened bin panel. This implies that you will have the freedom to rearrange them rather than having them ordered by clip name.

After that, edit the scene by placing the clips in the right order. To alter a clip's sorting order, click and drag it. The cursor symbol turns to a hand as you release your grip, and white bars appear to indicate the clip's landing location. Use the keyboard keys I and O to set each clip's in and out points. You can both click on one of your clips and use the keyboard shortcuts J, K, and L to play forward (L), pause (K), and play backward (L), respectively, or you can hover scrub through your clips. You may also play and pause videos with the Spacebar. A little blue bar with a tiny playhead shows up when you click on a clip in the trash window (see figure above). You can see which part of the clip is selected by looking at the In and Out points.

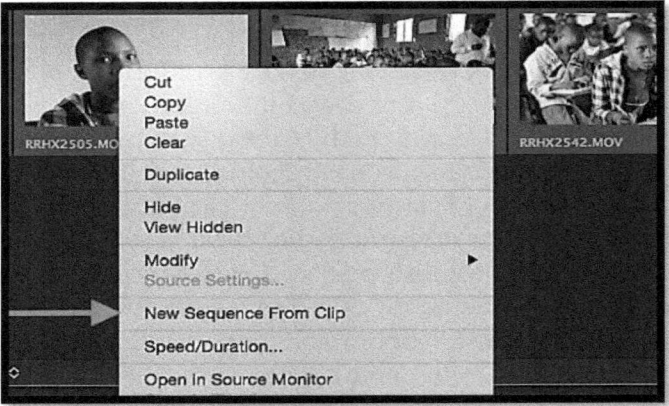

Lastly, select all of your clips by pressing CMD+A. Choose 'New Sequence From Clip' from the context menu when you right-click on one of them. This will produce an edit of your clips in the order you specify, as well as a new timeline with the same format and frame rate as the clip you have chosen. This is an easy way to arrange your clips and make a basic initial edit.

Editing from Three Points

The most accurate change an experienced editor can make is a three-point edit. Lastly, three marks are placed in the Timeline (also known as the Program Monitor) and Source Monitor to explain the three-point modification. Either two in points or one out point or two out points and one in point are your alternatives. The fourth point doesn't need to be mentioned because Adobe Premiere Pro will figure it out for you. You will use an in and out point to define the range of the modification. The most common choice is to place these locations inside a source clip. In other situations, though, you might want to define that range using the Timeline. The next step is to designate where the third point is located. Both the software and the source may experience this. Finding the In point is the most common method for figuring out where a clip should begin. A clip's end can likewise be specified with just an Out point.

This is an illustration of how to apply a three-point edit:

- You must first choose and open a sequence in order to change it.
- You must load a clip in order to use the Source Monitor. Write down the time you want to use.
- Click on the headers of the tracks you want to add or change.
- Drag source clip track indications to their headers in order to replace media tracks.
- In the Source and Program Monitors, select any three In and Out locations.
- Press the Insert or Overwrite buttons in the Source Monitor.

Something has changed.

Editing 360-Degree Videos

Understanding 360-Degree Video

With 360-degree video, an immersive multimedia format, viewers may experience a 360-degree panorama of a scene. Compared to standard videos with a fixed viewpoint, 360-degree films offer a more dynamic and captivating experience by capturing the entire surrounding area. You must first research 360-degree video's technology, production method, uses, and possible future developments in order to comprehend it.

- **Camera Technology:** To capture the entire field of vision, 360-degree films need sophisticated cameras with numerous lenses positioned correctly. The sophistication of these cameras ranges from straightforward dual-lens configurations to intricate six-lens or more lens combinations.
- **Stitching Software:** Several video feeds from various lenses are flawlessly combined using stitching software once footage has been captured. To guarantee that a panoramic image is coherent and distortion-free, this procedure is necessary.
- **360-Degree Video Formats:** Equirectangular and cube map projections are the two most popular 360-degree video formats. Equirectangular projection projects the spherical video onto a flat surface, while cube map projection employs six square faces to represent the spherical surroundings.

Creation Method

- **Pre-production:** Take into account the storytelling possibilities and difficulties of the immersive format when making a 360-degree video. Directors and content providers must choose how to direct the viewer's attention in the circular space.
- **Production Challenges:** Compared to regular filming, 360-degree video production calls for a distinct methodology. Since there is no set frame, everything within the camera's field of vision could be visible. Careful blocking, inventive use of space, and choreography are necessary for this.
- **Post-Production:** Stitched footage is edited to improve the story's visual appeal and coherence. Special effects, sound design, and other post-processing elements contribute to a polished result.

360 Degree Video Applications

- **Virtual Reality (VR) Experiences:** To enable viewers to completely immerse themselves, 360-degree films are frequently used in VR experiences. Training, education, gaming, and virtual travel can all benefit from this.
- **Marketing and Branding:** Businesses use 360-degree videos for immersive marketing campaigns, which let prospective buyers inspect products and destinations before buying.
- **Training and Simulation:** To replicate real-world situations and offer a secure and regulated learning environment, 360-degree films are utilized in healthcare, aviation, and military training.
- **Journalism and Documentaries:** To provide a more immersive view of news stories and events, journalists and documentarians employ 360-degree films.

Upcoming Developments

- **Better Resolution and Quality:** As camera technology develops, 360-degree video is probably going to have better clarity and resolution, which will make virtual experiences more realistic.
- **Interactivity and User Engagement:** By enabling viewers to investigate alternative stories and make decisions in real time that impact the plot, future developments may increase 360-degree video engagement. User engagement would increase as a result.
- **Integration of Artificial Intelligence (AI):** AI may automate tasks such as camera calibration and content editing, opening up the creative process to a wider audience.

360-Degree Video Editing

Step one: Turn on virtual reality in sequence settings

Like any other video, you can import your 360-degree video into Premiere. Here's how to manually activate VR in sequence settings, even though Premiere recognizes VR attributes when you import footage.

+ From the menu, select Sequence > Sequence Settings.
+ There will be a VR Properties section at the bottom of the dialog box.

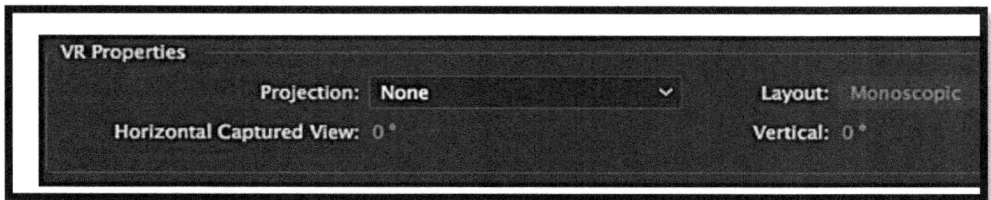

+ Choose a projection to activate virtual reality in your sequence. Only the equirectangular projection format is currently supported by Premiere Pro.

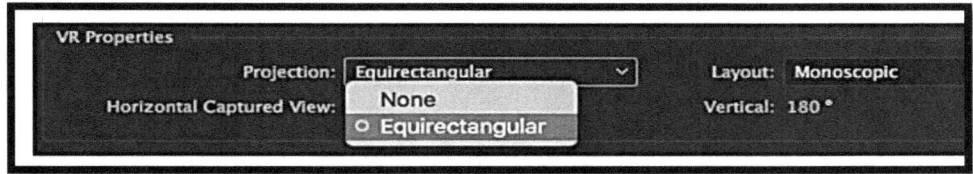

+ Next, choose a layout according to the kind of camera and footage you plan to shoot. This could be an over-under, side-by-side, or monochrome stereoscopic image. The sequence can only handle one sort of video at a time.

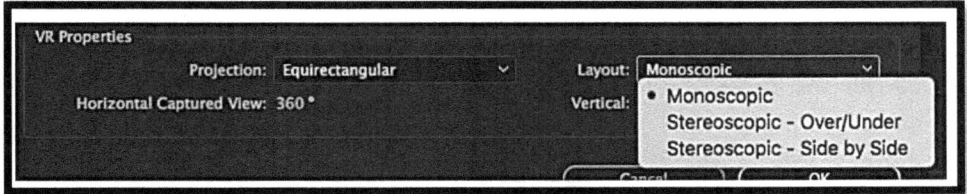

+ The number of degrees of view that are included in a single frame is customizable in the Horizontal and Vertical Captured vision choices. A full sphere, which is the default setting with 360 degrees horizontally and 180 degrees vertically, is what you typically desire.

⤴ You should be able to use your sequence on the VR Video display after selecting OK to preserve your modifications.

What Is Equirectangular Projection?

Think of an earth map, which is a flat depiction of a globe. Equirectangular projection, which converts latitude to Y and longitude to X coordinates, is merely used to unwrap the sphere.

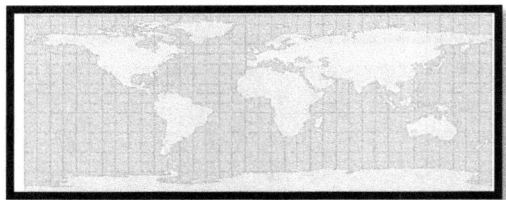

One common 360-degree video format that enables it to wrap into an immersive sphere is equirectangular footage. It can look like a twisted panorama when it's flat. You may alternate between equirectangular and VR perspectives when editing in Premiere. The unprocessed video will have an equirectangular shape.

Step two: Examine the VR Video Screen

Viewing the clips on the screen comes next after turning on VR editing for your sequence. You can watch your 360-degree video in one of two ways:

⤴ Right-click the monitor or choose the Settings button () on the right to activate VR Video.

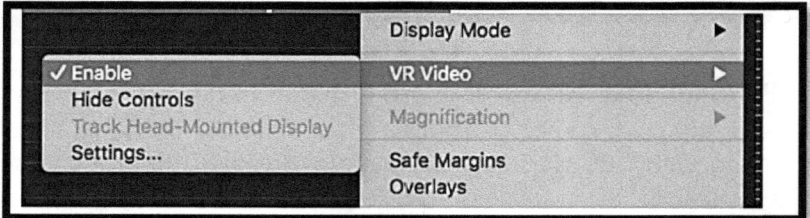

⊥ Drag the Toggle VR Video Display button to the toolbar by clicking the Editor Button (+).

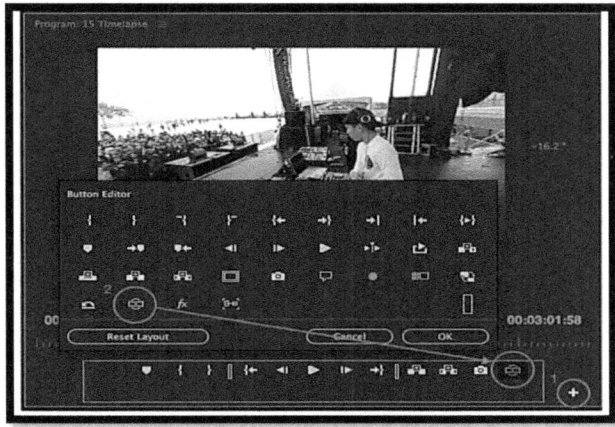

Go to VR Video > Settings after selecting the VR Video Display option. By adjusting the Monitor observe fields, you may choose which area of the sphere to view and create various viewing experiences when in VR Video Display mode. For instance, watching YouTube is simulated by 160 by 90 degrees. Note that these parameters affect the view window's aspect ratio. For instance, a 16:9 view window is displayed at 160 by 90 degrees.

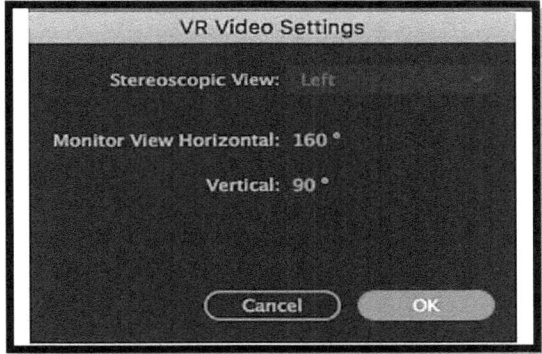

Step three: Adjust the Center Point and Edit the Video

After that, you may edit your 360-degree video just like you would any other video. This covers adding text, audio, images, color correction, slicing, trimming, and transitioning. Just be aware that the text will be fixed to a specific spot on the video and won't follow the viewer's head or attention naturally. Extending the text to a spherical viewpoint will cause some distortion. Additionally, warp stabilizers and other transformational effects won't work with 360-degree video.

A 360-degree video example of text distortion

The central location of the camera is another crucial factor. Unlike with a standard camera, you are unable to change the direction the viewer points. You can alter the shot's initial orientation, or center point, to draw attention to the topic. When you mix a lot of photos, you don't want people to turn around and see the problem again. **The easiest method for establishing the center point in Premiere is to use the Offset effect.**

- From the Effects panel, select Video Effects > Distort > Offset.
- Use the Offset effect on your clip in the timeline.
- The Effect Controls panel will open when you select a clip from the timeline.
- Drag the first number in the Shift Center left or right to pan the clip horizontally. Since the second number deviates from the vertical position, it should not be changed.

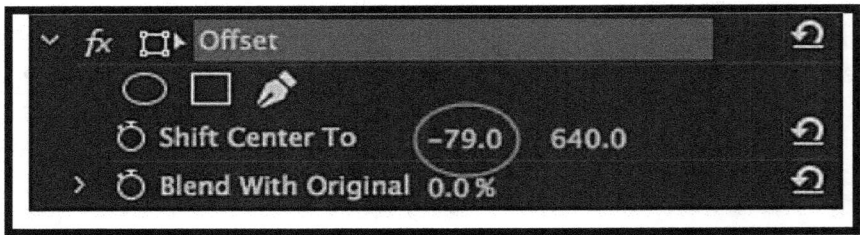

Keep in mind that after every shot in Premiere, the viewer's orientation is not instantly moved to the center. This implies that the viewer will likely overlook anything you were trying to emphasize in the middle of the image if they are still staring at the scene's back in the second frame.

Step four: Export

After choosing your timeline, press Ctrl/Cmd+M to export your video. Or go to the menu and choose File > Export > Media. The export window will open as a result. To make sure the Frame Layout is correct and the Video Is VR option is chosen, scroll to the bottom of the Video page after choosing your preferred codec.

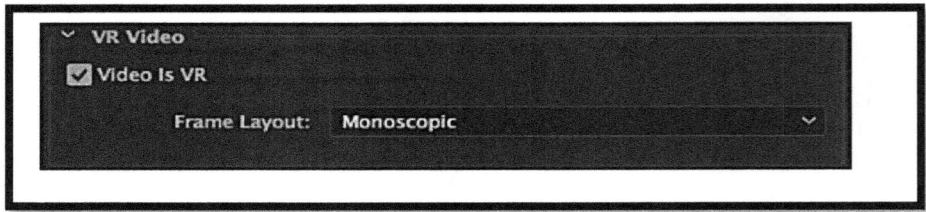

CHAPTER SEVEN
USING MARKERS AND CLIPS

Program Monitor Control Utilization

You can observe several significant distinctions between the Program Monitor and the Source Monitor.

What is a Program Monitor, exactly?

The frame that is now playing in your sequence is shown in the Program Monitor. The Timeline window shows the sequence as tracks and clip parts, while the Program Monitor displays the final video. The Timeline panel's time ruler and the Program Monitors are connected, with the former being a scaled-down counterpart of the latter.

Making use of the Program Monitor to add clips to a sequence

You already know that you can use the Source Monitor to select a partial clip and then drag, click, or press a key to add it to a sequence. A clip can also be added to a sequence by dragging it to the Program Monitor from the Source Monitor or Project panel. This causes a number of overlay visuals to show up in the Program Monitor, each of which represents a drop zone with a separate set of editing options for the action that follows.

Modify the Program Monitor

- At the beginning of the shot, at 00:00:13:00, position the Timeline's playhead. Since there isn't perfect movement constancy in this footage, let's include another HS Suit video segment.
- At the conclusion of the sequence, position the Timeline playhead anywhere over the Mid John shot. That would be around 00:00:20:00.
- Make a new In and Out point for the HS Suit clip in the Source Monitor. It should last roughly two seconds, so pick your favorite piece. The Source Monitor's lower-right section shows the duration that was chosen.
- Drag the Source Monitor clip onto the Program Monitor's Insert Before area.

Choosing the Resolution for Playback

Premiere Pro can play a variety of video formats, special effects, and other features in real-time without prerendering thanks to the Mercury Playback Engine. Mercury enhances performance by utilizing the computing capabilities of your machine. This implies that playing performance is affected by your CPU's speed (as well as its number of cores and kind), RAM's capacity, GPU's power, and storage device's speed. You can reduce the playback resolution to improve the smoothness of the video playback if your system is having trouble replaying each frame of your sequence (in the Program Monitor) or clips (in the Source Monitor). A hardware limitation is probably preventing your system from playing the movie if you experience stuttering, halting, and restarting while watching it. Keep in mind that it can be difficult to play high-resolution video files! A single frame of uncompressed full HD video is equivalent to about 8 million characters of text. For HD video playback, there are normally at least 24 frames per second, which adds out to 192 million characters per second. 4K video, sometimes referred to as UHD video, is four times higher! You won't be able to see every pixel in your photos if you lower the playback resolution, but it might greatly increase speed, which would greatly facilitate creative work. Since the Source Monitor and Program Monitor are typically smaller than the actual media size, video often has a greater quality than what can be shown. You might not always detect a change in the display as a result.

Steps to choose the resolution for playback

- Fill the Source monitor with the bin. The Source and Program Monitors have a Select Playback Resolution option in the lower right corner. Half-resolution is the playback resolution by default. Select it immediately if it hasn't been chosen before. In actuality, it has a quarter resolutions, which is half the horizontal and half the vertical resolution.
- Watch the video to observe how the quality varies when the resolution is reduced by half.
- To compare, rewatch the video with the resolution set to Full. It certainly appears to be comparable.
- Play the tape after reducing the resolution to 1/8; you'll notice a significant change. The images stay crisp even when the game is stopped. This is due to the fact that the pause resolution can be changed without affecting the playback resolution.
- Take into account lowering the resolution to 1/16. Premiere Pro analyzes every kind of material you work with, and if lowering resolution is more advantageous than the work involved, the option is turned off.
- 1/16 resolution can make a significant difference when working with extremely high-resolution content on a low-power device.
- To get ready for the remaining clips in this project, reset the value to 1/2. If your computer is powerful, you can choose to preview in full resolution and enhance the playing quality. This can be accomplished in another way. From the Settings menu in the Source Monitor or Program Monitor, select High-Quality Playback.
- The playback quality matches the file export quality when High-Quality Playback is chosen. Increased playback performance is exchanged for a slight quality loss when this option is disabled.

Resolution Paused

The Settings menus in the Source and Program Monitors can also be used to adjust the playback resolution. Paused Resolution is a second set of display resolution-related settings that may be found in each monitor's Settings menu. This option functions similarly to the playback resolution menu, except it only changes the resolution while the video is paused, as you might anticipate. Most editors choose to maintain Paused Resolution at Full. As a result, even if you are watching a lower-resolution movie, Premiere Pro will resume displaying a full-resolution image when you pause playback. The video will be displayed at its playback resolution when effects are being changed. Once you have finished adjusting the parameters, the pause resolution is engaged. Premiere Pro may make better use of your system hardware than some third-party special effects. Therefore, after adjusting the effect parameters, it can take a while for the image to refresh. While paused, you can reduce the resolution to expedite the process. The playback resolution and paused resolution settings do not affect the final quality when exporting to a file.

Reproducing virtual reality footage

Virtual reality headsets for the home aren't as inventive as they used to be. Premiere Pro offers built-in support for 360° and 180° video for VR headset display, as well as clip interpretation options, unique immersive video visual effects, desktop playback controls, integrated VR headset playback, and Ambisonics audio.

Making Use of Markers

It may be difficult to remember where you put a useful piece of a photograph or what you planned to do with it. If you could annotate clips and underline important sections for further watching, wouldn't that be helpful?

Markers: What Are They?

Markers let you point out and discuss certain moments in films and scenes. These temporal (time-based) indications are excellent for communicating with co-editors and staying organized. Markers are useful for both individual and group projects. Clips and sequences can have markers added to them.

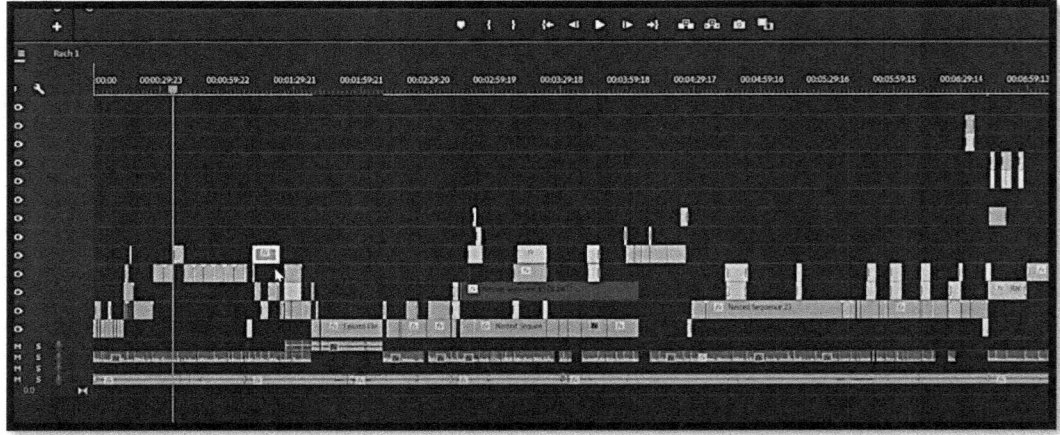

Analyzing the many types of markers

Similar to clips, markers are available in a range of colors and forms. You can alter a marker's type and color by double-clicking on it. **You can add a name, duration, and comments to this generic marker.**

+ **Chapter Marker:** A typical chapter marker can be made with the DVD and Blu-ray Disc production software.
+ Video distribution servers can divide content into chunks by using a segmentation marker.
+ **Web Link:** This marker is used by certain video formats to automatically load a webpage while the video is playing. Web link markers are included in the exported file when a sequence is exported to a supported format.
+ **Flash Cue Point:** This Adobe Animate marker is called Flash Cue Point. You can start working on your animation project while still editing your sequence by adding these cue points to Premiere Pro's Timeline.

This can be turned into a new kind of marking or used as a visual remembrance of a significant occasion.

+ Turn the Markers panel on. The Markers panel is linked to the Project panel by default. Choose Window > Markers, if it isn't already there.
+ A list of markers in chronological order is displayed in the Markers panel. Regardless of whether the Timeline, a sequence clip, or the Source Monitor are active (selected), markers for a sequence or clip show up in the same panel.
+ In the Markers panel, double-click the thumbnail of the marker. The Marker chat box opens as a result.
+ Observe how the Name box's insertion point is already flashing. Write something like, "Replace this image."
+ In the Duration box (blue numbers), type 400. To avoid closing the panel, do not press Enter or Return. Premiere Pro automatically adds punctuation, transforming

it to 00:00:04:00 (four seconds) when you click Tab to go on to the next field. To view the updated configuration, hit the Tab key now.

⁜ Click Enter/Return or Accept. The Timeline panel and Program Monitor now show the marker's duration. The text you entered in the Name area will appear when you zoom in on the Timeline.

⁜ Select Markers from the main menu bar at the top of the screen to see the commands that are available.

⁜ At the bottom of the Markers menu is the Ripple Sequence Markers command. When this option is selected, sequence markers will move in time with clips— editing techniques that alter a sequence's length and timing—as you insert and remove them. This setting keeps markers from shifting when clips are modified.

⁜ One of the menu's cleverly named commands is Copy Paste Includes Sequence Markers. If this option is enabled, all sequence markers inside the selection are also copied and pasted when you copy and paste a portion of a sequence that was chosen using In and Out points.

Transfer a Marker

Markers linked to a clip or sequence can be exported as a CSV (comma-separated values) file that spreadsheet editors can read, an HTML page with thumbnails, or a text file. **This is an excellent tool for reference and teamwork.**

⁜ To export markers, choose File > Export > Markers.

⁜ Using the Timeline panel to find clips. In addition to the Project panel, you may also search for clips in a certain order. To use the search options in the Project or Timeline panel, either click Edit > Find or press Command+F (macOS) or Ctrl+F (Windows), depending on whether the panel is active.

⁜ Premiere Pro highlights clips that fit your search parameters when it finds them in a sequence. Premiere Pro will highlight all matched clips if you choose Find All.

How to Change Marker Labels

Double-clicking a marker on the timeline will bring up the Marker Editor window. Certain jobs can be color-coded using color labels. You can also give each marker a name. Additional choices include enhancing the comment area with information and keywords to facilitate asset navigation. You can also change how long the marking lasts.

Use Marker Labels to Improve Your Video Editing Process

It's annoying when you forget to edit certain parts of a movie, but using markers can help you become a much better editor. Even though it isn't used much, this feature is among the most important to understand while using Adobe Premiere Pro. As you get more experienced with marks, the quality of your editing will improve. You can concentrate on mastering the other underutilized Premiere Pro features if you want to elevate your movie.

How to Remove an Adobe Premiere Pro Timeline Marker

- Double-clicking the clip in the project window will bring up the Source Monitor. This will allow you to relocate a marker within an existing clip in a sequence.
- Remove the marker icon from the time ruler on the Source Monitor. It should be noted that clip markers cannot be moved directly in the Timeline; instead, they must be moved in the Source Monitor.
- Drag a marker on the Timeline panel or the time ruler in the Program Monitor to move it in a sequence.
- Drag the current time indication to the marker's location after selecting the clip in the sequence to remove it.
- Make sure no clips are chosen before dragging the current-time indication to the marker in order to remove it from a sequence.
- Choose one of the submenu options after choosing Clear Clip Marker (or Clear Sequence Marker) from the Marker menu at the top of your workspace.
- When you select Present Marker, the marker is removed at that precise moment; when you select All Markers, all of the markers in the clip or sequence are removed; and when you select Numbered, a numbered marker is removed from a list of all markers.

Employing Track Locks and Sync

There are two methods for locking clips to tracks in the Timeline panel.
- Sync locks guarantee that, whether inserting or removing modifications, clips on other tracks stay in sync.
- Track locks prevent a track from being altered.

Making Use of Sync Locks

When an actor's lips move out of time with their voice, it's known as bad lip-syncing. Failure of this type of synchronization (sync) is readily apparent, whereas other sync problems could be harder to spot. The coordination of any two concurrent events is a crucial definition of synchronization. It could be as basic as a lower-third title that identifies the speaker, or it could be a musical event that matches a visual climax. **When numerous events take place simultaneously, synchronization takes place. (Using my files to work with)**

+ Find your sequence by opening the Sequences container.
+ Choose the Mid Suit clip from the available bin in the Source Monitor. Add a point of entry at around 01:15:35:18 and a point of departure at approximately 01:15:39:00.
+ Make sure there are no In or Out points at the beginning of the sequence and position the Timeline playhead there.
+ Click the Sync Lock button on the Video 2 track to disable it.
+ Verify that the Source V1 track is patched to the Timeline V1 track in your Timeline panel as it appears on the right (you can drag it into position or click to select a different location if necessary). The source track selection buttons need to be pressed, but the Timeline track header buttons are not crucial for the subsequent edit.

Making Use of Track Locks

In contrast to sync locks, track locks stop changes to a track. They are a great technique to preserve clips on specific tracks while working and prevent unwanted sequence changes. For instance, when you are importing individual video clips, you can lock your audio track. If the music track is locked and cannot be changed, you can lose sight of it while editing. A locked track's content cannot be changed, but it stays in the sequence. The Track Lock button is used to lock and unlock tracks. Clip sites are shown by diagonal lines on a locked track. Moving the audio clips would result in a loss of synchronization with the visual segments, even in this case where the sync locks are enabled.

Taking Care of Sequence Gaps

Up until recently, clips could only be added to a sequence; they couldn't be removed. The ability to reorder clips in a sequence and eliminate unnecessary parts is one benefit of nonlinear editing.

+ A lift edit will create a gap when removing clips or parts of clips, whereas an extract edit won't.
+ Although they operate in opposite directions, extract edits function similarly to insert edits. In a sequence, other clips move in to fill the void left by a deleted clip rather than moving out of the way to make room for a new clip.

- Zooming out of a lengthy, complex sequence may make it challenging to see small spaces between scenes. Choose Sequence > Go To Gap > Next In Sequence to have the next gap automatically determined.
- Once a gap between clips has been identified, you can remove it by selecting it (clicking it) and then using Backspace (Windows) or Eliminate (macOS).
- You can fix multiple gaps by choosing Sequence > fix Gap if you established In and Out points in the sequence and used the track targeting buttons to choose tracks. All that will be removed are the spaces between the marks.

Choosing Clips

Making choices is a crucial part of using Premiere Pro. The menu items you may access will vary depending on which panel you have set as active. **Choose your clips carefully before altering your sequences.**
- Each clip will contain at least two segments when working with audio and video clips in sequence: one audio segment and one or more video segments.
- Audio and video clip fragments from the same source media file are automatically connected when they are merged into a sequence. The other is automatically selected if you select one.
- By default, the Linked Selection button is active. Turn it off in the Timeline panel's upper-left corner to ignore the links between clips. Every clip linking is removed. You will only choose the audio clip you click on if there are numerous.
- Hold Option (macOS) or Alt (Windows) while selecting a series of clip segments to ignore connected selections without using the associated Selection button.

Choosing a clip or selection of clips

There are two methods for choosing clips inside a series.
- Use the In and Out points to choose time intervals.
- Choose the segments of the clip.

Additional choices

- Clicking on a clip from a series is the simplest method. By double-clicking, you may modify the In and Out locations (which will update in real time in the sequence) and access the sequence clip instance in the Source Monitor.
- The Selection tool (by default chosen in the Tools panel) is often used when adding choices. V is the keyboard shortcut for this tool.
- You can add or subtract sequence clip segments from the selection by holding down the Shift key while doing so. The chosen clips don't all need to be continuous.
- Drag the Selection tool across multiple clips to select them. To create a selection box, move the mouse pointer over an empty area of the Timeline panel and drag. You can drag the selection box over any clip, even if it's only partially there.

- The clip from the highest targeted track that the Timeline playhead crosses over can likewise be chosen automatically. This is particularly helpful for editing and effect setting with a keyboard. Choose Sequence > Selection Follows Playhead to activate the feature.
- Clips won't be chosen automatically during playback if this option is enabled.

Selecting each clip on a song

- Open the Timeline panel and press Command+A (macOS) or Ctrl+A (Windows) to pick every clip on each track.
- The Track Select Forward and Track Select Backward tools can be accessed with the keyboard commands A and Shift+A, respectively. By clicking and holding the Track Select Forward tool, you can use the Track Select Backward tool.

Clips dragging

Snap is located in the Timeline panel's upper left corner and is on by default. The clip segment edges automatically align when snapping is enabled. This straightforward but practical tool aids in the appropriate organization of clip segment frames. Snapping can be enabled or disabled with the S keyboard shortcut. You can press S to toggle snapping on and off while dragging, even if you've already begun moving an object to make adjustments. Learning whether snapping is on or off could be a helpful shortcut because it's easy to forget.

The actions are:
- Drag the Timeline, HS Suit's last footage a little to the right after selecting it. Just put a space before it because the sequence doesn't contain any further clips after this one. Not a single other clip has been affected.
- Drag the clip back to its original location after making sure the Snap option (blue) is selected. A portion of the footage will appear to jump into place at the last second if you move slowly. When this happens, you can be sure it's at the right place. Observe how the playhead and the clip change to the end of the cutaway shot on the Video 2 track.
- To make the two clips overlap, drag the clip to the left until its right edge touches the right edge of the previous clip. The new clip takes the place of the previous clip's finale when it is released. By default, the Overwrite editing mode is selected when dragging clips.
- The clip can be undone to return to its initial position.

Making a ripple delete edit and a delete

There are two comparable methods for removing clips by picking specific clip segments: Delete and Ripple Delete. **After selecting the second unwanted orange clip, Cutaways, with a single click, try the two alternatives below:**
- The selected clip or clips are removed when the Delete/Backspace key is pressed, leaving a space in their place. The lift edit is comparable to this.

- Shift+Delete (Windows) or Shift+Forward Delete (macOS) eliminates the chosen clips without leaving a space. Like an edit for an excerpt.
- On a Mac keyboard without a dedicated Forward Delete key, press and hold the Function (fn) key while using the Delete key.
- The outcomes are the same as those of Lift or Extract edits. By combining In and Out points with track-targeting settings, it is also feasible to remove or ripple certain segments of clips.
- Content is copied to the clipboard and may be positioned elsewhere in the sequence when extracting or lifting edits are used to eliminate material. When something is removed, it simply disappears.

Eliminating a Clip

Both the output of certain clips and the output of a full track can be turned on or off. Although they are not visible or audible, disabled clips stay in the sequence. When you want to compare many versions or performance takes recorded on different tracks, or when you want to analyze background layers, this tool is helpful for selectively obscuring parts of a complicated, multilayered sequence. **The actions are:**
- Right-click a clip and choose Enable to deselect or remove it.
- Avoid right-clicking the small clip FX indicator when you are right-clicking clips in a sequence because this will display options relating to effects instead of the standard clip settings. As you move through the sequence, you'll notice that the footage is still there but can no longer be viewed.
- To make the clip visible, right-click on it once more and choose Enable.

CHAPTER EIGHT
THE USE OF MOTION GRAPHICS

Motion Graphics

Motion graphics templates are special file formats created using After Effects or Premiere Pro. Because they provide customizable templates with easily adjustable settings that can be changed from within Premiere Pro, these templates are a great tool for editors using the application. They do a fantastic job of showcasing After Effects' motion graphics capabilities. To generate new titles and graphics, users can use the Type and Shape tools that are incorporated into Premiere Pro. These can then be exported as Motion Graphics templates for distribution or later usage. Additionally, Premiere Pro comes with pre-built templates that may be used right away, including sample Motion Graphics designs made in both After Effects and Premiere Pro. **Additionally, Premiere Pro expands editors' options and adaptability by enabling them to import Motion Graphics designs from a range of websites:**

- **Local Templates Folder:** Premiere Pro's Motion Graphics templates are readily accessible and usable by editors.
- **Creative Cloud Libraries:** These libraries contain templates that are easily available and uniform for use across several projects.
- **Adobe Stock:** A vast selection of Motion Graphics templates are available for editors to utilize in their work.

Along with the seamless integration of After Effects motion graphics capabilities and expanded creative options within Premiere Pro's editing environment, these import methods have greatly increased the amount of Motion Graphics templates available to Premiere Pro editors.

Install Motion Graphics Templates

You can use the Local Templates folder in the Graphics Template panel to save a Motion Graphics template to your PC. The Project panel does not include motion graphics templates, in contrast to media. The Graphics Templates Panel can be used to view and manage Motion Graphics Templates (MOGRTs). Go to Graphics Templates under Window.

- To install a template in the Local Templates folder, drag it into the Graphics Template panel browser. Alternatively, you can click the Install button in the lower right corner to install your MOGRTs.
- Click Open once you've found the Motion Graphics template folder.

After being copied to the Local Templates Folder, the template appears in the Graphics Template window.

Reminder: A dialog box asking you to overwrite or cancel the installation will show up if there is already a Motion Graphics template with the same name.

If a Motion Graphics template is not compatible with the version of your project you are trying to install, Premiere Pro alerts you. A motion graphics template won't work if it was made using an After Effects version that was later than this one.

The folder containing local templates

The Local Templates folder is the default place for installing MOGRTs or licensing them from Adobe Stock using the Graphics Templates Panel.

> - macOS: username/Library/Application Support/Adobe/Common/Motion Graphics Templates/
> - Windows: root://Users/username/AppData/Roaming/Adobe/Common/Motion Graphics Templates/

Take note:

- The Local Templates folder directory is hidden on macOS, while the AppData folder is hidden on Windows. To view these files, unhide them from your computer.
- If you try to install a Motion Graphics template that is the same name as one that is already in the Local Templates folder of Premiere Pro, a dialog box will show up. Terminating the installation or changing the current template are two options.

Premiere Pro will alert users if they attempt to install a Motion Graphics template that is not compatible with the version of the project they are working on. Compatibility problems occur when a Motion Graphics template is made using a version of After Effects that is older than the one used in the Premiere Pro project. If the Motion Graphics template has features or capabilities that the project version being used does not support, Premiere Pro will show an incompatibility alert.

Arrange templates for motion graphics

Establish a Library

Think of your computer as a huge bookcase that has all of your information, pictures, and videos. Similar to how you would arrange books in different areas of a library for convenient access, the video editing software Premiere Pro assists you in creating your own libraries to elegantly arrange and manage your video assets. To get started, picture the Premiere Pro Libraries panel as a separate area of your bookshelf that displays the collections of libraries you have built. **You can use this panel to create a new library or section to arrange your video content, as shown below:**
- First, confirm that you can navigate to 'Windows' and then 'Libraries' in Premiere Pro to reach the Libraries panel. Launching the library portion of your bookshelf is the same as activating the Libraries panel.

- By choosing the hamburger icon (three horizontal lines), you can choose Libraries. Choose 'Create New Library' from the menu that appears. It's like setting aside a new area of your bookshelves.
- To input the name of your new library, a text box will show up on the screen. Following
- Click the 'Create' button after entering the name. And presto! To arrange your video resources on your bookshelf, you have recently added a new component to your Libraries panel.
- **Assume you want to save a sizable picture or graphic in this just formed library. It can be included in this way:**
  - To save important graphics in Premiere Pro, use the Graphics Templates Panel, which functions similarly to a special drawer?
  - Right-click on a graphic to add it to your library, much like when you select a single image or item from the drawer.
  - Choose 'Copy to Library' and enter the name of the library to save the image. It's like placing an item or photograph in a newly built section of your bookcase.

The picture has been saved or sent to your newly arranged Premiere Pro library. Think of the Graphics Templates Panel section as a display where you can look at different Motion Graphics templates, similar to perusing a collection of amazing items for your movies.
You can perform the following tasks in this domain:
- Similar to looking for a certain item in a catalog, you can use keywords in the search box to find particular Motion Graphics templates.
- Hovering over these templates will allow you to preview them in a manner like to perusing a catalog.
- Similar to how products are arranged by name or usage frequency, templates can be arranged by title or most recent use.
- Like labeling or marking products in a catalog for improved identification, you may rename and tag these templates to make them easier to locate later. Similar to storing a page in a catalog, you can click the star icon to save a template as a favorite if you like it. This will make it easier to find later.
- Premiere Pro's libraries and panels make it simpler to find what you need, which streamlines video management and editing. This is similar to placing books or other items in different sections of a catalog or library to make them easier to find and identify.

Examine and control templates for motion graphics

- Motion Graphics templates are available for browsing in the Graphics Templates Panel. Both licensed Motion Graphics templates and premium, hand-picked Stock templates that don't need a license can be found and viewed using the Graphics Templates panel browser. You can do the following in the My Templates window.

- Using the search bar, you may quickly locate what you're looking for. To narrow down the templates that are available locally or throughout your libraries, use the checkboxes.
- To obtain animation samples for themes with video thumbnails, use the hover scrub function.
- Sort Motion Graphics templates according to their titles or most recent usage.
- Click the star to select the Motion Graphics template of your choice. Next, use the Favorites filter next to the search box to rapidly browse your favorites.
- To improve organization and searchability, rename and tag Motion Graphics templates using the Info View.

Adjust the MOGRT thumbnail dimensions

Note: You may also use the Libraries panel in Premiere Pro to import Motion Graphics templates from Adobe Stock or Creative Cloud Libraries.

Examine Several Libraries

Additionally, you can simultaneously examine templates from many libraries.
- All library results are displayed when All is selected.
- When switching to the library, only templates from it are shown.
- It is possible to choose more than one library at once. Every choice is reversed when All is selected.

Control Extra Folders

You can create new local paths or navigate to custom folders that have been assigned a route in Premiere Pro. Only the Local Templates Folder check box is visible if there isn't a custom folder. The Local list is where you may find a custom folder that you entered as a path in Premiere Pro. **To add new custom folders as paths, adhere to these guidelines:**
- Click the hamburger symbol next to the Graphics Templates window to create new routes.
- Select the Manage Additional Folders dialog box from the list that appears.
- In order to create a new folder, select Create. Click Select Folder once you've chosen a file. The Manage Additional Folders dialog box can now be used to access the folder.
- Click Remove once you've chosen the folder you want to remove.

Drag and drop between places

Similar to operating system files, MOGRTs can be copied or transferred. You can drag and drop MOGRTs between local folders on the same system, or you can copy them if they are on different drives. Additionally, MOGRTs can be moved from a local folder to a library. To help you stay organized, a blue outline will show where a MOGRT is now located in the library when you select it in the Graphics Templates tab.

Adding your disk's local directories

To handle MOGRTs on disk, just click the Add symbol in the Graphics Templates panel's top right corner. By heading to the My Templates browser, you can add a shared network folder, local folder, or cloud drive. Additionally, you may quickly find your personalized local folders on disk by right-clicking on the location in the Graphics Templates panel and choosing Reveal in Finder/Explorer. The actual folder containing the MOGRTs must be provided; if a parent folder containing MOGRTs is included under subfolders, the templates won't show up in the Graphics Templates panel. By selecting the Rename, Delete, and Show in Finder/Explorer options from the context menu, you may control your MOGRT disk folders from within the Graphics Templates panel. The folder on disk won't be affected if a location is changed or deleted from the Graphics Templates panel.

Taking Out the Default Templates

Help users get started with MOGRTs in Premiere Pro, we have a set of default templates in the Local Templates Folder. We are aware that some people would rather focus only on their belongings. **To get rid of these templates, just use these steps:**
- Right-click the Local Templates folder in the browser tree.
- Select Show in Explorer or Finder.
- Save the PrMogrtInstall13-0-0.txt file after removing every MOGRT from the Local Templates folder.

The MOGRTs will reappear when Premiere Pro restarts if you ever want to restore them. Just delete the.txt file.

Utilize Adobe Stock's Motion Graphics Templates

Premiere Pro can make use of a wide range of well-designed titles, lower thirds, transitions, and graphics from Adobe Stock. To choose and modify the exact image you desire without switching workspaces, navigate through Adobe Stock's Graphics Templates panel. To access Adobe Stock's Motion Graphics templates, navigate to Premiere Pro's Graphics Templates or Libraries panels.

Search Adobe Stock for Motion Graphics templates using the Graphics Templates Panel

Click the Browse option in the Graphics Templates window, and then choose Adobe Stock. Press Enter after entering your search term. The stock results, which look like pages in a large catalog, are the numerous Motion Graphics templates that are available for usage in your video productions. The size of the thumbnails you set, the number of templates, and the maximum number of pages that may be shown simultaneously in the browser panel all affect how many pages you view.

You can utilize and explore these stock findings as follows:
- Methods of Browsing:
  - To navigate between pages, use the 'previous' and 'next' arrows, just like in a catalog.
  - Like with an index, put the page number in the text edit box to view a specific page.
  - You can choose the License and Download button or drag a Motion Graphics template into your video project to license it.
  - Click the I icon beneath the image to get a preview of the animation or learn more about a template.
- Licensing and Downloading:
  - Click the License or Download icon and save the Motion Graphics template to the Local Templates folder to grant permission.
  - Once a Motion Graphics template has been chosen for your video project, you can include it into your sequence in the manner described below:
- Including Sequence Templates
  - Use the 'Browse' option in the Graphics Templates tab to view these templates. It's like looking through the catalog section.
  - In your sequence, drag and drop the appropriate template into a video track. This is comparable to picking out an item from the catalog and setting it on your desk.
  - Until the template is fully loaded, Premiere Pro may show offline content when you add it to a sequence. If the template calls for the missing fonts, you can install them.
  - After adding the template to your sequence, you can catalog by choosing the Edit option in the Graphics Templates panel.
  - As a result, you can utilize and change Motion Graphics templates in Premiere Pro's editing workspace just like you can when browsing the collection. These templates are available for you to view, license, and use in your video projects.
  - Make it look different. This is comparable to altering the characteristics of an object you choose from the

Include motion graphic templates to a sequence

- **Getting to the Templates:** Choose the 'Browse' option once the Graphics Templates window has opened. Some accessible templates are available on this page.
- **Including a Model in Your Sequence:** Drag your preferred template from the Graphics Templates window onto a video track in your sequence. It's like putting something on your desk after removing it from a shelf.
- **Status of Media Loading:** The media may appear to be 'offline' in Premiere Pro when you add the template to your sequence. This status indicates that the

template is currently being imported into your project. It's similar to having something prepared but holding off until it's completely available.

- **Restoring Missing Fonts (if required):** If the templates you've uploaded call for fonts that aren't on your computer, Premiere Pro will alert you about the fonts that are missing. You can fix this problem and guarantee that the template functions correctly by installing the necessary fonts.
- **Changing the Look of the Template:** Once the template has been incorporated into your sequence, you can modify its look and features. To make changes and enhancements to the item you have chosen from your shelf, pick the Edit option in the Graphics Templates panel. Here, you can modify different parts of the template to suit your project's requirements. Choosing, adding, and editing Motion Graphics templates for your video project is simple with Premiere Pro. Your editing workspace's Graphics Templates panel serves as a library of pre-made templates as well as a toolbox for creating your own.

Your Motion Graphics Template can be customized

You may easily alter Motion Graphics templates in Premiere Pro to suit the requirements of your project. Here's how to modify these templates step-by-step:

- **Choose the Template:** Choose the Motion Graphics template you want to use once you've finished creating your sequence.
- Go to the Graphics Templates settings window and choose Edit to change the properties as necessary.
- **Change Template Properties:** Depending on the kind of template you're using, your options will vary.
  - ➤ You can alter the source text, motion settings, and colors using the options provided by the template maker.
  - ➤ Modify elements such fake styles, fonts, and sizes.
  - ➤ In templates, control groups can have their attributes changed by expanding or contracting.
  - ➤ You can use templates to adjust the data values when working with spreadsheet data in TSV or CSV format.
  - ➤ You can use own media in place of pictures or videos by using replaceable media templates.
- **Real-time Updates:** The template instantaneously changes when the controls in the template attributes are changed.
- **Modify Template Duration:** To change how long a Motion Graphics template plays, select it in the timeline and drag the red arrows in the corners.

Revising Templates for Motion Graphics

After Effects motion graphics templates that are used in Premiere Pro scenes can be altered.

- Using Alt/Option, drag and drop the modified template onto the one that is currently in your sequence to update it.

+ Modifications to the template can be applied to specific cases or the project as a whole. Your changes are kept during the update process wherever possible.

Using the customizable Motion Graphics templates in Premiere Pro, you can easily modify visually appealing elements to suit project requirements. This feature ensures that editing is simple while maintaining the flexibility of your creative process.

Keyframing and Motion

Activating Clips

A clip inside the frame can be moved, rotated, and resized using the Motion effect. The Program Monitor may undergo numerous modifications. Only the controls for the clip that is presently selected are shown in the Effect Controls window. This clip could be a clip that was opened in the Source Monitor or a fragment of a sequence.

Modifying the Motion Effect

In a Premiere Pro sequence, effects are automatically added to each clip component. These are referred to as intrinsic or fixed effects. Motion is the term for one of these phenomena. To modify a clip's Motion effect, select it sequentially and navigate to the Effect Controls panel. To modify the Motion effect's parameters, expand it. You can alter the position, size, and rotation of a clip with the Motion effect. Look at how a clip was moved within a sequence using this effect.

+ Launch a project.
+ Either select Window > Workspaces > Effects from the Window menu or select Effects from the Workspaces panel. Reset the workspace.
+ Start your desired sequence if it isn't already open. There is only one clip in this short sequence.
+ Make sure Fit is selected in the Select Zoom Level menu on the Program Monitor.

The composition as a whole must be taken into account while setting visual effects. Only how the sequence is displayed is altered by this menu; the contents remain same. Zooming in or out to apply effects or notice small details in a picture may be useful, but you should usually leave this option set to Fit.

Make use of the preference

To make sure the clip animates into the frame, keyframes with varying values at different times have been inserted, along with adjustments to the clip's Position, Scale, and Rotation attributes.

Comprehending Motion Settings

These controls, in spite of their name, are immobile unless they are configured. By default, clips are positioned at their original size in the middle of the Program Monitor. Click the name of the panel after selecting the clip from the sequence to view it. Click the triangle next to Motion in the Effect Controls panel's Video Effects section to view the available options.

The choices are as follows:

+ **Position:** Line up the vertical (y) and horizontal (x) axes with the clip. The position is determined by measuring the distance from the top-left corner of the clip image to an anchor point, which is by default the center of the image. A 1280 x 720 clip would be positioned 640, 360 by default, which is halfway across and halfway down.

+ **Scale:** By default, clips are scaled to 100% of their original size, including Scale Height if Uniform Scale is not enabled. This includes Scale Height when Uniform Scale is deselected. Reduce this value to make a clip smaller. Photographs that are enlarged by 10,000 times will appear blurry and distorted.

+ **Scale Width:** Deselect Uniform Scale to get Scale Width. This lets you change the height and width of the clip separately.

+ **Rotation:** A picture can be rotated by a flat spin, much like when you look at a rotating turntable or carousel from above. Additionally, you can specify rotations or degrees. As an illustration, 450° = 1x90 (one complete 360° rotation plus an extra 90°). Clockwise rotation is caused by positive numbers, while counterclockwise rotation is caused by negative numbers.

+ Some controls will overlap or be obscured if the Effect Controls panel is too small. Adjust the panel's size as necessary before changing the effect parameters.

+ **Anchor Point:** The anchor point, which is in the center of the clip image by default, serves as the basis for rotation and position changes. Any location can be used for this, including a point outside the clip's image or a corner of the clip. For instance, if you change the Rotation option after setting the anchor point to the corner of the clip, the clip will revolve around that corner instead of the picture center. You might need to reposition the clip inside the frame if you shift the anchor point to the image.

+ **Anti-flicker Filter:** This filter works well with high-detail photos and video clips that include parallel lines, small lines, or jagged edges, as these can result in moiré effects. Such fine-grained images sometimes flicker when moving. To minimize flickering and add a small blur, set this value to 1.00.

Modifying the Rotation, Size, and Position of a Clip

Multiple independent configuration changes can be combined with the Motion effect. In the following example, you will utilize Motion to create a behind-the-scenes documentary's opening by sequentially changing the parameters for numerous clips.

Modifying Position

To begin, let's use keyframes to move a layer around. Making changes to the clip positioning is the first stage.

The image will begin off-screen and scroll across the screen from right to left.

- Launch the sequence of your choice. Go over the order to familiarize yourself with the specifics. Several of the tracks in the series had their output turned off. These tunes will be used in the future.
- Move the Timeline panel's playhead to the start of the series.
- Adjust Fit to the Zoom Level of the Program Monitor. To choose the first video clip from the V3 track, click once. To see the thumbnails more clearly, you can choose to increase the track height.
- After you select a clip, the Effect Controls window shows the effect controls for that clip.
- Select the Toggle Animation stopwatch button for Position (the icon should turn blue) in the Effect Controls panel. In the Effect Controls panel, this creates a keyframe at the current playhead position and activates keyframing for this preset. Because the keyframe symbol is placed to the first frame of the clip, it is somewhat concealed.
- Every time you adjust the position of the playhead, Premiere Pro will automatically generate a keyframe if animation for Position is enabled.
- There are two numbers on the Position slider. They stand for the values on the x and y axes, respectively. To start the Position setting, click the blue number and type -640 as the x-axis value (the first number).
- The V1 and V2 tracks are seen below as the clip shifts off-screen to the left. Since track V2 is currently empty, the full screen is occupied by the Map.jpg clip from track V1.
- Advance the playhead to the chosen clip's last frame (00:00:4:23). Either the Timeline or Effect Controls panels can be used for this.

Modifying the Clip Size

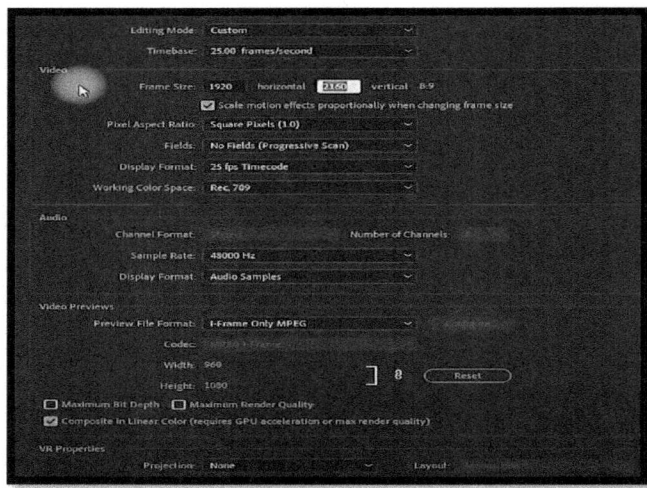

The size of the items in a sequence can be changed in a variety of ways. By default, items added to a sequence are shown at 100% of their initial size. **There are multiple methods to adjust a clip image if its size differs from that of the sequence frame:**

- In the Effect Controls box, adjust the Scale attribute of the Graphics > Vector Motion or Video > Motion effects.
- To adjust the frame size, right-click on the sequence clip and choose Set To Frame Size. This modifies the Video > Motion effect's Scale property to make the clip fit inside the frame. Scale is still adjustable.
- Select Scale to Frame Size with a right-click on the sequence clip. With the exception of Premiere Pro resizing the image to the new (often lower) resolution, this has the same effect as the Set to Frame Size option. Even if the original clip was of high quality, the image can still look fuzzy even if you use the Motion > Scale option to scale it back up.
- You may also select Scale to Frame Size or Set to Frame Size automatically by heading to Premiere Pro > Preferences > Media > Default Media Scaling (macOS) or Edit > Preferences > Media > Default Media Scaling (Windows). The option does not affect previously imported things, but it does apply to newly imported assets.

Using Interpolation Keyframes

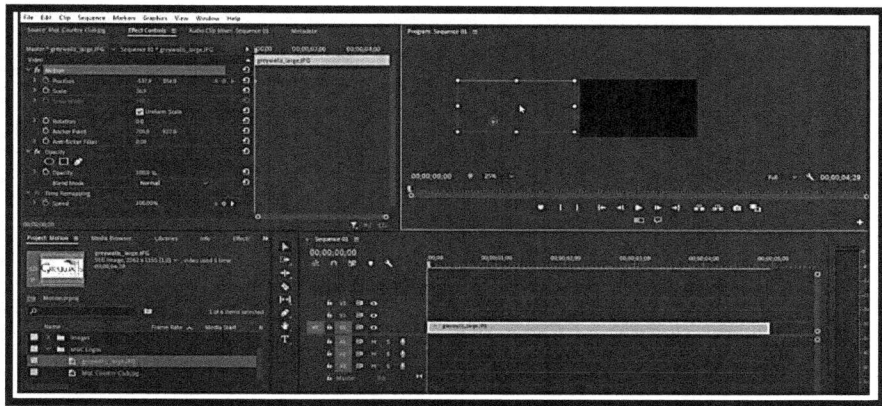

The word "keyframe" originates from traditional animation, where the main artist would sketch the most important (or key) poses. From one keyframe to the next, assistant animators would then draw the individual frames that represented each stage of the animation. You are the master animator when using Premiere Pro, and the computer interpolates values between the keyframes you supply.

Modify the interpolation technique for keyframes

One of the most beneficial yet sometimes overlooked aspects of keyframes is interpolation. This is a creative approach to explain the specific trip from point A to point

B. There are five interpolation algorithms in Premiere Pro. Altering the procedure could produce a different animation. **Any interpolation method can be accessed by right-clicking on a keyframe icon.**

- **Linear:** For keyframes, linear interpolation is the default method. It keeps the rate of change between keyframes constant. The first keyframe marks the beginning of changes, which continue at a steady pace until the following keyframe. The second and third keyframes' rates of change swiftly follow, and so on. This can look very mechanical, yet it can also be effective and even fast.
- Compared to interframe keyframes, bezier provides the greatest versatility. The contour of the value graph or motion route on either side of the keyframe can be altered by adjusting the manual handles on Bezier keyframes, which are named after the French engineer Pierre Bézier. The Bezier handles that show up when you select a keyframe can be used to generate modifications with acute angles or smooth curves. For instance, you could have an object move gently to a spot on the screen before suddenly reversing course.
- The rate of change throughout the frame is constant with Auto Bezier keyframes. When the settings are altered, they are automatically updated. This is a fast and dependable way to fix Bezier keyframes.
- **Continuous Bezier:** This option enables manual control, much like Auto Bezier. Transitions on the motion or value route will always be seamless, but you can use control handles to alter the Bezier curve's shape on both sides of the keyframe.
- **Hold:** Only temporal (time-based) characteristics are covered by this functionality. Over time, hold-style keyframes maintain their value without undergoing a smooth transition. When creating staccato motions or a quick disappearance of an object, this is helpful. The value of the first keyframe is kept when the Hold style is applied until the subsequent hold keyframe is reached, at which point the value instantly changes.

Using the Effect of Auto Reframe

There were several ratios before 16:9 was adopted as the standard delivery aspect ratio for internet video distribution platforms and television broadcasts. 1.78:1, or 1.78 times wider than tall, is a frequent term used to describe this standard. For motion pictures that are released in theaters, the two typical aspect ratios are 1.85:1 and 2.39:1. To satisfy a variety of conventional video distribution needs, big film companies usually produce several versions of a movie with various aspect ratios and color standards. However, they are often near 169 or 43 dimensions. Significantly varied aspect ratios are once again in demand due to the growth of popular social networking sites, especially on smartphones. You can repeat scenes in Premiere Pro by using the Auto Reframe option. It is possible to automate the process of changing a whole sequence's aspect ratio. Before applying and customizing the Auto Reframe effect for each clip—which automatically maintains areas of interest, such faces, on-screen—Premiere Pro examines the images in your film. Clicking build in this dialog box causes Premiere Pro to build a new sequence depending on the options you choose. The initial sequence will remain unaltered. **The conditions are as follows:**

  + **Series Name:** Give the new sequence a name. By default, the old name is associated with the new aspect ratio.
  + **Target Aspect Ratio:** Indicate which aspect ratio is preferred. Numerous sequences with various aspect ratios can be produced by repeating this method.
  + **Motion Tracking:** Specify how many keyframes will be utilized to track motion during the scene. It is advised to use Speedier movements for faster action and Slower Motion for slower, more fluid movements.
  + **Clip Nesting:** Choose if you want to nest clips. Each clip can only have one Motion effect, and unless you nest the clips, any motion keyframes that are already there will be overwritten in the new sequence. Your video's transition effects will be eliminated if you overlay it.

Adding Motion Effects to a Silhouette

There are various motion-controlling effects in Premiere Pro. You could wish there were more options, even though the Motion effect is the most readily available. You can increase object control (including 3D rotation) by using the Transform and Basic 3D effects. With one exception—fixed effects like Motion, Opacity, and Time Remapping always appear last—the order in which visual effects are applied matches the order in which they are displayed in the Effect Controls panel. When using lighting effects or effects that alter a clip's form or placement, this could lead to issues. You will learn how to blend effects in this exercise to achieve results that look natural.

CHAPTER NINE
INCLUDING TRANSITIONS

Transition Effects: What Are They?

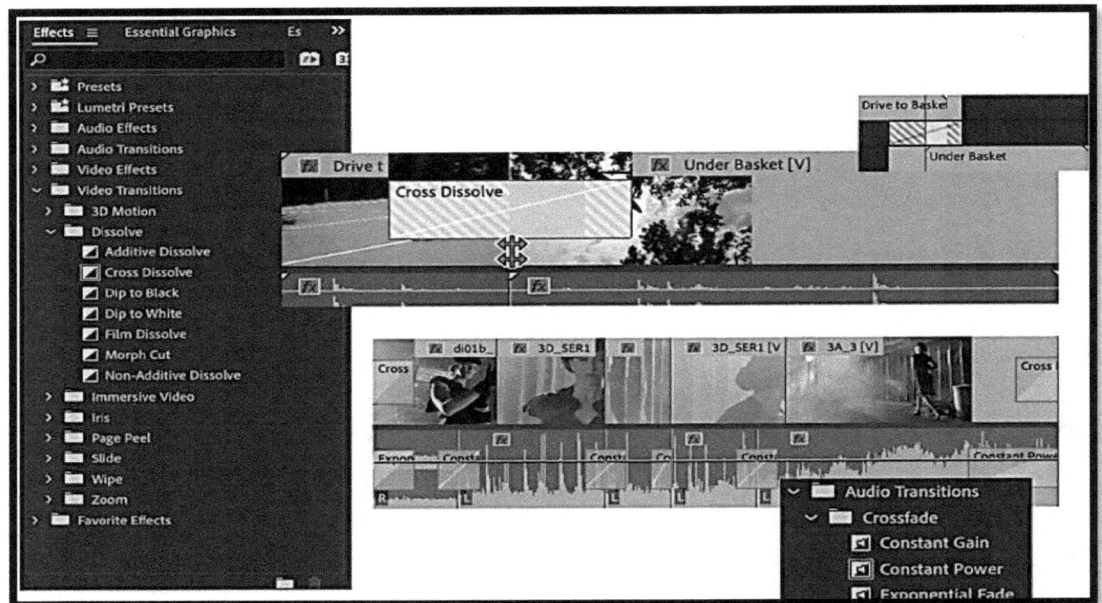

For connecting adjacent clips in a series, Adobe Premiere Pro offers a variety of special effects and pre-made animations. The audience can go from one scene to another with the use of these transitions, which include dissolves, page wipes, and color changes. Transitions can be used to signal a significant shift in the plot as well as to make the change between two segments easier. Adding transitions to your project is an art. Simply drag the selected transition from the Effects panel into the timeline's cut between two clips to use them. Their placement, length, and settings—such as motion, direction, and beginning and ending points—are where the skill lies. The Timeline panel has certain transition settings that can be changed, although the Effect Controls panel usually allows for more accurate adjustments. To see the parameters for each transition effect in the Effect Controls window, select it. The Effect Controls panel has a useful A/B timeline display (more on that later) in addition to the many parameters for each transition. This makes it simple to adjust the length of transitions, adjust their timing in relation to an edit point, and apply transitions to clips that lack sufficient head or tail frames, or extra content to overlap at the clip's head or tail.

Knowing When to Employ Transitions

Similar to screenwriting, transitions are a fundamental narrative component in video editing. They are effective when they help the audience comprehend the plot.

+ You can go forward in time or switch between indoor and outdoor settings in a video. To convey to the viewer a change in location, time, or a character's point of view, an animation transition, fade to black, or dissolve can be employed.

+ A scene is said to be over when it fades to darkness at the conclusion. The difficulty with transitions is being careful, which typically means being restricted, unless, of course, the desired creative outcome is a total lack of restraint.

+ Regardless of their taste in art, your audience will trust your choices if they seem well-planned and powerful. Knowing whether transition effects are appropriate and improper requires knowledge and experience. Less is usually better when in doubt.

+ A well-established visual language is recognized and responded to by modern audiences. Your viewers will know they are watching a character's dream right away, for instance, if a character nods off and the screen goes out of focus but everything in the frame shines wonderfully. You might be able to make more imaginative choices if you take the time to master this kind of visual language.

A Clip Handle's Significance

You need to know about edit points and handles in order to comprehend transition effects. The transition from one clip to the next is known as the edit point in a sequence. This is sometimes referred to as a cut, but it can also be called an edit. Similar to two bricks adjacent to each other, Premiere Pro uses vertical lines to indicate the end of one clip and the start of the next.

+ An in point and an out point were used to select the proper location when a clip was first edited into a sequence. The unused portions at the start and finish of the clip remain visible but are hidden in the Timeline window when you edit the chosen clip segment into a sequence. These extra parts are referred to as handles or clip handles.

+ Between the clip's initial start and the In point you choose, there is a handle. Furthermore, a handle joins a clip's original end to the Out point that you specify. The Source Monitor's time ruler indicates how much footage is in your hands.

+ You might have simply put the In and Out points at the start or finish of the tape, or you might not have used them at all. In this scenario, one end of the cassette would either have completely unused content or no unused media at all.

+ You've reached the end of the original clip and there are no more frames left if you notice a tiny triangle in the upper-right or upper-left corner of the clip in the Timeline panel.

Because handles naturally overlap the incoming and outgoing clips, they are necessary for transition effects to function.

Including Transition Effects in Videos

There are numerous video transition effects available in Premiere Pro. The great majority of the options are included in the Effects panel's Video Transitions section. To find further transitions, locate the Video Effects > Transition group in the Effects panel. However, the purpose of these effects is to gradually expose the visual content of the clip between the beginning and end frames, and they are meant to be applied throughout the entire clip. Text and images can be superimposed with ease using this category.

Linking two clips together using a transition

Let's include some transitions. You may observe the end result by repeating the procedure as you move through the phases.

+ Because the Plus symbol is commonly found on the same key, it is simple to remember that pressing the = key (if your keyboard has one) zooms in on an English-language keyboard.

+ Press the equals symbol (=) key two or three times to zoom in close after positioning the Timeline playhead between clips 1 and 2. The navigator at the bottom of the Timeline panel can be used to zoom in if the = key is absent from your keyboard.

+ Over the edit point between clips 1 and 2, apply the Dip to White transition effect from the Effects panel's Dissolve group. There are three sites where the impact will be corrected. Rather than at the end of the first clip or the start of the second, make sure the effect is in line with the modifications midway through.

+ To view the contents of the Slide video transition group, click the triangle in the Effects panel. Between clips two and three, drape the Push transition across the edit point of the sequence.

+ To learn how the transition works, play through it. Then, switch the playhead to the cut between clips 2 and 3 by using the Up Arrow key on your keyboard. To move the Timeline playhead to the previous or next edit on certain tracks, use the Up and Down Arrow keys as keyboard shortcuts.

+ If you are unable to see a panel, it is always listed in the Window menu. To choose the Push transition effect symbol, click it once in the Timeline panel and then open the Effect Controls panel.

+ Click the small direction control triangle to the right of the A/B thumbnail in the upper left corner of the Effect Controls panel to alter the direction of the clip from West To East to East To West.

+ In the Push transition effect, the direction of each little white triangle changes. Hovering the cursor over a triangle will display a tool tip explaining the option. Play through the transition in the Timeline window to see the result.

+ In the Effects panel's Video Transitions section, enlarge the 3D Motion group. At the edit point, use the Flip over transition effect between clips three and four.

- To evaluate the sequence, play it through from beginning to end. This process makes it clear why transitions should be used sparingly.
- Between clips two and three, position the Split transition from the Slide group above the Push effect symbol. The duration of the new transition effect is the same as that of the old one.
- Select the Split transition effect icon from the Timeline to see the parameters in the Effect Controls panel. In this panel, set the Border Width to 7 and the Anti-aliasing Quality to Medium to produce a thin black border between the two clips.

The default transition effect is applied to many clips

Usually, editors produce a photomontage, which might appear better with transitions between the individual images. It's easy to apply transitions between two or three photographs, but if there are 100, it will take a long time. By letting you choose a preset transition effect, Premiere Pro makes it easy to automate this procedure.

The actions are:
- From the Project panel, find and launch the Slideshow sequence. This sequence's photos are arranged in a certain order. Keep in mind that the music clip's beginning and ending already have an in-and-out fade created by an audio crossfade with Constant Power.
- When the Timeline window is open, press the spacebar to play the sequence. Each clip is separated by a pause. You can utilize the Keyboard Shortcuts dialog box to designate a replacement key if you find a helpful keyboard shortcut that calls for a key that isn't on your keyboard.
- Use the backslash () key to zoom out of the Timeline window to see the full sequence. If you don't have a key on your keyboard, you can slide the navigator on the right side of the Timeline panel to change the zoom.
- Adjust the V1 track's height to view clip thumbnails (you can drag the line in the track header that separates V1 and V2).
- Draw a marquee around each clip using the Selection tool. The first clip you choose will be shifted if you drag the marquee outside of the clips on an empty timeline track zone.
- Both audio-only and video-only transition effects are now available in the Sequence menu.

Adjusting a Transition using A/B Mode

You can split a single video clip into two by using the A/B editing option when you review the transition effect settings in the Effect Controls panel. Two independent clips on different tracks with a transition between them are now shown instead of the two continuous and connected clips on a single timeline track. This lets you change the transition variables, including the head and tail frames (or handles).

Modifying the Effect Controls Panel's Settings

All transitions can be altered in Premiere Pro. The transition effect parameters and the outgoing and incoming clip handles (unused media in the original clip) are shown in the Effect Controls panel. **Let's modify the changeover:**

- Select the Transitions sequence once more in the Timeline panel.
- Click the transition effect icon after positioning the Timeline's playhead above the Split transition you made between clips two and three.
- On the Effect Controls tab, select the Show Actual Sources option to examine frames from real clips. This facilitates evaluating the upcoming adjustments.
- Choose Start at Cut from the Alignment menu in the Effect Controls panel. The changed location is reflected by updating the transition icon in the Effect Controls panel's timeline and sequence.
- Click the little Play the Transition button in the Effect Controls panel's top-left corner to see a preview of the transition.
- Modify the transition's duration. To apply the new setting, click the blue Duration numbers in the Effect Controls panel, type 300, and then click away from the numbers or press the Tab key. Premiere Pro will automatically change 300 to 00:00:03:00, or three seconds, by adding the proper punctuation.
- The Alignment menu now reads Custom Start as the influence now lasts past the beginning of the subsequent transition effect. The start time is automatically adjusted by Premiere Pro to account for the new transition time. Look at the timeline in the Effect Controls panel on the right.
- Play through the transition in the Timeline window to see the change. Since these automated adjustments could be little, you should always use the impact tool to confirm the effects of any new settings. In this manner, you may verify that the recently exposed content from the clip handles—which was concealed until you applied the transition effect—is acceptable to you. Even though Premiere Pro automatically adjusts effect timing when necessary, it is still crucial to verify the transition before moving further.

Including Effects for Audio Transitions

By eliminating undesired audio pops and cuts, audio transitions can greatly enhance a sequence's soundtrack. Crossfade transitions can significantly reduce difference between parts, and audiences are often more aware of audio irregularities than of the audio's overall quality.

Constructing a cross-fade

Three distinct crossfade styles are available.

- **Constant Gain:** To switch between sections, the Constant Gain crossfade employs a steady audio gain (volume). Some editors find this transition helpful, even though it causes the listener to perceive a little drop in audio volume. When you only want a dip out and in between two clips rather than a lot of mixing, it is quite helpful.

+ **Constant Power:** Constant power is frequently used in audio transitions. It produces a soft, seamless change from one audio sample to another. Constant Power's crossfade functions similarly to a dissolve in a video. The footage of the departure starts out slowly before accelerating toward the end. When you want to smoothly blend audio between two segments without experiencing a significant drop in volume, you need to use this crossfade.

+ **Exponential Fade:** This change produces a smooth transition between sections. To fade in and out sounds, use the logarithmic curve. To produce a one-sided transition, several editors employ the Exponential Fade effect (e.g., fading in a clip from quiet at the beginning or finish of a program).

Putting Audio Transitions into Practice

An audio crossfade can be applied to a sequence in a number of ways. Similar to a video transition effect, an audio transition effect can be dragged, but there are a few shortcuts that can help expedite the process. The duration of an audio transition is automatically expressed in frames or seconds. Click Premiere Pro > Preferences > Timeline (macOS) or Edit > Preferences > Timeline (Windows) to modify the preset duration.

The actions are:

+ Open the Audio series first. There are multiple audio samples in the sequence.
+ To review the material, play the sequence again.
+ Go to the Audio Transitions > Crossfade group in the Effects panel.
+ To begin the first audio clip, drag the Exponential Fade transition.
+ Go on to the sequence's conclusion.
+ Select Apply Default Transitions after performing a right-click on the right edge of the final clip in the sequence.
+ Right-click while holding Option (macOS) or Alt (Windows) and choose the audio clip to make a basic audio transition.
+ A default audio and video transition is applied at the end of the clip.
+ To alter a transition's duration, drag its edge on the Timeline. Listen to the outcome after dragging to make the newly created audio transition larger.
+ Add an opening Cross Dissolve transition effect to the sequence's first video clip to complete the project. To deselect the transition effect you have just customized, press Esc.
+ Press Command+D (macOS) or Ctrl+D (Windows) after moving the playhead to the start of the sequence to add the default video transition. Now you have a black start fade and a black end fade.
+ Using the Selection tool, highlight every audio edit between the clips on track Audio 1 by pressing Command+Option (macOS) or Ctrl+Alt (Windows). Take care not to choose any video clips; instead, drag from beneath the audio clips to prevent inadvertently choosing video clips. You can isolate the transitions while

making a selection by momentarily separating the audio and video clips with the Option (macOS) or Alt (Windows) keys.

+ The preset audio transitions from the selection can be applied by pressing Shift+Command+D (macOS) or Shift+Ctrl+D (Windows). Using this shortcut, all chosen clips will have the default transition effect applied. Premiere Pro will only apply audio transition effects because you have only chosen audio clips.

+ It's possible that you used the keyboard shortcut Shift+D to initiate an audio-only transition. However, depending on the clip types you select, you can choose the type of transition effect to apply if you use the Command (macOS) or Ctrl (Windows) keys.

CHAPTER TEN
USING AUDIO

You will still have a lot of post-production work to do even if you follow all the required precautions to record high-quality audio. When you put everything together in Premiere Pro, this obligation still exists. This can be a little arbitrary because there are so many different levels of excellent audio. For instance, even though a lot of people think that an MP3 sounds fantastic, an audiophile's definition can mention subtleties that the general public would find unimportant. Let's put all of that aside and discuss the many steps required in creating high-quality audio.

Think about the following:

+ **Keep an eye on those levels:** When editing in Premiere pro, pay attention to the audio meters. Whether your sound is appropriate or not will be communicated to you. As seen above, speaking at a decibel level of -12 is regarded as best practice. The sound will clip or suffer irreversible damage at any higher level; at any lower level, the dynamic range will be inadequate.

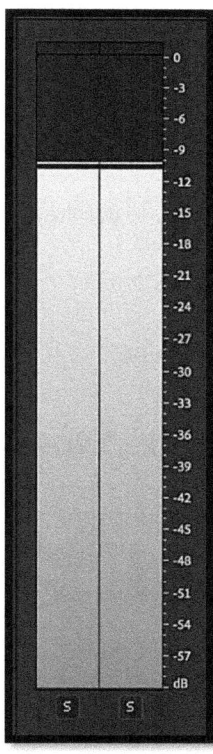

+ **Modify ambient sound:** Lower sound is frequently produced by background and ambient audio levels. As a result, when ambient sound is recorded at an abnormally loud volume, it is either not attenuated or is raised to the same level as the conversation, creating a faux soundscape. Instead, ambient noise shouldn't be higher than -18 dB.

+ **Verify that the levels complement one another:** To create a unified soundscape, adjust the volumes of conversation, performance, and background noise. In other words, audio levels need to be in sync. Hearing a voice that is too high or too low in relation to another is the most disagreeable thing there is. According to Yoda, "You have to adjust."

Bringing in Audio

+ **Launch Premiere Pro:**
  ➢ On your computer, launch Adobe Premiere Pro.
+ **Import Files:**
  ➢ Go to the top menu on the screen.
  ➢ Click "File."
+ **Choose Import:**
  ➢ From the dropdown menu, choose the Import option.
  ➢ This action opens a file selection window.
+ **Find audio files:**
  ➢ To find audio files, look through the directory structure on your computer.
+ **Choose audio files:**
  ➢ Choose the audio files that you want to add to Premiere Pro.
  ➢ You can choose many audio files at once by clicking on each one while holding down the Ctrl key (Command key for macOS).
+ **Import files:**
  ➢ Select audio files and click the Import button in the file selection box to import them.
  ➢ This operation adds audio files to the Premiere Pro project, allowing for modification and use.

Note on Compressed Audio File Types

+ Upon import, Premiere Pro will decompress compressed audio files, such as MP3 or WMA.
+ Premiere Pro might need to resample audio for compatibility, depending on your output settings.
+ For higher quality, use uncompressed or CD audio versions of audio clips wherever you can. Although Premiere Pro has a high-quality resampler, uncompressed files usually produce superior results.

Adjusting Audio Levels

It is uncommon that recorded audio levels do not need to be changed. Premiere Pro provides a range of solutions to this problem. You can modify audio levels in a variety of ways.

- **Proceed to the audio track's rubber band:** Proceed to the audio track's rubber band, which is positioned halfway through it. This is the easiest alteration to make and is suitable for an emergency fix. Changing tracks accurately can be difficult and time-consuming.

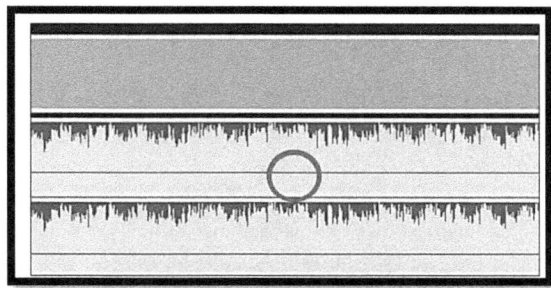

- **Audio Mixer:** This tool allows you to have a lot of control over the overall sound of your project and is comparable to a virtual studio mixing board.
- **Clip Mixer:** Compared to the rubber band function, the Clip Mixer offers noticeably more precise control over the clip.
- **Pen tool:** The Toolbox tool, which is circled in the figure below, allows you to create keyframes and alter the sound as you raise or decrease them using the audio track in the timeline once more.

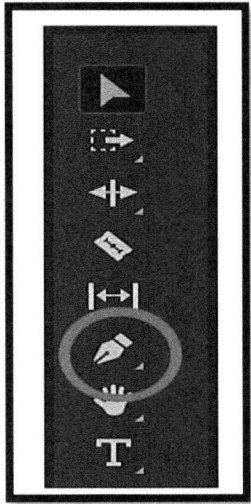

Comprehending Audio Mixers

Outstanding audio accompanies outstanding video, so make sure the audio levels on each channel are perfect. This is akin to fine-tuning video snippets. The Audio Clip Mixer and the Audio Track Mixer allow you to adjust the audio quality. Each is unique even though they have the same names, look the same, and have different audio levels. You can use the Audio Track Mixer to alter the overall audio levels as well as the levels of each audio track individually. The virtual mixing board, which also displays activity in the meters, has sliders for adjusting each track. The mixer creates extra sliders for every track when more are added. The goal here is to make sure that the track levels don't peak in red or exhibit abnormally low activity, which would be too high or too low. You can use the slider in either direction to change the audio level. A number appears beneath the slider when you adjust a track's level, signifying that the track is now at that level. You can directly adjust the audio level in this box by entering a negative integer to lower the loudness. Next to the updated track, this data is also shown on the timeline. While accounting for the changes in the other channels, the master control modifies the sequence's overall level. **The following information will help you understand the Audio Mixer, a virtual studio audio mixer that lets you change the volume of each audio track separately.**

+ **Track:** A single audio clip that can be utilized as a voiceover or music track independently or in addition to the video.
+ **Levels:** The music's audio volume and intensity.
+ **Sliders:** Each track features sliders. When it is raised, its levels increase, and when it is lowered, they decrease.
+ **dB:** Decibels, which is the sound measurement unit.
+ **Proper audio levels:** Maintain a volume between -6 and -12 dB for conversation and between -16 and -22 dB for ambient sound.
+ **Red indicator:** When audio levels transcend 0 dB, the meter's top light will turn red. In other words, not good.
+ **Mute:** This feature lets you turn off a track by pressing a button.

More details regarding the sliders

Let's look at the letters above each slider: M, S, and R.
+ **M:** The music is now turned off.
+ **S:** When you solo, the opposite occurs. Clicking it mutes all other tracks so you can only hear that one.
+ **R:** You can record directly onto the track with this one.

Above the main control, there is another control that simply says "Read." Clicking on it brings up a list of options.
+ **Off:** Do not include any keyframes.
+ **Read:** The default mode plays audio channels based on the master or individual song parameters.

- **Lock:** To preserve level changes during playback, hold down the Lock button. It remains where you left it when you release it.
- **Touch:** During playback, touch captures level adjustments. The remaining time is reset to the default if you let it go.
- **Write:** Use a slider to adjust the levels of keyframes that are recorded on your timeline while it is playing. It takes the place of previously published levels. Pressing the spacebar initiates the recording process in this mode.

Mixer for Audio Clips

In contrast, the Audio Clip Mixer modifies the individual clip underneath the playhead instead of the track's overall levels. The number of tracks on the timeline that are shown as tracks in the panel behaves and controls identically. The only difference is the volume of the audio, which changes from clip to clip.

Audio Mixing

To get the sound you want in your video, the audio mix is essential. Adjust the volume settings and make sure the other audio channels match them to have a sufficient amount of sound.

Make sure those levels are correct

First things first. Let's get the sound into range first and foremost. Make sure you can see the audio meters. You can use this technique to determine if the levels are too high or low.

What you can do in that situation is as follows.
- **Modify the schedule:** Drag the rubber band line up or down to adjust the timeline loudness.

- **Make use of the audio mixer:** Throughout the entire track, use the Audio Mixer to change the levels.
- **Edit individual clips:** You can alter certain tracks using the Clip Mixer.

Take into account the following while modifying the volume levels.

- **Avoid peaking audio levels:** Avoid peaking audio levels since this may result in clipping. It sounds like a tap due to the distortion. Make sure that every track level is within range to prevent this problem.
- **Use Gain:** As seen in the image below, right-click the clip and choose Audio Gain to apply gain. Change the number. Keep in mind that the initial volume was 0.0 dB. The volume rises when the level is set to a positive number and falls when it is set to a negative value.
- **Create keyframes:** To correct a clip's volume levels that can be too loud or too quiet, use keyframes. You can adjust the volume by dragging the keyframes once they have been set.

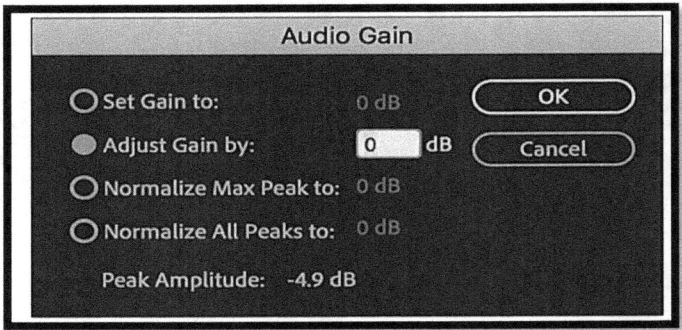

Making Diverse Audio Levels Simpler

A few of the clips have an odd balance that is simultaneously too loud and too quiet. **Here is a straightforward method for resolving the issue, though there are additional options.**

- Navigate to the Hard Limiter section of the Effects Panel after selecting the Audio Effects area. All you have to do is enter it into the search field.

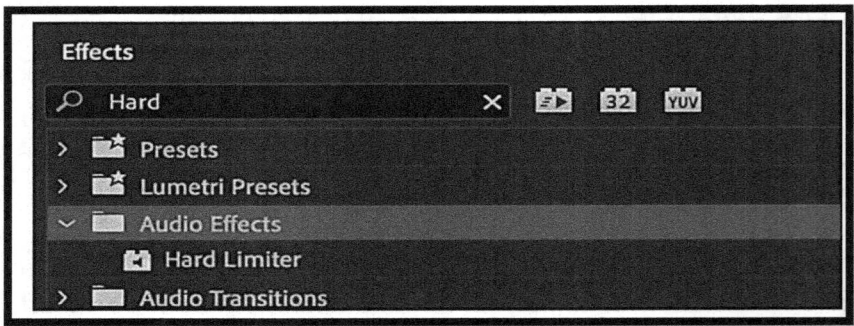

✛ Navigate to Effect Controls and scroll to locate the Hard Limiter. Press the Edit button. The Clip FX Editor will then open.

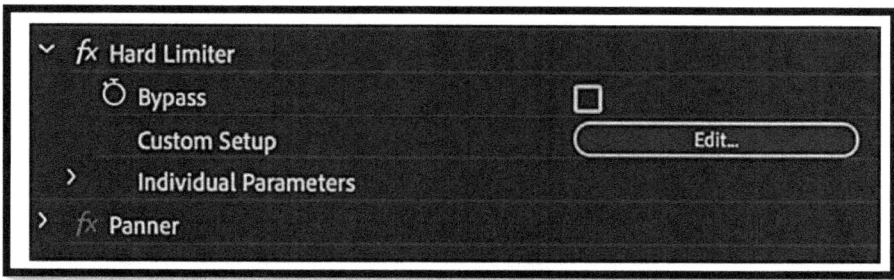

✛ Set the -0.1 dB level to -12 on the Maximum Amplitude slider.

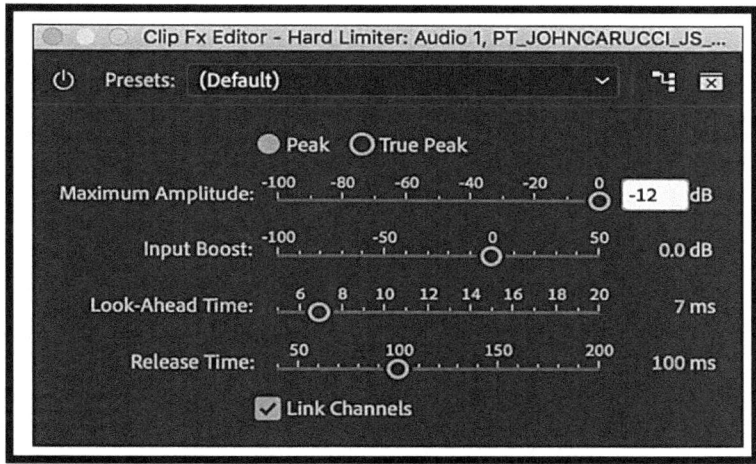

✛ The levels of the video will be balanced as a result. By right-clicking on clips and choosing Paste attributes, you can copy and paste characteristics to them. You can use this to copy and paste features from other clips.

Starting with Audio Recording

Regardless of Premiere Pro's audio correction features, nothing can replace the appreciation of the mutually beneficial link between audio and video recording. The first step is to use the most efficient method to capture the scene's audio. Even in the best of situations, you will still need to do audio work for your edit. Think about someone who takes good care of their teeth. Their dental appointments will still be necessary, but they won't be as stressful as those of those who disregard their oral health.

Pay attention to the sound in the area

Keep in mind that the symbiotic relationship between audio and visual quality will remain merely a concept if you do not take the necessary actions. Audio recording is crucial in this situation. In certain situations, it is sufficient to frame your photo around the background noise in the area. In other situations, you might think about employing a certain kind of microphone technique. A shotgun microphone, sometimes referred to as an interference-type line microphone, is necessary in some circumstances while a directional microphone is required in others. The most precise audio reproduction during an event can occasionally be achieved by connecting a camera to a soundboard. Getting a flawless sound recording is the icing on the cake, or whatever dessert you decide to have. **Here are some things to think about: When adjusting the volume levels, keep the following in mind.**

+ **Prevent the peaking of audio levels:** High levels can result in clipping. This seems to be an unfixable tap-like distortion. Make sure each track's levels fall within a reasonable range to prevent this problem.
+ **Have faith in your ears:** Sunglasses can pick up a variety of sounds, so have faith in your ears. Listen for a moment before pressing the Record button. It will pay off.
+ **Avoid attempting to record talk from a distance:** To prevent picking up undesired sounds, keep the subject close to the camera when recording dialogue. Although it is unlikely to be exceptional, the sound quality will still be bearable. Instead, place a wireless type or shotgun microphone closer to the subject.
+ **Get close to the subject:** The subject's voice will record and rise above competing background noises the closer they are to the microphone. It is impossible to overstate this recommendation. More of the speaker's voice will be recorded the closer they are to the microphone.
+ **Exercise caution in noisy areas:** even in excellent settings, the microphone can pick up anything. This implies that you can get a lot of things you don't need and a small amount of what you want. A few examples of locations that look fantastic in films but are really challenging to film are depicted in the image below. These include busy locations, train stations, and airports.

101

+ **Make use of a shotgun microphone:** To record background noise and natural sounds in the environment, use a shotgun microphone. The whoosh of a babbling brook, the monotonous tones of an assembly line, and the sounds of automobile traffic are a few of the sounds that are audible. When utilized with talking heads, these mics are also helpful, but they need to be positioned four to seven feet away from the camera.

+ **Verify that the levels are not excessively high:** To prevent clipping, which can result in irreparable distortion, record audio at the proper volumes.

Simple Audio Editing

Including Sound Effects

In a Premiere Pro production, you can incorporate external audio tools, like as VST plug-ins. You **must follow these steps in order to use the plug-ins that you have installed on your computer in Premiere Pro.**

+ Start by going to the Premiere Pro Preferences, which have crucial settings that control a lot of the program's functionality. If you're using Windows, select Edit from the top menu bar to bring up the Preferences dialog box. When you get there, choose Preferences from the drop-down option. Click Premiere Pro in the top menu bar, then choose Preferences to bring up the Preferences menu. Users of Mac OS will be able to access the Preferences menu as a result.

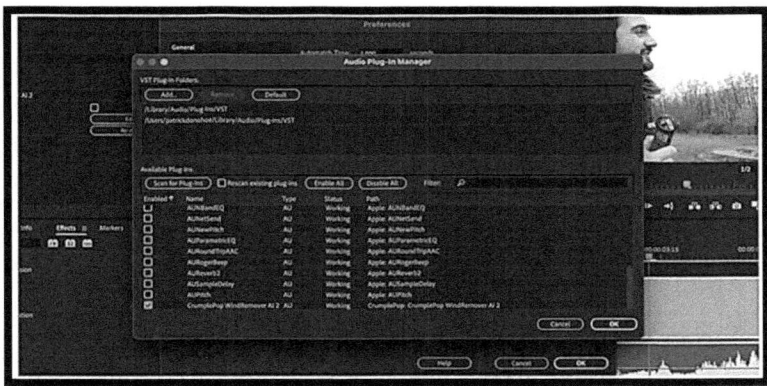

+ To use the different plug-ins that come with Premiere Pro, enter the Preferences dialogue box and scroll down until you find the Plug-in Manager option.

+ The Add option is located within the Plug-in Manager. You can look for the precise folder on your computer that contains your Virtual Studio Technology (VST) plug-ins if you choose this option.

+ Click the Scan for plug-ins button when you've finished choosing the folder containing your VST plug-ins. Premiere Pro will search the folder you've provided and import all of the plug-ins it finds into its system as a result of this action. When the scan is finished, a list of all the imported plug-ins will appear in the Plug-in Manager window.

+ The status of each item in the imported plug-ins list will be indicated. Ideally, the status would be functioning, meaning that Premiere Pro has successfully found the plug-in and it is operating as intended.

+ Click the OK button in the Plug-in Manager window to complete the configuration. You can save your settings and verify that the VST plug-ins have been successfully integrated into Premiere Pro by taking this step, which will close the Plug-in Manager dialogue box.

All of your VST audio effects will be easily accessible and used straight from Adobe Premiere Pro's Effects Control panel once these steps are finished. You can use all of your effects this way. This makes it possible to quickly access a wide variety of audio effects and apply them to video projects, which enhances the overall quality of your editing process and gives you more creative expression possibilities.

How to Use Premiere Pro's Audio Effects

The most important sound panel in Adobe Premiere Pro is the Effect Controls panel, where you may find your sound effects.

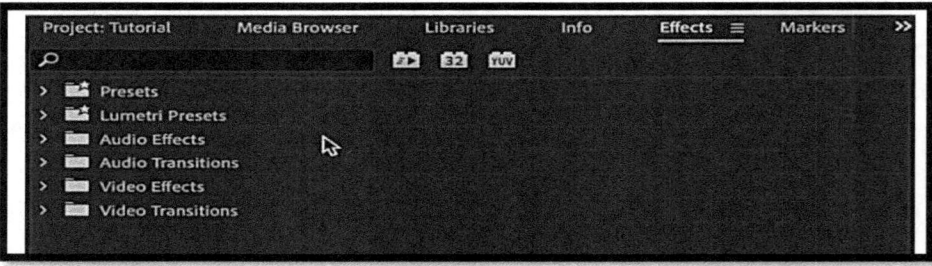

+ **Using Audio Tools in the Effects Panel:** Open Adobe Premiere Pro's Effects panel to begin improving your audio. This can be done by searching for a particular sound effect to apply to your audio clip or by navigating through the Effects panel. You can alter and enhance your audio tracks with the abundance of audio tools and effects available in the Effects panel.

+ **Sound Effects Application for Audio Clips:** There are several ways to apply a sound effect to an audio clip in your project after you've located it in the Effects panel. You have two options: either click or drag the symbol of the effect from the Effects panel straight onto the Timeline panel's audio clip that you want to modify. Another option is to double-click the sound effect that appears in the Effect Controls panel after selecting an audio clip from the Timeline panel. This will instantly add the sound effect to the chosen audio clip.

+ **Modifying Audio Settings:** You can fine-tune and modify an audio effect's parameters after applying it. This enables you to alter the effect to suit your tastes or the project's specifications. Access the Effect settings panel, which includes a comprehensive list of parameters and options unique to the applied audio effect. To create the appropriate audio change, you can precisely adjust parameters like volume, pitch, equalization, and other effect-specific variables using this panel.

Adding Several Effects to One Clip

In Adobe Premiere Pro, use these procedures to add multiple effects to a single audio clip:
+ To highlight or choose the audio clip, locate it in the Timeline window and click on it. You can choose an audio clip in this way.
+ Go to the Effect Controls panel to choose multiple effects. Once there, decide the effects you want to use. By clicking on the desired effects while holding down the Control key (on Windows) or the Command key (on Mac), you can choose from a variety of effects in this menu.
+ Holding down the Control key (on Windows) or the Command key (on Mac) allows you to drag the effects to the audio clip after choosing the appropriate combination of effects in the Effect Controls panel. Next, click and drag the selected set of effects onto the audio clip you want to modify in the Timeline window. By applying all of the specified effects to the selected audio clip simultaneously, this operation enables you to layer and modify a variety of effects to achieve the desired audio output.

How to Get Rid of Premiere Pro Audio Effects

Eliminate Specific Effects from a Video

+ Select the audio clip from which you want to eliminate one or more audio effects to get started. This is the first step in determining which audio clip is wanted. By going to the Timeline panel and choosing the particular audio clip that has the desired effects, you can eliminate them.
+ Open the Effects Controls Panel: To further customize the effects, open the Effects Controls panel after choosing the audio clip in the Timeline. A list of the effects that have been applied to the clip you have chosen will appear in this box.
+ Eliminating Particular Effects: Click on the effects you wish to remove in the Effects Controls menu. This will enable you to eliminate specific impacts. You can select multiple effects by holding down the Control key (Windows) or the Command key (Mac) as you click on each effect. The Remove Selected Effect option on the effects panel allows you to remove the effects as soon as you've selected them. As an alternative, you can eliminate the effects you've selected by pressing the Backspace or delete key on your keyboard.

Eliminating Every Effect in a Clip

- Choose an audio clip in the Timeline panel to remove all of the effects that have been applied to it. This will enable you to reverse every consequence without incurring any penalty.
- Right-click on the selected clip in the Timeline window to remove all effects. Choose Remove Effects from the list of alternatives when the contextual menu displays. A dialog box will appear once you finish this step, asking you to confirm that you want to delete every effect from the clip you choose.
- A list of the audio editing effects applied to the clip will appear in the dialog box once you give your approval for the effects to be removed. Either choose which effects you wish to eliminate, or click the Select All option to eliminate every effect connected to the clip. Once your selections are complete, click the OK button. All audio effects that have been applied to the clip will be erased as a result of this procedure, which will eliminate all of the designated effect kinds.

Improving the Quality of the Audio

Crucial Sound Panel Methods

Audio quality in video production is rarely flawless. You'll probably need to use audio effects in post-production to fix a few mistakes and enhance the sound quality, especially when singing, because audiences are quite sensitive to flaws in the human voice. Not all audio frequencies can be accurately reproduced by all audio equipment. **For instance, compared to larger speakers, heavy bass notes never sound the same on a laptop.**

- Use studio monitor speakers or high-quality headphones to listen to your audio instead of adjusting the sound to compensate for a malfunction in your playback equipment. You can be confident that you will provide your audience a consistent sound since professional audio-monitoring equipment is meticulously adjusted to guarantee that all frequencies play evenly, a phenomenon known as a flat response.
- Using subpar speakers to listen to music could also be beneficial. By doing this, you can make sure that a sizable portion of the audio is audible and that distortion from low-frequency sounds is avoided.

Among the many useful effects in Premiere Pro's Effects panel are the ones listed below:

- **Parametric Equalizer:** This device makes it possible to precisely alter the volume of sounds at specific frequencies. An audio recording's presence can be enhanced by studio reverb. It may, for instance, replicate the ambiance of a bigger space.
- **Delay:** Audio may echo noticeably or softly as a result of this effect.
- **Bass:** A clip's low-frequency content is impacted by the bass effect. Narration clips, especially those with male voices, perform well with it.
- **Treble:** This effect modifies the upper frequency range of the audio clip.

Try different things to learn more about Premiere Pro's audio effects. Since these effects are non-destructive, the original audio files are not changed. Additionally, you have the option to add as many effects as you wish to a clip, adjust their parameters, listen to them, then remove them and begin again. Similar to how you would with transition effects, drag effects from the Effects panel into clips. To access the effects controls, select a clip in the Effect Controls panel.

Modifying the Audio of Conversations

There are many choices available for altering conversation sounds under the Essential Sound panel.

+ Select one or more clips from a sequence and a tag that matches the audio type of each clip in order to use the Essential Sound panel.
+ The tools appropriate for that kind of material are shown when a tag is selected. With good reason, conversation audio has the most options. Your conversation audio is probably the most crucial, although ambient sound files and music-prepared special effects (SFX) are usually pre-mixed and ready to use.
+ Every adjustment you make in the Essential Sound panel alters the settings and applies one or more audio effects to the chosen clips. In a way, the Essential Sound panel is the ideal quick fix for getting amazing results with basic settings. You can select a clip and adjust the effect parameters in the Effect Controls panel after making adjustments in the Essential Sound panel.

Fixing Audio

No matter how hard you try to capture clear audio on location, there's a good chance that some of your footage will include undesirable background noise. For modifying spoken passages, the Essential Sound panel provides a number of options. **Look through the Repair category to see what solutions are available for fixing the chat.**

+ Cut down on background noises such as hissing, rustling clothing, and air conditioners.
+ Cut down on low-frequency noises, such as wind and motor noise.
+ To lessen hum and electrical interference, use DeHum. In North and South America, this is 60 Hz; in Europe, Asia, and Africa, it is 50 Hz. You might have heard this disagreeable but readily removable noise if your microphone cable was close to a power cord.
+ Reduce reflected noise to enhance speech clarity. Several clips can benefit from one or more of these cleaning techniques, and you will often combine them. Some of the sound may be reflected to the microphone as reverb when recorded in a setting with plenty of reflective surfaces.

Improving Clarity

Three easy methods to enhance the clarity of spoken audio are provided by the Essential Sound panel's Clarity area:

+ **Dynamics:** The loudness difference between an audio recording's loudest and softest passages is referred to as dynamic range. It can be made higher or lower.

- **EQ:** Modifies the loudness (amplitude) at specific frequencies. Selecting the right parameters is made simpler with presets.
- **Enhance speaking:** Choose a male or female voice for particular frequencies to improve speaking clarity.

Try all three options because different configurations will result in better recordings of conversations.

CHAPTER ELEVEN
WORKFLOW IMPROVEMENT

Utilizing Templates to Increase Productivity

+ Double-click the downloaded Premiere edit template. The blank template will appear when Premiere Pro is launched.

Footnote: To customize these blank templates to your liking, simply drag & drop your materials into them.

+ Select the Media Placeholder, Titles, and Logo folders from the Project menu. The majority of templates will employ a similar language, though not exactly the same.

+ Open the Media Placeholder folder to get started. Media compositions will be numbered based on where they appear in the video sequence.

+ The simplest method is to begin with Media Placeholder 1 and proceed sequentially down the list.

+ To see the timeline's initial Media Placeholder composition, double-click.

+ From the project browser, drag the selected material to the timeline.

+ Select your clip from the timeline and trim the ends to display just a section of it.

+ By modifying the Scale, Position, and Rotation settings as necessary, you can reframe your material.

+ Keep adding images and video clips to every media output. The sequence in the timeline can be closed after you're satisfied with the way your movie plays.

+ Choose Text from the drop-down menu once you've finished inserting media placeholders. The order in which the Text Placeholder compositions will reappear in the video determines their number.

+ To open Text 1, double-click on it.

+ Double-click the media viewer after choosing the Title layer from the timeline to change your text.

+ Change the headline and make any necessary typographic adjustments.

+ After going over each title contest, make any necessary text changes.

+ The last step is to submit your logo to the Logo Placeholder contest. This is done in the same manner as the media and titles, as you might anticipate.

Keep in mind that your logo asset will require a high-quality PNG image with a transparent backdrop.

Methods for Saving Time

Editing is just the process of aligning jigsaw pieces to achieve the best possible fit. Sometimes the puzzle pieces are really easy to work with and fit together perfectly, even though it can seem like you are pressing slightly matching parts that do not fit and the problem just seems to be right. You have to continue, though, since you are running out of time. In any case, you need to continue being effective and productive in order to overcome any editing obstacles. Here are some things you can do in Adobe Premiere to keep motivated.

+ **Get Everything Organized First:** This includes maintaining appropriate folder organization and color-coding labels. Another step you can add to your workflow is creating a.zip file that has all of your bins, a Premiere project, and any recurring elements, including logos, photo assets, and bottom thirds.

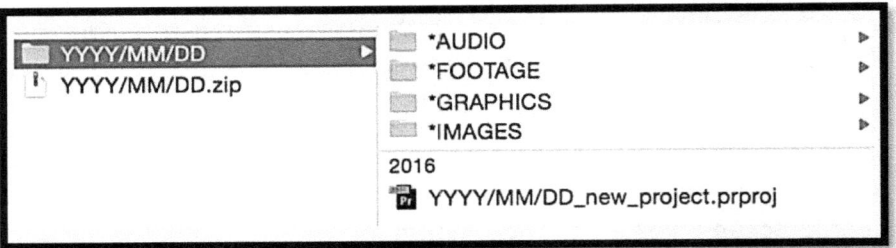

By doing this, you can save time because your folder containing all of your assets and sub-folders is formed when you unzip the file. After that, you may drag the root folder into your freshly created project.

+ **Make Use of Proxies:** Particularly on older models, large file transfers and rendering delays can be very annoying and slow down a computer. Proxy files, which are smaller (in terms of file size rather than resolution) and sometimes the codec, can help you avoid this; you can replace them after your assembly cut is finished.

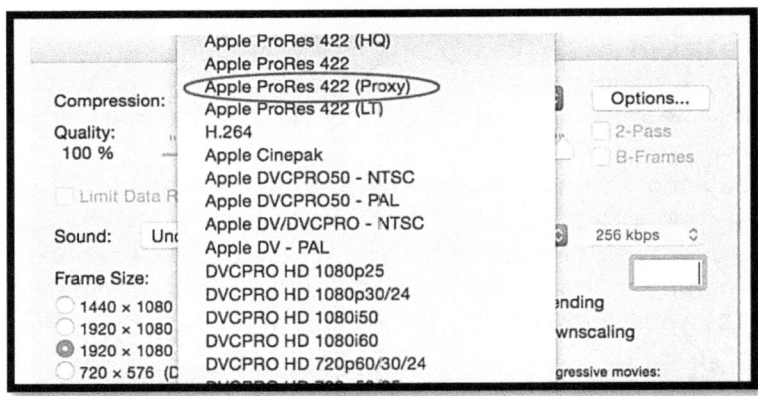

This speeds up processing while you work, but it takes longer initially because you have to convert them before you can start editing. To convert your files into a format that is comparable to your final files but has a lower bit rate, codec, or container, just use a conversion program (I strongly suggest the great and free MPEG Streamclip).

Simply re-link (or swap out) the smaller proxies with their originals after your assembly upgrade are finished. If you maintain the same frame rate and aspect ratio, everything will function!

+ **Adhere to Your Media:** Premiere might not be the ideal option for your workflow, even though it supports a large variety of frame rates, aspect ratios, and file types. Because it requires a lot of processing power for your computer to identify and optimize them for your period, you can speed up the process by keeping everything the same, just like with large files.

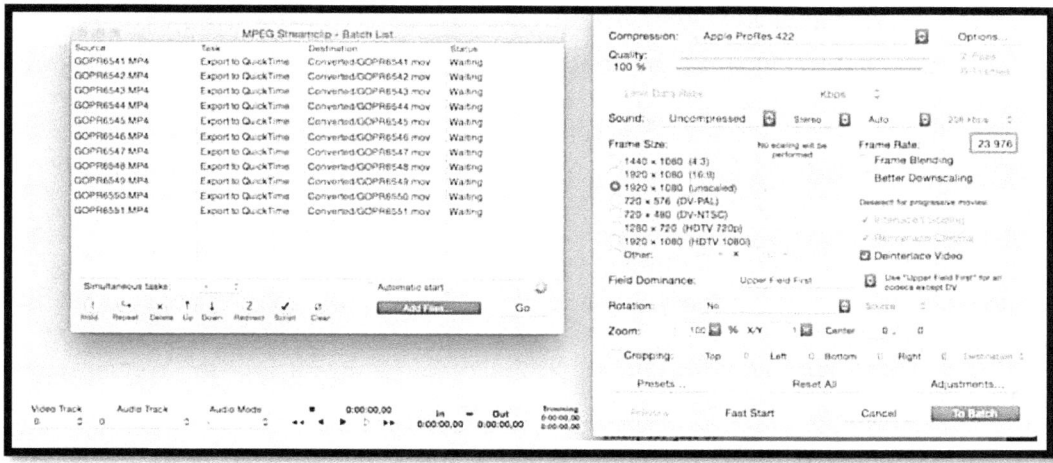

Once more, it will take more work up front, but it will guarantee that no frames are missing, trimming is done, or unwanted black bars appear. Arranging your files according to your preferences before you start is more efficient than wasting time modifying clips after you have started working.

+ **Apply master clip effects:** You can be far more productive if you combine all of your effects into a single file instead of copying and pasting them into each cut piece. Simply open the file in the source monitor or project panel, then drag it across to apply an effect. Every segment of the master clip utilized in the sequence will immediately receive all of your changes.

110

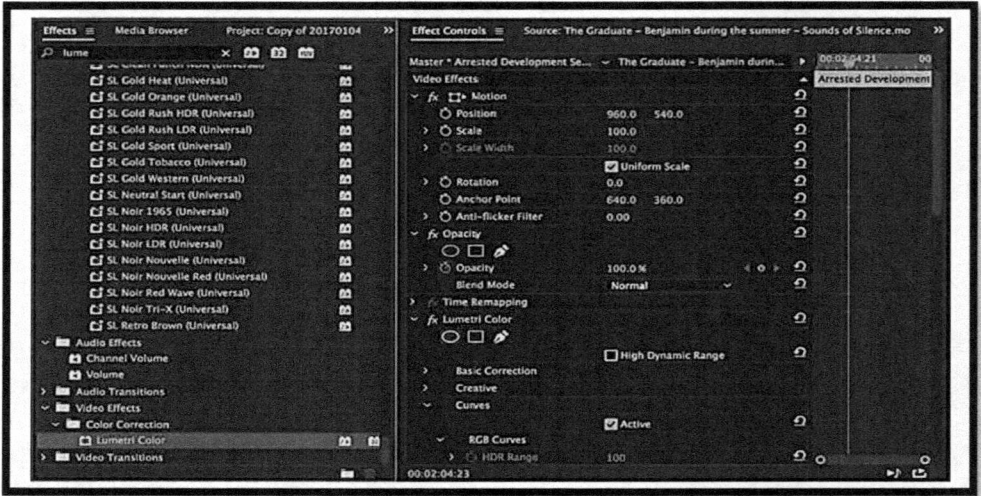

⊥ **DIY Voiceover:** You can be productive and record the voiceover yourself in the interim because it's often something you know will happen later when you work on the edit. This can help you time your script edits even if you don't have the graphics ready. You can listen to determine the ideal tone, emotion, and intonation before making any necessary adjustments if you are hiring the voice actor directly.

⊥ **The Shortcut That Changes Everything:** Naturally, you can use the many keyboard shortcuts offered to go through your changes gradually. My editing style was drastically altered by the ~ button, which makes the current window fill the screen. You can view a full-screen preview and explore the program panel fast by pressing ~. Make a big push for the timeline so you can make any minor adjustments that are required. To see your files in full-screen mode in the media browser, press ~.

⊥ **Color Presets and Lumetri Looks:** Adobe added a great tool to Premiere a while back: the Lumetri color panel. This panel is part of Premiere, so you may use it to reduce the time you spend bouncing between editing and color correction/grading tools. It's a great tool for adding a certain look to your project.

⊥ **In order to preserve your export presets, Make use of Adobe Media Encoder:** Making some presets is the next step to increasing your productivity after you've mastered exporting your project. Choosing that preset from the dropdown menu and exporting your projects in the same manner is the easiest method. You may access your choices whenever you want by saving them. Additionally, you might have to edit a virtual reality video or create deliverables that adhere to certain bitrates or file sizes.

Additionally, Adobe Media Encoder allows you to convert files, export numerous files from various sequences, and establish watch folders that automatically encode to the format of your choice. The AME is a highly useful tool for handling conversion tasks while you work on other parts of your edit. It may be used separately or through your export window.

+ **Dynamically Link:** The first time I used a dynamic link to produce real-time visual effects for my video was another one of my editing highlights! Although it requires the other software to function, it is a really helpful tool. At the most basic level, you can construct titles, bottom thirds, and live text. Additionally, you may perform rotoscoping, keyframing, and explosions.

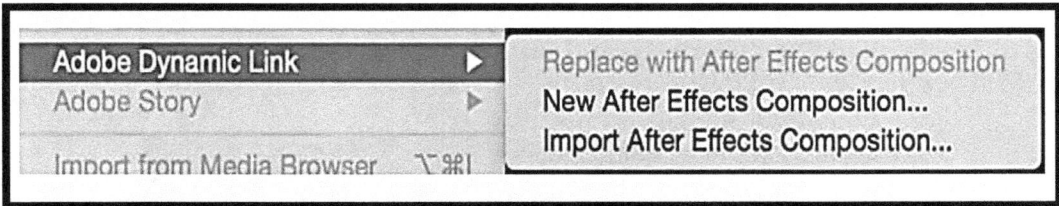

Using dynamic linking essentially removes the requirement to export your movie in order to verify that your visual effects are functioning. Without a doubt, everyone has had to redo an image because it didn't seem right or was two to three frames too long or short. You can stay on course while managing all of that using dynamic linking. The only thing to remember is that this procedure requires a lot of CPU power to run efficiently, so be aware of your computer's capabilities.

Utilizing the Button Editor

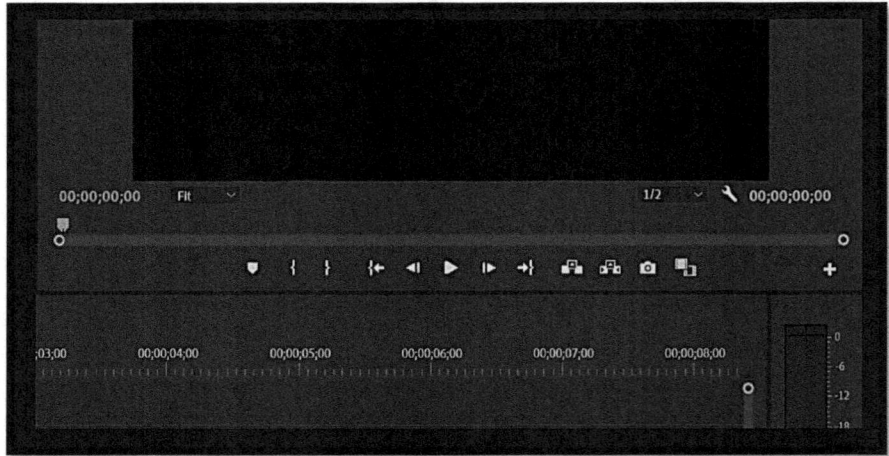

Underneath the Source and Program monitors are all Premieres' transport controls. You can explore each clip frame by frame with the jogging controls in addition to your usual playback settings. Additionally, there is a toggle to enable and disable Comparison View, as well as a button for setting markers. The lift and extract buttons in the Program panel take the place of the Insert and Overwrite buttons next to the transport controls in the Source monitor. If necessary, a still image can be taken using the Export Frame button on both monitors. Clicking the little plus symbol in the lower right corner of the screen will bring up Premiere's button editor. You can further customize your Premiere workspace by selecting the other button options.

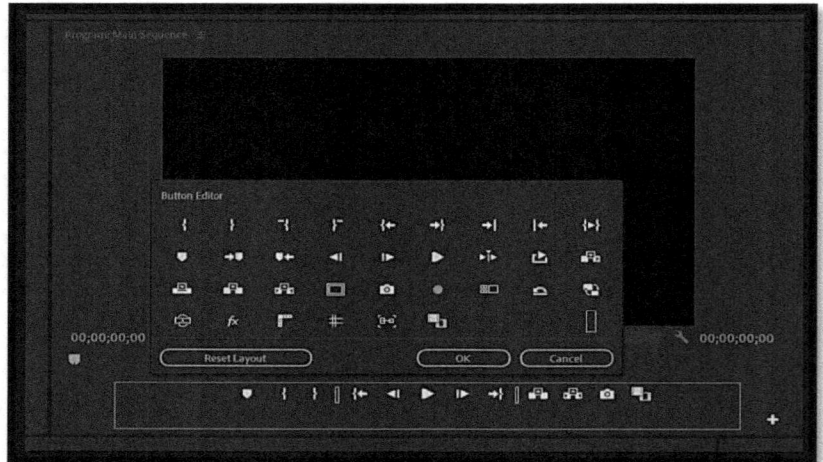

After activating the Button Editor, you may drag buttons into the button bar to add them. By dragging them to the Button Editor Option panel, you can eliminate those that are automatically there. To proceed with your session, click OK if you are OK with the layout.

A List of Keyboard Shortcuts and Premiere Buttons

Hovering over any of these buttons will reveal its name in a tooltip; some buttons function more obviously than others. What does Toggle Proxies mean to most of us, but what about some of these other terms? What is Play Around meant to be, after all? **The following is a list of Premiere buttons, arranged according to look, and their standard keyboard shortcuts:**

- **Mark In (I):** Establish the timeline or clip as the starting point for your modifications. This indicates to the system where your edit or selection starts.
- **Mark Out (O):** Indicate where your edits will cease. This indicates the point on the timeline or clip where your selection or alteration ends.
- **Clear In (Ctrl + Shift + I):** Take away the initial position you established. If you wish to begin your selection or modification from a different location, you can use this to reset the In point.
- Use Ctrl + Shift + O to clear out, which removes the Out point you previously established. This enables you to modify or eliminate the edit's end point.
- **Press Shift + I to go to In:** Leap to the marked In point. For easy navigation, the playhead goes to the precise beginning point.
- **Press Shift + O to Go to Out:** Fast-forward to the timeline's Out point. This is helpful for determining the end of your edit or selection.
- **Select the Next Edit Point (Down Arrow):** Advance to the timeline's subsequent cut or transition. This makes it easier to move on to the next segment of your video.
- **Use the Up Arrow to Go to Previous Edit Point:** Return to your timeline's most recent cut or transition. This is useful for going over previous edits again.
- Play the video in between your in and out points to get a sneak peek. Only that portion of your timeline or clip is played.
- **Add Marker (M):** Give your timeline or clip a marker. Markers make it easier to recall particular scenes or passages for future editing.
- **Press Shift + M to Go to Next Marker:** Advance to the following marker on your timeline. This makes navigating marked points simple.
- **Use Ctrl + Shift + M to Go to Previous Marker:** Return to your timeline's previous marker. It's helpful for verifying previously noted points.
- **Step Back One Frame (Left Arrow):** To make exact edits and modifications, move the playhead back one frame.
- **Step Forward One Frame (Right Arrow):** For in-depth adjustments, advance one frame at a time.
- **Play-Stop Toggle (Spacebar):** To play or pause your video, press the Spacebar. Playback can be quickly started and stopped using this method.

- **Play Around (Shift + K):** Perform a brief sequence both prior to and following the playhead. This makes it easier for you to understand the background of a certain idea.
- **Loop Playback:** Program a segment to repeat repeatedly. This is excellent for often verifying adjustments or effects.
- **Insert (Comma):** Without erasing anything, add content to your timeline from the Source monitor. It advances already-existing content.
- **Overwrite (Period):** Use the information from the Source monitor to replace stuff on your timeline. By doing this, the old clip gets replaced with the new one.
- **Lift (Semicolon):** Leave a space after removing a specific portion of the timeline. Your clipboard has a copy of the deleted portion.
- **Extract (Apostrophe):** Close the gap and remove a chosen portion of the timeline. Everything immediately moves to fill the available area.
- **Safe Margins:** To prevent vital content from being cut off on various displays, activate the guides that indicate where it should remain.
- **Export Frame:** Capture the current frame by pressing Ctrl + Shift + E. Ideal for reference photos or thumbnails.
- **Multi-Camera Record On/Off (0):** Press a button to begin or end real-time multi-camera cut recording.
- **Toggle Multi-Camera View (Shift + 0):** In a multi-camera configuration, switch between various camera perspectives.
- **Revert Trim Session:** While the trim tool is still operational, undo the trimming you have completed.
- **Change Proxies:** Alternate between high-resolution video and low-resolution proxies. Using proxies during editing improves playback quality.
- **Toggle VR Video Display:** To edit virtual reality footage, turn on or off VR mode.
- **Global FX Mute:** To improve playback during editing, temporarily disable all effects.
- To show rulers on your editing screen, press Ctrl + R. For accurate positioning, use them to align items.
- **Show Guides:** Toggle guides on or off by pressing Ctrl + Semicolon. These assist you in precisely placing components in your film.
- **Snap in Program Monitor (Ctrl + Shift + Semicolon):** To make alignment simpler, snap objects to designated locations, such as the center or guides.
- **Comparison View:** Side-by-side comparison of two frames. It facilitates consistent modifications or color matching.

At last, we reach the mysterious and very little Space entrance. This is a placeholder that gives you some leeway between sets of related buttons so you may fine-tune the look of your button bar.

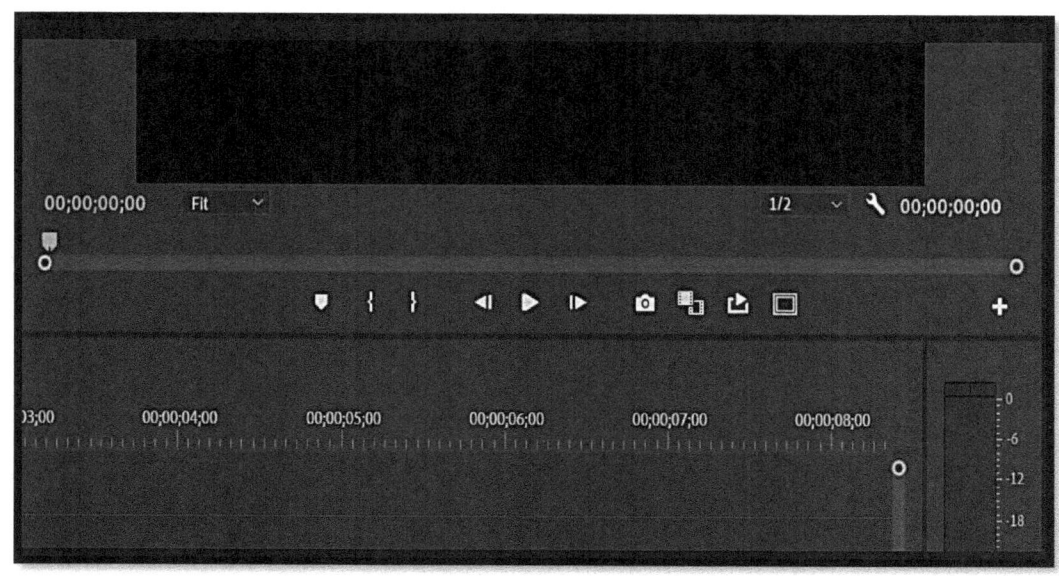

CHAPTER TWELVE
THE USE OF VIDEO EFFECTS

Using Visual Effects

You know how to apply effects and change their parameters already. Similar to an audio effect, a visual effect can be double-clicked in the Effects panel after selecting a clip (or many clips) or dragged onto a clip. A single clip can have several effects applied to it, with unexpected consequences. A collection of clips can be given effects by using adjustment layers. The abundance of options available in Premiere Pro for choosing video effects could seem daunting. Additionally, a wide range of extra effects are sold or given away by third-party merchants. The methods for applying, modifying, and removing effects are simple and uniform, despite the fact that the variety of effects and their controls might be intricate.

Effects That Are Permanently Modified

Upon adding a clip to a sequence, a number of effects are applied automatically. All clips should have fixed effects, commonly referred to as intrinsic effects, which are controls for geometry, opacity, speed, and audio. Although fixed effects are applied automatically, clips' appearance remains unchanged until their settings are altered.

Among the consequences are:
+ **Motion:** A clip can move, rotate, and scale thanks to the Motion effect. Moreover, shimmering borders on active objects can be removed with Anti-flicker Filter. This is crucial when reducing the size of an interlaced or high-resolution source, as Premiere Pro must resample the image.
+ **Opacity:** Modify the clip's opacity using the Opacity effect. Additionally, you can generate visual effects from many layers of pictures or video by using specific mix modes.
+ **Time Remapping:** Manage freeze frames, playback direction, and speed. Think of it as an enhanced version of the Timeline panel's Clip Speed/Duration settings. There is a relationship between the two controls.

Premiere Pro shows the panner controls, channel volume, and volume if a clip contains audio.

Using the Navigation in the Effects Panel

Premiere Pro offers standard effects that alter a video clip's appearance in addition to fixed video effects. To help with navigation, effects like distortion, keying, and time are categorized because there are so many. Adding third-party effects will increase your options. The exception is the obsolete category, where some effects are still available in Premiere Pro for compatibility with older project files even if they have been replaced by better-designed, more recent versions. Since these effects might be eliminated in later versions, it is advised to refrain from using them in brand-new projects. There is a bin for each category in the Effects panel. **You can make additional bins in the Effects panel to store duplicate effects and make them easier to locate, just like in the Project panel.**

- In the Effects window, expand the Video Effects category. The keyboard shortcut to open the Effects panel is Shift+7.
- On the bottom of the panel, click the New Custom Bin button. In the Effects panel, the new custom bin may be found at the bottom of the list (you may need to scroll down to see it).
- Just click a container once to choose it.
- Click directly on the bin's name (Custom Bin 01) to choose it.
- Favorite Effects should be the new name. To duplicate several effects, expand different video effect categories and drag them into the Favorite Effects bin. To make dragging effects simpler, you might need to modify the panel. Select the effects that you like. You can add or remove effects from a custom bin at any time. Use the Delete Custom Items option to get rid of duplicate effects.

Using the Master Clip Effect

In the Project panel, you may also apply effects to clips. In the same way, you employ the same visual effects. The effects that are applied to the clips on the Project panel are known as master clip effects, and the clips themselves are called master clips. The effects you apply to the master clip will be carried over to each clip or clip segment you add to a sequence using master clip effects. You can use master clip effects to update sequences even after adding clips to them; this is a great technique to modify multiple clip segments at once. For instance, you can change a clip's color in the Project panel to match the other camera angles in a scene. The adjustment will be made automatically if you utilize this clip or a portion of it repeatedly. A master clip effect can be used to quickly match the colors, even if the correction is made after the scene has been changed.

The master clip effect can be applied by:

- Start the Effects sequence that you want.
- Position the Timeline panel's playhead above the first instance of the clip. We must first access the sequence clip's original master clip in the Source Monitor before we can apply an effect to it. It is pointless to double-click the clip in the sequence because it will start the instance.
- After choosing the clip, hit F. This is the keyboard shortcut for Match Frame. At the current frame in the Program Monitor, it launches the original master clip in the Source Monitor. Since you will often need to check master clips when evaluating sequences, either to view an un-effected version of a clip or to assess alternative content, this is a helpful shortcut to keep in mind.
- You can now see the effects of the modifications as they happen because the same clip is open in both the Source Monitor (the master clip) and the Program Monitor (the sequence segment).
- To discover the Cinespace 100 Lumetri Look effect preset quickly, type 100 into the search box in the Effects panel.

- In the Source Monitor, drag the Cinespace 100 effect. The master clip is given this effect.
- To explore the different effect options, pick the Effect Controls panel after selecting the Source Monitor to make it the active panel.

Making Use of Effects Preset

Although there are several pre-made presets for particular uses, making your own presets is where the real power of effects lies, particularly if you choose to utilize the identical effect arrangement later. Many effects and animation keyframes can be found in a single preset.

Making use of built-in presets

Common chores, like adding a picture-in-picture effect or making a stunning transition, are made easier by the effect presets included with Premiere Pro.

- Launch and examine the preset order. The background texture is highlighted in this sequence, which consists of a single clip with a delayed start. Let's make the opening of the picture more visually appealing by using a preset.
- To remove the Search box, click the X at the top of the Effects panel. The Solarize In preset can be found under Presets > Solarizes.
- Drag the Solarize to get ready for the clip of the sequence.
- Watch the video again to see how the Solarize effect evolves from the start.
- After choosing the video from the Timeline panel, examine its parameters in the Effect Controls panel. There are two keyframes that are fairly close together. To see them better, zoom in using the navigator at the bottom of the timeline in the Effect Controls panel.
- Drag the second keyframe to the Effect Controls panel to modify the effect. The length of the effect is prolonged, softening the shot's opening.
- Turn off the Solarize effect and play about with the Effects box's other settings or mix and match other presets.

Using the Command to Render and Replace

When working with high-resolution media on a low-power device, you may find that the content regularly skips frames during previewing. Frame drops can also occur while working with intricate third-party visual effects that do not support GPU acceleration or dynamically connected After Effects compositions. You might wish to use the proxy technique, which lets you alternate between playing media files in full and low resolution, if all of your content is of very high quality. **You can quickly replace the original item in the sequence by creating new media files if only one or two of the clips are hard to play.**

- Right-click a segment of a sequence clip and choose Render and Replace to swap it out with a simpler version that is easier to play.
- The settings in the Render and Replace dialog box are comparable to those in the proxy workflow.

The primary setups are as follows:

➤ **Source:** Create a new media file that is the same size and frame rate as the source media, presets, or sequence. Not every frame size can be used with CineForm presets. It is usually sufficient to use one of the QuickTime ProRes settings.

➤ **Format:** Select the file extension of your choice. Different codecs are accessible through a variety of file types.

➤ **Preset:** Choose one. Either one of the many well-known choices or a custom preset made with Adobe Media Encoder can be used. Premiere Pro will incorporate the effects into the new file if you choose the Include Video Effects option, preventing you from adjusting their settings in the Effect Controls window.

➤ Click OK after selecting a preset and the new file's location to replace the sequence clip.

➤ The previous media file is no longer linked to the rendered and modified clip. This implies that Premiere Pro will not display modifications made to an After Effects composition using a dynamic connection. Right-click on the clip and choose Restore Unrendered to restore the link to the original item.

CHAPTER THIRTEEN
EXTENSIVE EDITING METHODS
Changing Media and Clips

Changing out one sequence clip for another is a typical practice when experimenting with alternative edits.

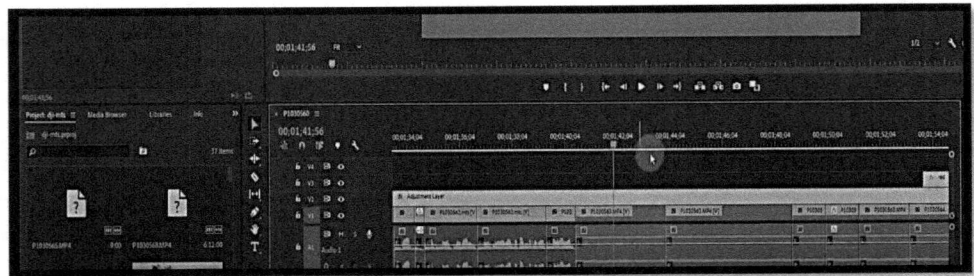

This might call for a worldwide update, like adding a more recent animated logo to an older file. Additionally, you can choose to swap out a clip from the available garbage for one from a sequence, such an actor's performance. The strategy you use will depend on the task at hand.

In a Premiere Pro sequence, changing a clip

Let's say you want to change a clip in a series while keeping the keyframes, motion effects, and filters. **This technique is widely used to swap out one cutaway shot for another; it's a fast way to switch viewpoints without losing clip characteristics.**

+ Enter the clips in point in the Project window; if not, Premiere Pro will use the first frame.
+ Drag the clip from the Source or Project panel to the Sequence panel while holding down Alt (for Windows) or Option (for Mac). Release the mouse button once the clip has been highlighted. The clip is altered without losing any of its characteristics.
+ You can drag and drop a replacement clip from the Project panel. Once the clip is selected in Icon view, you may create an In by pressing I after using hover scrub to locate the appropriate In point. Select Replace with Clip > From Bin from the menu when you right-click on the sequence clip you want to change.

Use Source Frame Matching instead of Edit

If you want to swap out a shot in Premiere Pro with a comparable one, try this method. Replace Edit ignores the In and Out points but considers the sequence and the playhead's position in the Source Monitor. To locate the identical spot in a different take, move the playhead over a word or action in the sequence. Select Replace with Clip > From Source Monitor > Match Frame after performing a right-click on the clip in the Sequence. The clip is altered without losing any of its characteristics.

Changes to the Project's Clip

Customers frequently send you updated files, or you can be swapping out a placeholder clip.
- In a Premiere Pro project, right-click the clip and choose Replace to swap out footage.
- In every segment, new footage takes the place of earlier video. The clip is altered without losing any of its characteristics.

Nesting a Sequence

One sequence has been nested inside another. One way to break up a big project into smaller, more manageable parts is to design different sequences for each component. Each sequence can then be dragged into a new master sequence, complete with clips, images, layers, different audio/video tracks, and effects. While nested sequences behave and look like individual audio/video clips, their content can be updated and changed within the main sequence. Although nesting sequences is a difficult post-production procedure, it could be a useful tool for your workflow if you can understand how to treat sequences as clips.

By nesting a sequence, you can:
Simplify editing by dividing intricate sequences into discrete parts. By doing this, you can prevent arguments and unintentionally altering clips, which could destroy your edit.
- Make it possible to apply an effect to numerous clips in one step.
- Sequences can be used as a source for other sequences. For a multi-part series, for instance, you may make a single intro sequence that is used at the beginning of every episode.
- All nested sequences will be updated instantly if the introductory sequence's content changes.
- Gives you the ability to arrange your source material similarly to how you would add bins in the Project panel.
- Use transitions as a single entity across numerous clips.
- The Insert and Overwrite Sequences as Nests or Individual Clips button located in the upper-left corner of the Timeline panel can be used to nest sequences.
- When changing one sequence into another, enabling this option will add the Source Sequence as a single nested sequence clip to the Main Sequence.
- All of the source sequence's clips are included in the nested sequence clip, which shares the same name.
- Changes made to the contents of nested sequences will be dynamically applied throughout the sequence.

122

Adding an inner sequence

Reusing a previously modified sequence is one application of use nesting. A revised opening title will now be inserted into a series.

- Verify that the option to stack sequences is selected by opening the sequence.
- At the beginning of the series, set an In point.
- To view the contents of the Open sequence in the Timeline panel, double-click on it in the Project panel.
- The Timeline panel shows the source track indicators for a clip or sequence, enabling you to set up track patching, whether you choose it from the Project panel or open it in the Source Monitor.
- Click once to select the open sequence in the Project panel. Click on a sequence's name in the Timeline tab to view it.
- Verify that the sequence track and source track V1 are in sync. A video Verify that Audio 1 is patched to source track A1.
- Sequences function similarly to clips when nested, so you can use your preferred option to change one sequence into another.
- Use the Comma (,) key to perform an insert edit. You have provided an In point in the sequence, which will be used for timing, so it doesn't matter where the Timeline playhead is. Double-clicking a nested sequence in the Project or Timeline panels will open it in a new Timeline panel within the same panel group as the current series, allowing you to change its contents.
- Press Ctrl+Z (Windows) or Command+Z (macOS) to reverse the previous change. Next, right-click the time ruler in the Timeline panel and choose "clear on and out."

Disable the sequence nesting function

- Drag your sequence selection Open from the Project panel to the beginning of the series in the Timeline panel (Windows) while holding down Command (macOS) or Ctrl. This also does an insert edit.
- The clips that make up the sequence are added to the existing sequence by Premiere Pro. The sequence has nothing to do with these extra clip occurrences. Furthermore, this sequence's contents remain unchanged.

Carrying Out Routine Trimming

The portion of a clip that is used in a sequence can be altered in a variety of ways. Trimming is the conventional term for this. By restoring or deleting content, the chosen portion of the original clip can be made shorter or longer during cutting. While some cutting methods simply impact a single clip, others have the potential to alter the interaction between multiple clips or even two adjacent segments.

About Trimming in the Source Monitor

In the Project panel, a clip that has been transformed into a sequence manifests as an independent instance from the original clip. A sequence clip can be viewed in the Source Monitor by double-clicking on it in the Timeline panel. The In and Out points can be changed once the clip has been accessed in the Source Monitor. The video will be added to the sequence. The navigator will automatically zoom in on the current selection when you open a sequence clip segment in the Source Monitor.

Explore all of the available clip content using the navigator

The Source Monitor's current In and Out points can be changed in two basic ways.

+ **Include more In and Out points:** Add new In and Out points to the Source Monitor in place of the current options. You cannot move the In or Out point in that way if there is another clip in the sequence that comes before or after the current one.

+ **Drag In and Out Points:** Hover your cursor over the Source Monitor's small timeline at the bottom to drag in and out points. The pointer contains two-way arrows and turns red and black when trimming is available. The In/Out point can now be changed by dragging left or right.

+ The current clip in the sequence cannot be enlarged in that direction if it is next to another clip.

The Program Monitor's trimming

Use the Program Monitor Trim mode if you want to trim more accurately. In addition to offering specific correction features, Premiere Pro shows the departing and incoming frames of the trim you're working on. The sequence will loop around the selected modification if you press the spacebar while the Program Monitor is in Trim mode. This implies that you can rapidly view the outcome and alter the timing of an edit at any time.

Three sorts of trimming are possible with the Program Monitor Trim mode selections. Among them are:

+ **Regular trim:** Removes one edit point from the chosen clip. Only one side of the edit point is trimmed using this method. No other clips are affected, but it shifts the specified edit point either earlier or later in the sequence.

+ **Ripple trim:** Similar to regular trim, this trim eventually shifts one of the edit points of the chosen clip. Only one side of the edit point is trimmed using this method. Clips are moved to fill in gaps or create space if editing lengthens them after the edit.

+ **Roll trim:** This feature advances the head of the adjacent clip (the beginning) as well as the tail of one clip (the finish). It lets you adjust an edit point's length (assuming handles are present). The length of the sequence doesn't change, and there isn't any pause.

Access to trim mode in the Program Monitor

The controls alter to make trimming easier while the Program Monitor is in trim mode. First, choose an edit point between two clips to activate Trim mode. Three options are offered.

+ Double-click an edit point (the left or right end of a clip) on the timeline using the selection or trimming tools. Alternatively, you can use the Selection tool to drag a rectangle around adjustments while holding Command (macOS) or Ctrl (Windows) to select adjustments and enter Trim mode.

+ When the blue right Timeline track appears, press Shift+T. The next available editing point will be reached by the playhead.

+ Use the Rolling Edit or Ripple Edit tools to drag one or more edits.

Two video clips are shown when the Program Monitor Trim mode is in use. The left-hand box shows the outgoing clip, also referred to as the A side. The incoming video clip, sometimes referred to as the B side, is displayed in the area on the right.

CHAPTER FOURTEEN
ADVANCED AUDIO EDITING

Premiere Pro Audio Effects that You Must Utilize

About DeNoise

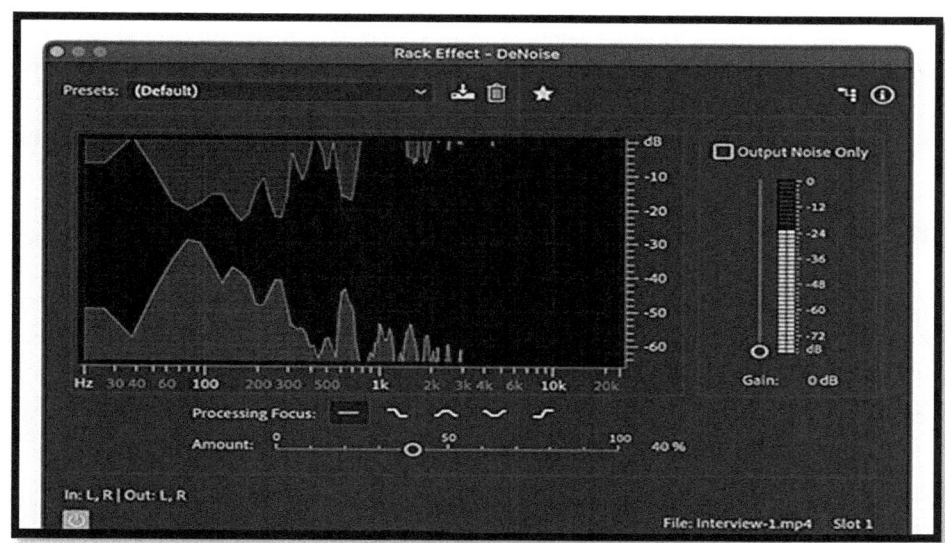

One of the most frequent problems that arises when working with audio is probably background noise. It happens often and is always difficult to get rid of. Because you simply need to use a slider to choose how much noise reduction you want to apply, Premiere Pro's built-in DeNoiser is simple to set up. Lowering the slider will lessen the amount of noise, but be cautious because your voice will also be impacted. Continuous noises from your electrical devices, such fans, air conditioners, and hums, can be eliminated using DeNoise. AudioDenoise's artificial intelligence removes sophisticated background noise that other plug-ins cannot because of its state-of-the-art technology. Its ability to identify and eliminate even the smallest sounds while preserving speech makes this possible. The quality of the sound can be improved by simply changing the basic parameters.

A DeEsser

For voice recordings, you will often use a sound effect called a DeEsser. It will assist you in lessening the sibilance that words that contain the consonants s, sh, ch, or t produce. Although speech is its primary usage, additional high frequencies and loud noises in your audio clips may benefit from its assistance. When using DeEsser, you can select between a broadband mode that compresses all frequencies uniformly and a multiband option that compresses the sibilance spectrum. You can adjust when the compressor is active, set the frequency band where the sibilance is more severe, and output the sibilance to fine-tune your audio.

The Delay

The repetition of an audio stream at millisecond intervals is known as a delay effect. It is capable of producing a wide variety of sound effects. When layering audio to produce more complex sound effects in your movies, the delay is commonly used. By varying the delay between the left and right channels, this is accomplished. It's ideal for creating mood-enhancing echo sounds. You may change the delay period, feedback, and delay spread with Premiere Pro's Analog Delay effect, which mimics a conventional delay using tape and tube warmth distortion. You can also select the delay spread.

The Flanger

Additionally, the Flanger effect adds a small delay (less than twenty milliseconds) to the audio stream while altering the speed of the original audio source. It is also known as the sweeping effect or the jet-plane effect. It creates an odd hallucinatory noise. But for sound design purposes, the Flanger effect can be a useful tool for altering audio. It is commonly used to create distorted rock guitars in music production. It can make your audio sound strange, so use it sparingly.

The chorus

With the help of short delays and minimal feedback, the Chorus effect can create the impression that a sound is being played repeatedly. Duplicating the sound at a similar frequency and timing accomplishes this. The Chorus audio effect can be used to record voices, produce crowded noises from a single audio track, or create stereo gaps in mono audio.

Phaser

Sometimes people mistake the effect Phaser for Flanger. It is applied to an audio source in order to phase-shift it before mixing it with the source. After selecting one of the signals, it passes it through filters that change the audio stream's level. You can hear the sound traveling both toward and away from you when these signals are mixed.

Reverberation

By adding an echo, the reverb effect gives the audio a more realistic feel. Convolution, studio, and surround reverb are the three reverb effect types available in Premiere Pro.

- **Convolution Reverb:** This technology faithfully captures reverberation in a variety of environments, including music halls and closets. Your computer needs to have a lot of processing power.
- **Studio Reverb:** This technique mimics the sound of an acoustic environment. It takes a lot less processing than the other two types of reverb.
- **Surround Reverb:** This effect was created especially for music and is only compatible with 5.1 audio sources. For those in the film industry, a surround reverb effect is an essential tool since it produces the dramatic effect that makes movies come to life.

Effects of Pitch Shifters

Voices with high or low pitches can be created with the Pitch Shifter effect. When only one person is recording various conversations, you can use the Pitch Shifter to make it seem like many people are speaking. For sounds other than voices, a pitch changer can be used. An essential component of a sound designer's work is experimentation!

Distortion

Distortion is a technique used in sound design to enhance or completely change an audio source. You can imitate muffled microphones and overdriven amplifiers, produce a growling sound, or combine all of these effects by adding saturation to your audio clip. When used sparingly, distortion is a great way to give an audio recording depth and warmth.

EQ Parametric

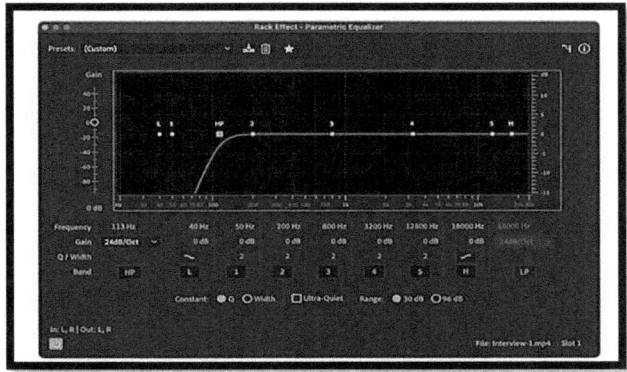

A single audio sample's frequencies can be adjusted using parametric equalization to produce a variety of tones. It is possible to apply cinematic effects and clean up vocal recordings. It's common to find presets that mimic a voice on an old-fashioned telephone or radio. These configurations can be intriguing.

Lowpass and Highpass filters

Frequencies that are either above or below a preset cutoff frequency can be eliminated using highpass and lowpass filters. On the other hand, a lowpass filter will increase the number of low frequencies displayed, while a highpass filter will concentrate high frequencies while decreasing lower frequencies. By using these effects, you can emphasize the most relevant audio frequencies in your music and achieve a more balanced sound. By combining these filters with reverb, you may create unique layers in your audio mixing and achieve great results.

Mastering

You may optimize audio files for their intended use, such as internet streaming, DVDs, or movie theaters, with Premiere Pro's mastering effect. Once you've completed layering and audio editing your tracks and clips, use this effect as the last step. The output volume will be adjusted by the mastering effect to stay below zero dB and prevent clipping. This will enable most audio devices to play your video. It is important to remember that the Track Mixer should only be used on the Master track. It is not appropriate to apply this to specific tracks or clips.

How to Use Premiere Pro to Cut Music to Complement Your Video

Section 1: Music 101

It is essential that we review the different time signatures and have a basic understanding of the language of music before we start. Additionally, one of the most often used time signatures in music is 4/4. This indicates that there are four beats in each subsequent measure. Four, eight, twelve, or sixteen measures are common ways to write the phrase. Therefore, we can use a straightforward formula to figure out where the audio has to be cut. For instance, you can easily identify the song shift by identifying the peaks of the curve and then using the razor tool to cut the frame if the beginning of your song includes eight measures but you only need four. As we make changes, keep this scenario in mind!

Section 2: Adapting Your Music to the Video

First Step: Assessing Your Audio for Editing
+ **Start by bringing in the audio:** Drag the audio file onto your video editing program's timeline from your source or library. Place it beneath the layer of video that you are working on at the moment. You can browse the Motion Array library's extensive collection of stock music if you require a track for your project.
+ **Assess the Length of the Audio Clip and the Beat Points:** Record the length of the audio clip and listen for beat points and rhythmic patterns in the sound waves.

This comment aids in comprehending the song's speed and structure. Because they will direct your editing process, these elements are essential to keep in mind.

+ **Imagining the Concluding Objective:** One of the most important steps is to visualize the final result of your edited audio. In order to smoothly integrate the music into the timeline and make sure that it is in line with the video's topic, it is intended to be purposefully chopped at particular moments.

Step 2: Accurately Editing and Cutting Your Music Track:

+ **Adopting the 4/4 Time Signature:** It's crucial to keep in mind that the 4/4 time signature is a helpful tool while you're editing your music track.

+ **Starting the Review Process:** Commence at the start of the audio clip and align it with the start of the video that you are using. Timing the start of the music track with the start of the video helps to create a seamless transition between the audio and visual elements.

+ **Applying Beat Counting to Accurate Cuts:** Perform a segmented music analysis. You can separate the music into portions by measuring the beats and making exact cuts with the razor tool at the end of each beat, for instance, if the first section comprises eight measures but you only need four.

+ **Segmentation:** After completing these cuts, the audio will be divided into two parts, each consisting of four measures.

+ **Emphasizing and Eliminating Extra Measures:** Choose which extra measurements need to be eliminated. To make your music track the length it needs, remove or cut them.

+ **Techniques for Handling Timeline Gaps:** After removing unnecessary portions, you might observe gaps in the timeline. These gaps need not be concerning; they can be filled by moving and changing the modified parts at a later stage.

+ Making use of ripple editing Use the delete function along with the ALT key (or Option on a Mac) to perform a ripple edit. By reinstalling the music track and modifying the chronology, this technique ensures a seamless transition between the different pieces.

+ **Talk about changes in tempo.** Look for instances where the rhythm or tempo shifts as you play the song again. Make sure to keep the length of each segment, which is four bars, constant while you carefully cut these parts with the razor.

+ **Repeating Procedures for Changes in Tempo:** Repeat the aforementioned steps each time the tempo or beat changes during the song to ensure that the edit is coordinated and harmonic.

+ **Approaching the Final Scene:** Keep editing until the music track is the right length, and then line it up with the cut of the video.

+ **Aligning the Final Note:** It's crucial to make sure that the video's ending harmonizes with the last note of the song. This will ensure that your video ends in a comprehensive and engaging way.

Step 3: Audio Editing Smoothness

+ **Identifying Sound Anomalies:** When editing, you may come into situations when a single note or abrupt sound disrupts the fluidity and flow of your audio cuts.

- **Getting to the Audio Transition Features:** To fix this problem, go to your editing program's Effects section and find the Audio Transitions. To combine audio components without any disruptions, just look for the cross-fade indicator.
- **Applying Cross Fades:** This comprises giving the audio recording's clipped portions the cross-fade effect. Any sudden audio changes between these segments can be lessened with the use of this transition effect.
- **Modifying the Cross Fade Settings:** Make careful to change the Delay settings to four frames after applying the Cross Fade effect (the default value is frequently one frame). This upgrade reduces the possibility of abrupt gaps or leaps in the audio by enabling more seamless and organic transitions between audio cuts.
- **Application Consistency:** Use the Cross Fade effect consistently throughout the music track where you've made cuts. The audio flows smoothly and consistently across the edited sections thanks to the application of this consistent method. Additionally, apply a four-frame delay for each Cross Fade effect to achieve the best possible smoothness.

Using Audio in Your Movie

In addition to cleaning your teeth, you will most likely drink orange juice. However, it is quite improbable that you would perform each one in succession, and even if you did, the outcome would not be enjoyable. Video clips can say the same thing. Even if the individual video might sound excellent, you will discover that they do not blend together as smoothly as you had hoped when you play them all together. Because the camera microphone picked up the natural sound on channel 2, there may be a level mismatch, unexpected noises that don't go well with the edit, or a dirty sound. This might cause distractions. The good news is that Premiere Pro makes fixing any of these problems—and more—simple.

Track linking and unlinking

Typically, when you add a video to your timeline, it consists of two tracks that move in unison. Some earlier formats may only contain a single monaural track; in other forms, stereo is integrated into a single track; and in still other formats, a single stereo track will include two stereo audio channels. In any event, it's encouraging that your audio and video tracks were successfully combined and synchronized. Otherwise, your video may look like a poorly dubbed movie if you are not careful. In other words, the video and audio will not work together. However, there are occasions when you may choose to purposefully cut the audio and video apart. Double-click the clip, then choose an In and Out point in the Source Monitor. The entire clip (audio and video) or just a portion of it can now be dragged onto the timeline. Click the Drag Video Only button (the first circle in the image at the bottom of this page) to drag just the video. You can drag only audio by simply pressing the Drag Audio Only button (the second one in the example).

Track unlinking

The process is quite easy if you already have the complete track in the timeline and want to separate the audio and video tracks.
Here's how:
- ┿ Select the video that you want to take off the timeline.
- ┿ Choose Unlink from the pop-up menu that appears when you right-click the clip. Another option is to choose Clip > Unlink.

The audio and video tracks are now distinct and can be added one at a time.

Relinking videos

It is possible to rejoin the disconnected clips. Just remember that you should select them collectively first.
Here's how:
- ┿ Verify that the elements of the clip you choose are on the timeline.
- ┿ You have two options: either right-click on the clip or select Link from the pop-up menu after selecting Clip > Link.

At this point, the audio and video tracks are combined into a single, moveable object.

Utilize Reverb to Close out a Song

How to Give a Song Reverb

Imagine that you have a song that you would like to conclude before it ends on its own. For audio editing, there are numerous options. To make it impossible to tell the two apart, one of them is splicing the actual end into the start of the same beat. But it's not implausible that the song's conclusion might leave you feeling let down right away. If this is the case, you can finish your song at any place you like in the next area. **To do this, take the actions listed below.**

1. **Track down the Beat:** Start by determining when you want the music to stop. Place it in a place where reverb can be added, then adjust the level manually and apply the reverb effect. After finishing, make sure the overall effect is harmonious. Once the ideal song conclusion has been defined, you can start using this strategy. It is important to keep in mind that creating a song's natural finale on the first beat is far simpler. What do we make of that? The beats of the song are as follows:

- 1,2,3,4
- 1,2,3,4
- 1,2,3,4
- 1,2,34

To find out what you are hearing, listen to the first one as well. On the first beat, the music starts. What follows?

2. **Putting the Song to Rest:** Select the desired portion of the song and cut it until it reaches the conclusion of the audio file. It may not sound right now, but that's okay. Making it sound right only requires a little effort. Next, select your file's final part and begin expanding it to the finish. Keep doing this until you get to the moment right before the song's next rhythm or main theme appears. Think about extending a brief segment—just a few milliseconds—to a very long duration. However, since you can only enhance what already there, think about if you enjoy the sound that is there right now. Make sure to stop recording before the finish if there is a part of the audio file that you do not like or that could ruin the finale. The location should then be clipped right after the downbeat, which is often the moment when the audio volume in that area increases the highest. Both your main audio part and the small section that has been cut off should now be visible. You will take your clip and nest it now, but nothing should sound out of place. You can right-click to access Nest.

3. **Closing the Video:** The video clip needs to be positioned in the proper order at this point. Holding down the Alt or Option keys while in the main sequence will solve the issue if you find that the song's ending cannot be extended any further. Make a copy of the clip on a different layer, turn it off, and then enlarge it as big as you can. Additionally, it's advised that you begin this phase with a fade-out and finish it by lowering the intensity to zero. It doesn't have to be too long, but letting it fade out naturally now can help cover up any severe cut-offs that might happen when you add the reverb later. You'll see that the nested sequence has been further expanded when you go back to your original composition.

4. **Add the Reverb Effect:** Now is the moment to add the Reverb Effect, which will resonate throughout your finished song and gives you a lot of creative freedom. You can apply the Studio Reverb Effect to your project after finding it in the Effects panel. To add it to the nested series, just drag & drop it. Now you can put it into practice and start to see its impact. You can't notice anything different right away, but we'll go over the precise characteristics and quantities to get you where you need to be.

5. **Changing the Reverb Controls:** Click on the audio clip you want to change, then choose the Effects Controls option. To access your Reverb Controls, you must press the edit button. The primary characteristic that will be in charge of delivering you is referred to as deterioration. Although your mileage will differ, we advise setting it between 5500 and 6500. Try 5500 to start, and adjust as necessary. Are you beginning to like the sound of it? I'm hoping the music is nearly done. There are a few things you may do to make your efforts more effective if you're still not satisfied. The sliders allow you to adjust the Dry and Wet output levels. The following explanation could account for this phenomenon: Your sound will bounce outward more if it is moist. The wettest output could not maintain the tone you want to achieve with your song, even if you think it's the finest choice. It appears that this Acoustic Indie Folk song in our repertoire would sound best with a dry output of 34 and a wet output of 26. Try listening to what sounds best at various times, though. Every new song will be different.

6. **Include the Final Details:** Lastly, you want to make your sound as spacious and complete as possible. The slider might be the cause of the low end being eliminated given the track's initial settings. It's possible that the low frequencies in this area are being physically eliminated by the low-frequency reduction. Therefore, you will be able to keep more of the deep bass sound the lower you drop it. Additionally, after you've finished that, make sure to tweak the Diffusion, Width Damping, and Room Size settings until you're satisfied with the sound. In order to finish the music with the reverb effect, the next step is to add a rapid and steady Power Fade. Just be sure it's fast enough so that the next beat doesn't drag the music back in.

Using the Crucial Sound Panel

Up until now, you have only been able to partially satisfy your requirements by altering the track levels on the timeline or making little adjustments to the audio using the mixers. However, using the Essential Sound tab places you in a different category. You would leave with a ton of hats, including one that said "Audio Engineer," if this panel were a hat store. Since it reimagines the difficulty of integrating several audio sources into an easy-to-use collection of transformative tools, it is worthy of the term. It's like the ability to use your favorite spreadsheet to do math or the discovery of autofocus for cameras.

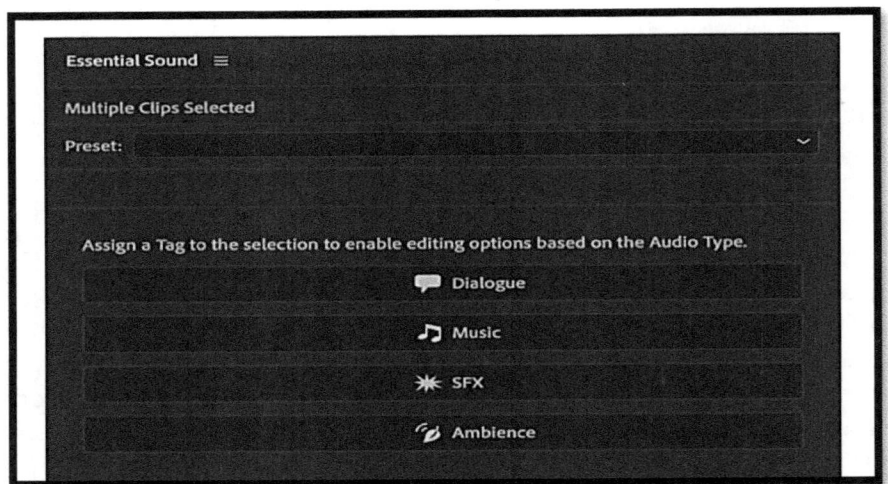

With just a few keystrokes or movements, this program can flawlessly blend a variety of audio genres across the entire film, including conversation, music, and natural sound. By going to Window, then Audio, you may locate this special Workspaces feature.

Making Use of the Crucial Sound Panel

Located on the right side of the workstation, this all-in-one panel offers a convenient location for your audio needs. It is perfect for audio mixing tasks because it provides a large variety of mixing techniques and repair options. These preset options, which are arranged into four basic categories—conversation, music, sound effects, and ambiance—allow you to classify your audio files. You can change the settings for each group when you assign a set of chosen clips. These adjustments include adding compression or equalization, lowering background noise, and leveling out the various recordings. Nevertheless, this does not imply that you can only use these choices. Imagine that you will mix your clips in the Essential Sound panel, then make any necessary modifications in the Audio Track Mixer. You can use standard techniques to apply the finishing touches when the fundamental modifications are finished. For instance, if your footage has conversation, you can use the conversation tab in the Essential Sound panel to adjust the sound by removing noise, rumble, hum, and ess noises, among other adjustments.

Using the Essential Sound Panel's Audio Tracks

Depending on the type of track, Premiere Pro will assign a distinct color label to each one you add to the timeline. For instance, camera tracks are colored blue, video tracks are colored green, still photos are colored pink, and so on. By choosing Labels from the Premiere Pro settings menu, you can alter the colors. You can modify each kind of audio track by assigning these tracks to one another in this panel.

135

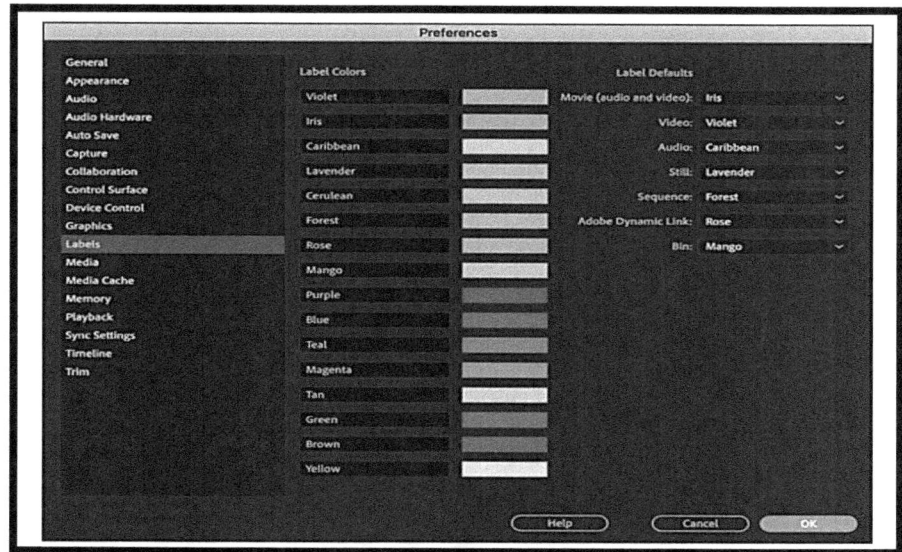

Being organized is essential

Since your audio components will be used for various purposes, it is a good idea to arrange your audio clips according to each category. Following the selection of an audio type, the Essential Sound panel offers access to a number of parameter groups for basic tasks like EQ and compression as well as background noise reduction. **Audio clips can be arranged using the tags shown below.**

    ⚓ The parts that your talking heads speak are called dialogue.

    ⚓ **Music:** The soundtrack or any other musical selections you make.

    ⚓ **SFX:** Any extra sound effects you incorporate into the mix.

    ⚓ **Ambience:** The scene's sound design, which includes cutaways and setups.

Assigning roles to audio tracks

The Essential Sound panel's capabilities can help you swiftly balance different audio genres, such music and sound effects, once you've laid out your movie on the timeline. The first step is to choose the kinds of sounds you want to use in the movie. Click the relevant option once you've made your selections. Right now, anything you do will have an impact on all of the songs you've chosen.

Exploring the presets for dialogue

You'll probably utilize the conversation presets the most because they let you apply standard operations to a collection of footage. Why not, then? Interview subjects, scene actors, and narrators can all significantly lengthen your movie.

Audio Tools Reset

- To access the tools panel, check the box next to the group you are working on. Click the Clear Audio Type button in the top-right corner to switch panels. Let's see how well the activities under this tab work. Select the Dialogue checkbox in the Essential Sound tab after determining which clips to modify. The panel appears with buttons and sub-menus associated with this option, as seen below.

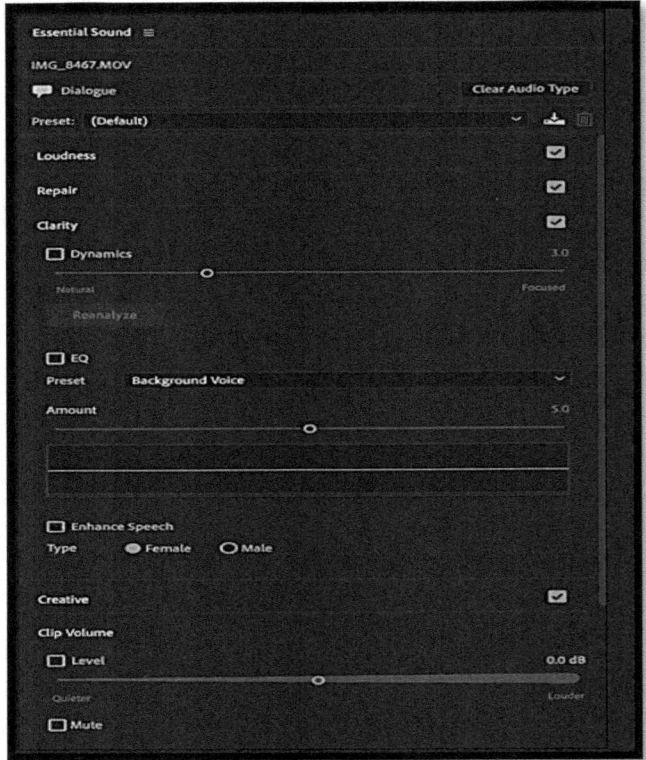

What they do is as follows:
- **Preset:** Presets can be used to duplicate sound from specific sources or situations or to guarantee consistency.
- **Volume:** Auto-Match settings are revealed when the Volume button is pressed. To guarantee that every clip sounds the same, this tool automatically modifies their levels.
- **Repair:** This option shows you how to change the audio in your movie, including the EQ, esses, and noise.
- **Clarity:** These options adjust human voice loudness and frequency in addition to other factors that affect track clarity. Audio can be changed by a variety of factors.
- **Creative:** Using presets, you may give your video presence.

✦ **Clip Volume:** The slider allows you to change the music's volume or turn it off.

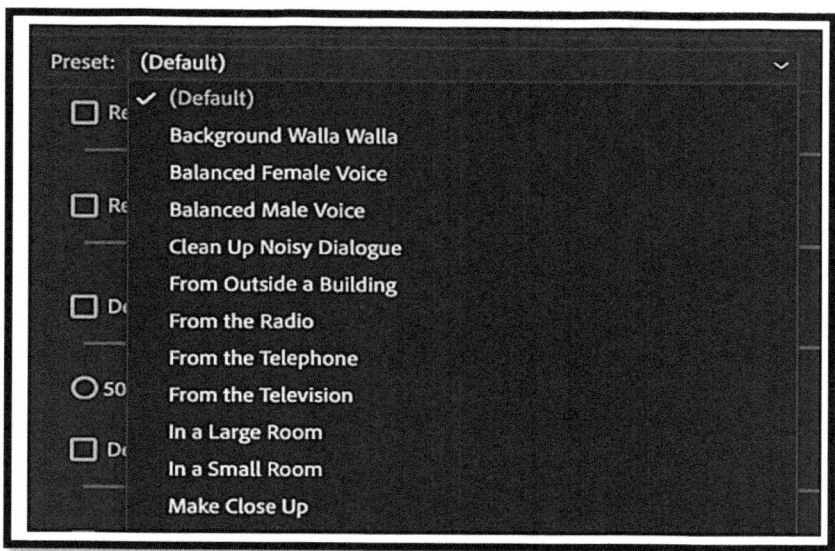

Controls for Clarity

The following can be changed with the Clarity controls:
  ✦ **Dynamics:** Modify the intensity and naturalness range.
  ✦ **EQ:** This feature modifies recording frequencies according to external conditions, phone usage, and background.
  ✦ **Improve Speech:** Modify the human voice's frequency.
  ✦ **Creative:** Offers pre-sets for the site of the conversation, including a small room, an outdoor space, a church, etc.

Examining the Music Selection

You can adjust the volume of a track using the Music option just like you do with the Dialogue option. But it also does something else, which is to duck—that is, duck the sound. Some words, such as this one, can be interpreted as attempts to sidestep or avoid (duck) noises. However, it is not what it suggests. Instead, you can use this function to change the volume of a particular track while other tracks are playing. When you arrange the clips on the timeline and select Generate Keyframes, this function creates keyframes that lower the music levels so that the conversation and foreground noises can be heard. This is because you want the music to stop when people are talking.

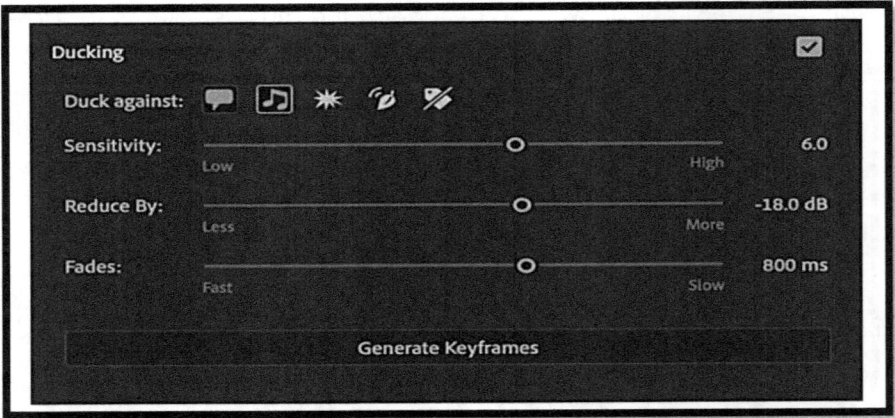

Impacting the Sound Effects Track

You may create illusions like music coming from a particular spot in the stereo field or the atmosphere of a field or room with the right amount of reverberation and reflections if you can use Premiere Pro to add false sound effects (SFX) to your audio.

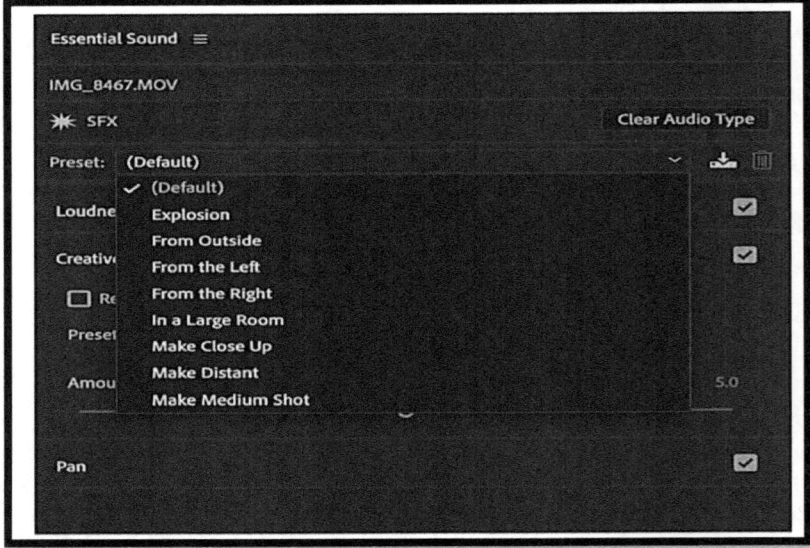

To enhance your audio with SFX:
+ The effects clip should be added to the timeline.
+ Select the clip and select SFX under the Essential Sound tab.
+ To alter the effect, select the Reverb checkbox under Creative.
+ Choose a Reverb configuration that satisfies your needs.

Modifying the Scene

As the name suggests this group of tools aids in controlling background noise and natural sound in a given setting. The pull-down menu in the first image and the Creative menu options in the second illustrate the range of settings in which this function can be utilized to create fake echo and reverberation.

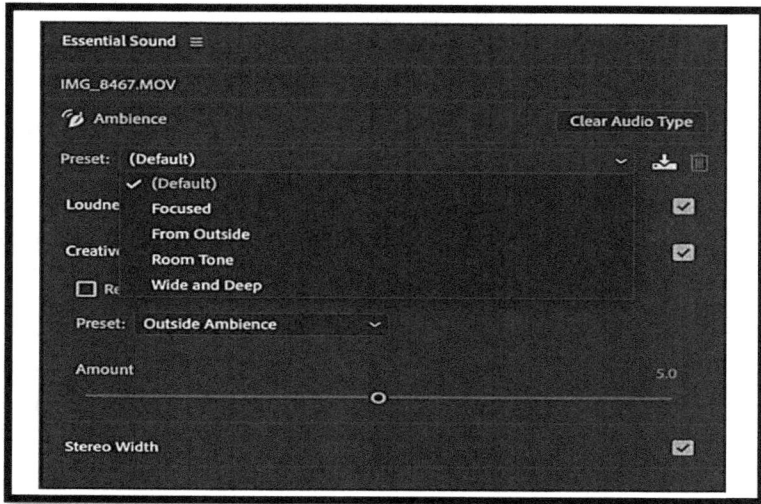

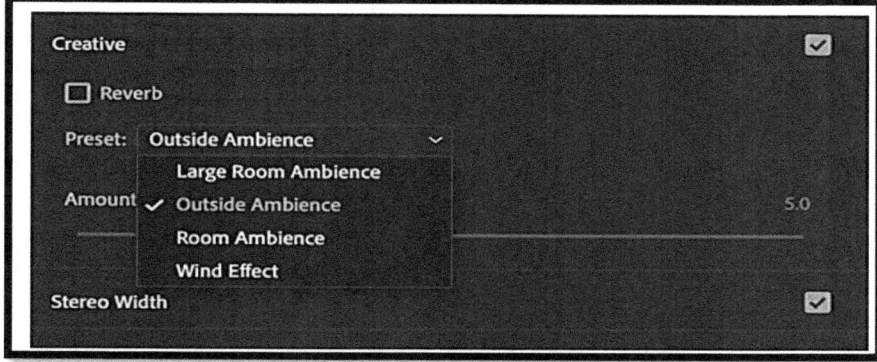

Enhancing the sound of voices

An essential step in the editing process is fine-tuning the chat audio. Regretfully, different clips have different audio capture. Although there are sporadic differences in speech volume, noise and hiss problems are the most common. Numerous methods for resolving audio problems can be found in the Repair tab (found beneath the Dialogue option on the Essential Sound panel).

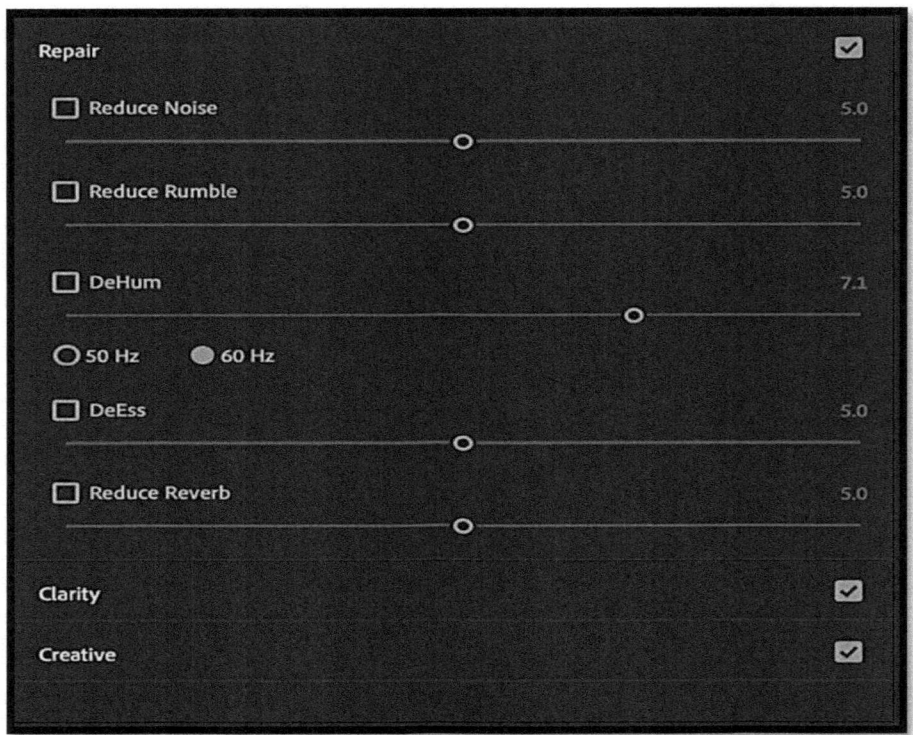

The following is what the repair controls do:

- **Reduce Noise:** Cuts down on distracting background noise, such as microphone noise, clicks, and studio floor noise. The amount of noise reduction needed depends on the kind of background noise and the permitted quality loss for the remaining signal.
- **Reduce Rumble:** Rumble noise, which is very low-frequency and occurs below 80 Hz, is reduced by this function. Action cams and turntable motor noise are examples of this kind of noise.
- **DeHum:** This method lessens or gets rid of hum, a single-frequency noise that is prevalent throughout North and South America, Europe, Asia, and Africa and ranges between 50 and 60 Hz. For instance, electrical interference from power lines that are too near audio cables might produce this kind of noise. You can change the hum level based on the clip.
- **DeEss:** DeEss eliminates high-frequency, abrasive sounds like sibilance in voice recordings that produce s-sounds due to breathing or air movement between the microphone and the vocalist's lips.
- **Reduce Reverb:** This method eliminates or lessens reverb in audio recordings. This software allows you to use real recordings from multiple sources to make them seem to be from the same location.

CHAPTER FIFTEEN
CORRECTION OF COLOR AND GRADING

Comprehending Display Color Management

Compared to televisions and movie projectors, computer monitors frequently use a different technique to show color. You can almost ensure that your audience will be viewing your films on a computer screen that is comparable to your own, and that the colors and brightness levels of your photos will be the same if you are producing them for online distribution. A viewing strategy that is suitable for the type of screen is required when displaying video on a TV or a movie theater screen. Professional colorists can use certain display technology to review their work. They will use a projector that looks like the one in a movie theater to show the image on a screen for review if they are making a film for theaters. In some situations, computer screens can reproduce color more accurately than televisions. Premiere Pro may alter the way video is displayed in the Source Monitor and Program Monitors to mimic how colors appear on a television screen if you have enabled GPU acceleration and are using this kind of computer monitor.

+ Compatible displays will be immediately detected by Premiere Pro. In Premiere Pro > Preferences > General (macOS) or Edit > Preferences > General (Windows), choose Display Color Management to activate this option.

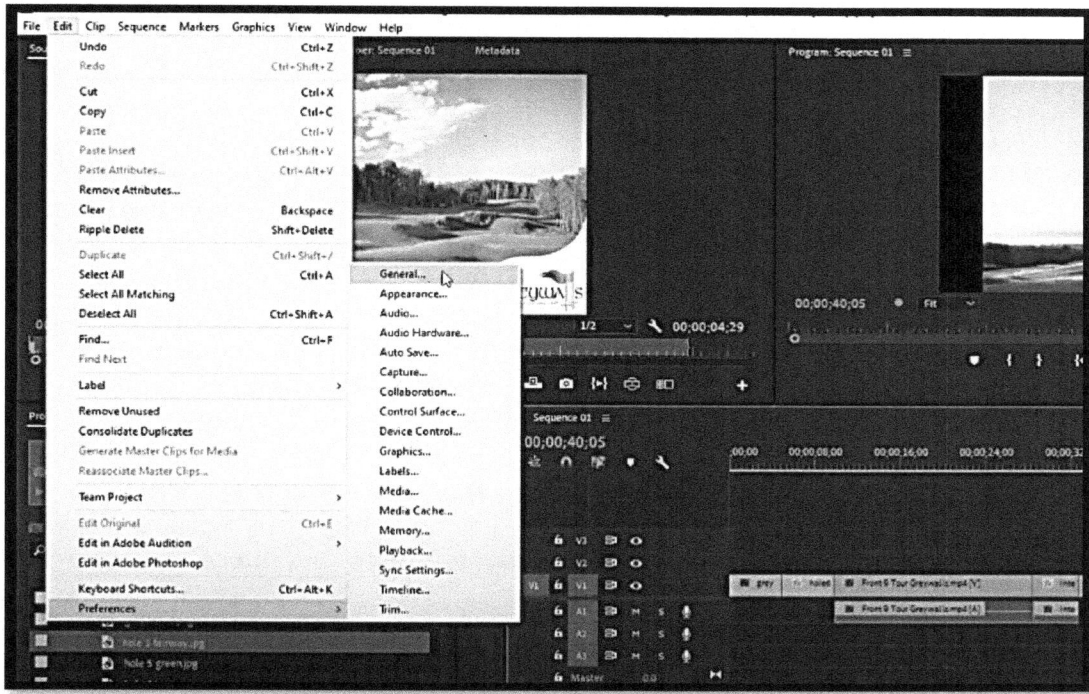

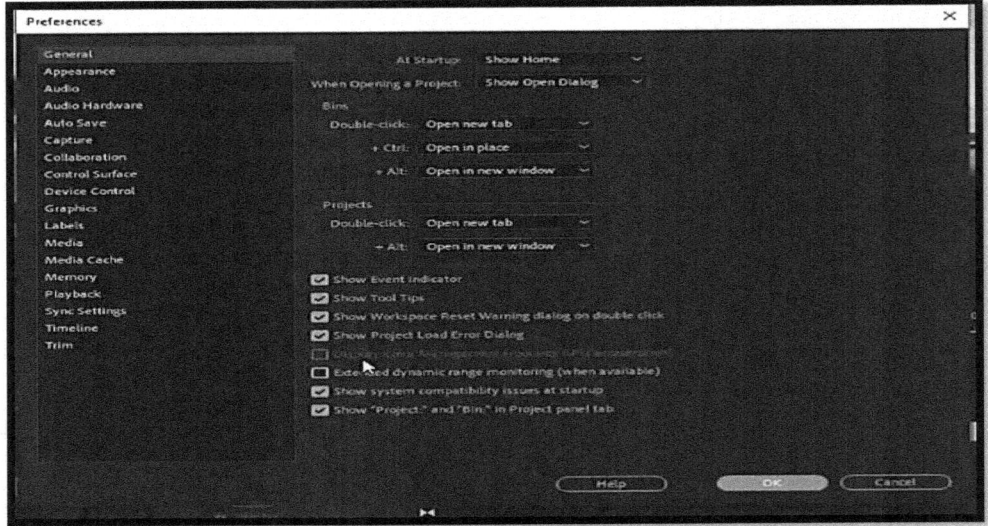

Workflow for general color correction

Now that you have chosen the Color workplace, it is a good idea to change your perspective. Once your clips are in position, evaluate them more on how well they blend and appear than on the volume of events and action. When working with color, there are two primary steps.

 + Verify that the color, brightness, and contrast of the clips in each scene are consistent, showing that the same camera, location, and time were used to capture them.
 + Give everything a unique appearance, such a certain tint or tone.

It's typical to approach each of these goals separately and in this way, even if you'll need the same tools to accomplish them. The continuity will be broken if two clips from the same scenario have different colors.

Observing the Color workplace

The Lumetri Color panel, which has numerous sections with color tweaking options, is part of the Color workspace. Additionally, it integrates the Source Monitor and the Lumetri Scopes panel. Numerous tools for image analysis are accessible through the Lumetri Scopes panel. The remaining screen real estate is used by the Program Monitor, Timeline panel, Project panel, Tools, and Audio Meters. **The Timeline panel contracts to make room for the Lumetri Color panel.**

 + To see it, select the Lumetri Scopes panel. There are more display settings available on the panel than by default.
 + To view the scopes, choose Presets > Vectorscope YUV/Parade RGB/Waveform YC by performing a right-click in the middle of the Lumetri Scopes window.

- The clip with the highest targeted score is chosen if there are clips on several track-targeted tracks.
- This workspace is more about finishing tasks than it is about planning or reviewing your work, even though you can open and close any panel at any time.
- The Lumetri Color panel will automatically choose sequence clips on tracks with track targeting enabled when you scrub the playhead over certain tracks.
- This feature is crucial since, similar to other effects, modifications made in the Lumetri Color panel are always applied to the selected clip. When you apply a modification, the Timeline panel's playhead will automatically select the next clip for you to work on.
- You can turn on or off automatic clip selection by selecting Sequence > Selection Follows Playhead.

A general view of the Lumetri Color panel

The Effects panel provides access to the Lumetri Color effect, which has all of the settings and choices found in the Lumetri Color panel. The Effect Controls panel displays its controls next to those for any other effect. The chosen clip takes on the Lumetri Color effect the first time you use the Lumetri Color panel. Any Lumetri Color effects that have already been applied have their parameters changed as you work on the footage. The Lumetri Colour panel functions somewhat as a remote control for the Lumetri Colour effect settings in the Effect Controls panel. Like any other effect, Lumetri Color effects may be copied and pasted from one clip to another, presets can be made, and the Effect Controls panel can be used to adjust the settings.

Making Use of Comparison View

These are the most crucial actions to take when attempting to alter the color of something:
- **Color grading:** This process eliminates color casts or brightness issues, aligns shots in a sequence to make them appear to be from the same video that was captured at the same time and location, or ensures that they satisfy an internal standard for final delivery.
- **Color grading:** This technique determines how each shot, scene, or entire sequence should seem. You might want to compare two shots side by side before making any color corrections. This is particularly useful when the two photos were taken in different locations since, although the colors may differ, the general tone should remain the same. The Comparison View button could be difficult to see in some panels.
- In the Program Monitor's lower right corner, click the two arrows. 3. Select Comparison View from the resulting menu.
- You can use the Source Monitor as a reference for side-by-side comparison by dragging your current sequence from the Project panel onto it, but switching the

Program Monitor to Comparison view is a simpler method. Click the "Comparation View" button on the PC monitor to begin doing this immediately.

Updated controls

- **Reference frame:** Also known as the automatic color matching frame of reference frame.
- **Reference position:** The timecode of the reference frame.
- **Playhead position:** The timecode of the current frame.
- **Snap or Frame Comparison:** Alternate between referring to the status of the current frame and the preceding frame. The latter option keeps your eyes from getting accustomed to the finished output by allowing you to view the before and after continuously while working with effects.
- **Side by Side:** Examine the two images separately and compare them.
- **Vertically Divided:** See the two images on a single screen that is divided vertically and features a movable separator.
- **Horizontal Split:** This option has a horizontal separator but is otherwise the same as Vertical Split.
- By flipping the sides, you can alter the images on the left and right.
- **Current frame:** The frame you're working on right now.

Complementary Colors

The Lumetri Color panel's ability to instantly match the colors of two clips is among its greatest and fastest features.

- In the Color Wheels & Match area of the Lumetri Color screen, click the Apply Match button. Next, switch to the Comparison view in the Program Monitor and select a current frame and a reference frame.
- It won't always be ideal; you may need to experiment with other reference and current frame selections to find a better match. However, the outcome is frequently sufficiently similar that you can make additional adjustments while still adhering to the first automatic repair. Premiere Pro saves a great deal of time if the color is accurate 80% of the time.

Let's try our current sequence:

- The reference frame must be set to 00:00:00, carrying over from the previous task.
- Move the playhead to the beginning of the final clip in the row after scrolling through the Timeline panel. It's simple to navigate between the series' clips by pressing the Up and down button keys.
- These are snippets taken from various scenes in the same film. Although it's not necessary, it would be preferable if the colors matched precisely. Remember to choose Face Detection from the Lumetri Color panel. This will assist Premiere Pro in identifying faces and selecting appropriate tones.

- When you select a clip from the Lumetri Color tab and click the Apply Match button, Premiere Pro fixes the clip's color.
- The distinction is obvious. However, your eyes will probably adjust to the new frame's appearance in due time. Turn the Color Wheels & Match check box on and off frequently to highlight the difference.
- Click the Comparison View icon to return to the standard playing view in the Program Monitor.
- The Lumetri Color panel's automatic color-matching feature is unlikely to find an exact match because people's perceptions of color vary depending on their environment. However, you can still alter all of the previously made modifications to improve the outcome.

Examining the Impact of Color Adjustment

There are numerous additional well-liked color effects that you should become familiar with in addition to color changes using the Lumetri Color panel. Keyframes allow you to adjust the parameters over time, just like the other effects. If you adjust the parameters in the Effect Controls tab, the Lumetri Color effect functions in the same manner. The search box at the top of the Effects panel is always a good place to look for an effect. Applying an effect to a clip with a good variety of colors, highlights, and shadows, then adjusting all the settings to see what occurs, is a good approach to learn how to use it. As you become more proficient with Premiere Pro, this occurs frequently. In some situations, you may not be able to predict which effect will be most effective. Depending on your preferred method of using Premiere Pro, there are frequently multiple ways to do the same task. It is advised that you experiment with various effects to see what you can achieve. To see how colors, highlights, and shadows affect various kinds of content, pick a video that uses a variety of these effects.

Resolving Exposure Issues

Let's examine a few clips that exhibit brightness problems and determine how to use the Lumetri Color panel to resolve them.
- Verify that you are in the Color section and return to the saved version if necessary.
- Launch the Color Work application.
- To quickly turn off all other scopes and start the waveform show on its own, right-click on the Lumetri Scopes panel or go to the Settings menu and choose Presets > Waveform RGB.
- Last time, you can choose Waveform Type > YC No Chroma from the Settings menu or right-click on the Lumetri Scopes panel. The waveform on the screen is altered to use the conventional broadcast TV range in this way, which is a good standard for the majority of video applications.
- The playhead ought to be placed on the series' opening clip.

- This piece is smokey; full exposure is indicated by 100 IRE (on the left side of the waveform) and no exposure is indicated by 0 IRE.
- Click the Basic Correction heading to view that section of the Lumetri Color panel. Change the shot using the Exposure and Contrast settings, and watch the waveform display to ensure it doesn't become excessively bright or dark.
- Displaying a frame from a later segment of the tape on the screen will yield the greatest results. There is a fairly noticeable stretch at 00:00:07:19. Reduce the Exposure to 0.6 and increase the Contrast to 60.

Fixing an Underexposed Picture

Now let's experiment with an improperly exposed image.
- Go to the Effects section.
- The second clip in the Color Work sequence should have the timeline's playhead. This video clip may appear to be fine at first sight.
- To view the waveform for this clip, use the Lumetri Scopes panel. Near the line at the bottom of the graphic that reads "0 IRE," there are numerous black dots. There are multiple applications for the Lumetri Scopes panel. It is always accessible via the Window menu.
- Locate the Brightness & Contrast effect by selecting the Effects tab. The effect can be added to the video.
- To relocate the Lumetri Scopes panel to a new set of panels on the left side of the Program Monitor, drag the panel name down and to the right. In this manner, the Lumetri Scopes panel, the Program Monitor panel, and the Effect Controls panel are all visible simultaneously.
- You can adjust the brightness using the Brightness setting in the Effect Controls menu. Instead of clicking on the blue number and entering a new one, you may see the change occur gradually. As you drag, notice how the entire design rises. The brightness of the image is effectively emphasized, but the shadows remain flat. The dark shadows become gray thanks to your efforts. You can see how flat the image remains if you increase the brightness to 100 and slightly crop the highlights.

Fixing Overexposed Images

- In Timeline, move the playhead to the fifth clip in the sequence. The majority of the pictures have been destroyed by fire. Burned-out bright areas lack definition, much like the flat shadows in the second clip of the series. Therefore, the character's face and hair will be the only features that seem gray when the brightness is reduced.
- To increase the contrast range, try using the Lumetri Color panel. Although you might get good results, the video will appear to have been edited.

Fixing Color Offset

Your eyes automatically detect any changes in the color of the light surrounding you. Because of tungsten light, you have a very unique skill that allows you to see white as white even when it is orange. Cameras can automatically adjust their white balance in response to changes in light, much like your eyes can. Whether you are filming indoors or outside (where the light is bluer), white objects will appear white if the conditions are correct. Because the settings that are meant to adjust the white balance automatically don't always work, professional shooters frequently choose to adjust it manually. You may obtain some intriguing outcomes if you adjust the white balance incorrectly. The most common source of color balance issues in clips is improper camera calibration.

Making Use of Special Color Effects

The Effects tab contains a variety of expressive effects that you can apply to the colors in your video.

Making Use of Gaussian Blur

Although it's not a color adjustment effect, adding a little shading can make your adjustments appear less harsh and give the image a more realistic appearance. Premiere Pro features some motion effects, as you can see. Most people choose Gaussian Blur. It adds a smoother, more realistic appearance to a photograph.

Making use of stylized effects

The Stylize effect group offers several dramatic alternatives. Some of them, like the Mosaic effect, will be used with an effect mask for more pragmatic purposes, such as concealing someone's face. With the Solarize effect, you may add style to images or opening sequences by altering the backplate colors.

Including Color Adjustments Based on Files

The Looks list you previously experimented with is integrated into the Lumetri Color panel. As you are aware, there are some Lumetri color options in the Effects tab to get you started. **All of these have the Lumetri Color effect.**

- The Lumetri effect allows you to use one of the built-in presets or a current LOOK, LUT, or CUBE file to make minor, subtle color adjustments in your video.
- You can utilize a LOOK or LUT file as a starting point for your color adjustments. Cameras and position markers are increasingly using this kind of color reference file. When altering footage after the fact, it is beneficial to maintain the same standard.
- Locate the Basic Correction section of the Lumetri Color panel, then select the Input LUT option. To use an existing LOOK, LUT, or CUBE file, select Browse next.

CHAPTER SIXTEEN
UNDERSTANDING GRAPHICS AND TITLES

Premiere Pro can do some amazing things when you incorporate titles and motion graphics into your edit. Still unsure? Consider watching a nameless film. You'll undoubtedly come to the conclusion that something is still lacking. However, it's difficult to fathom not waiting for the movie title or closing credits to appear when you consider how text is employed in movies and television shows. On-screen identities are also required for new scenes and movies. How would you be able to identify the talking heads without the essential middle third? Next are the times and places of the scene. As a result, it is difficult to envision completing an edit without these crucial components.

Comprehending Titles and Motion Graphics

Title cards can have a significant impact on your film, but there may be other methods to engage the viewer. By including intricate visuals that you can drag and drop into the timeline to make them appear as though they were created in After Effects, Premiere Pro fundamentally altered the way you play. Since the Graphics Templates panel was added, more advancement has been made. To make your presentation more engaging, you can use the tools and visuals here to reorganize the text onstage, add movement, and personalize your message.

Finding your way around the Graphics Templates panel

In Premiere Pro, loading a particular section speeds up the process, but this is also the case for a lot of other functions. Therefore, before you add a movie title, use a lower third to draw attention to a subject, or create an intriguing opening sequence, you must choose the appropriate workspace. Navigating to Window > Workspace > Captions and Graphics will accomplish this. This section contains the Graphics Templates panel, which is located on the right side of the workstation. It offers all the tools you need to type anything you want on the screen. In terms of names and images, this panel performs as promised. It also includes pre-set themes, your graphics, and the Adobe Library. You may obtain the titles and graphics you require by using the Graphics Templates panel, which provides you with a robust approach.

Examining the templates

The Edit and Browse sections are located at the top of the Graphics Templates panel. By searching through the names that are included with the program, you can download other pictures and locate the one you want. It's time to fill the timeline with content after selecting a title and dragging it in. On the Edit tab, you can then add keyframes, modify, and alter the information that will appear in your image or title. The Graphics Templates category allows you to easily search for, browse, and download motion graphics. With a few easy steps, you can instantly add some flair to your film by changing a picture. You can now create the types of graphics that were previously limited to After Effects thanks to this relatively recent capability. This panel displays every motion graphic available on your PC, in Adobe Creative Cloud, and in Adobe Stock. What is motion graphics, in your opinion? These are motion-based images, which can be quite captivating. Consider it the title of an anime.

Making use of text-to-speech

It's not always better to talk about it. I can't help but think of the scene from The Office when a broke Michael Scott exclaims, "I declare bankruptcy," as if speaking those words will make it happen. Unfortunately, it didn't. However, Premiere Pro has a new Speech to Text feature that instantly converts spoken words in your video into editable text, allowing you to utilize it for things like subtitles and transcripts. **You can benefit from this functionality in the following ways:**

+ **Transcripts your video:** After arranging your clips on the timeline, you can quickly create a transcription of your video by selecting a segment or the entire edit and clicking a few times.
+ **Turn on closed captioning:** Your video will sync with the conversation's pace after processing, much like closed captioning on a flat-screen TV.
+ **Various languages are supported:** In addition to American and UK English, this feature is currently available in 13 other languages, including Spanish, Italian, Hindi, and Mandarin.
+ **Style captions:** After finishing the transcription, you can improve your text by adding more individuality and flair. Try it in the real world.

Making a Transcript

Transcribing is the most time-consuming part of creating a news article, interview, social media post, or anything else that requires copy. This technique is quicker now that Premiere Pro has Speech to Text. Make sure to select the new Graphics Workspace and Captions option so you can activate it. **This is one way to use it.**

+ Selecting Windows > Text will bring up the Text Panel. Click on Transcript on the panel's left side.

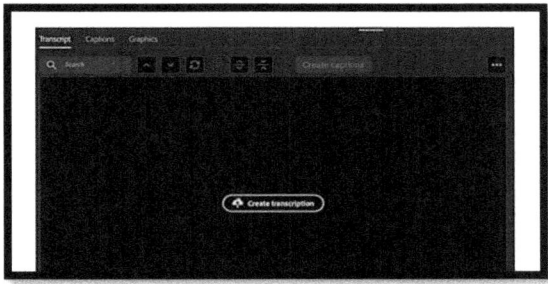

- Select the portion of the timeline that needs to be copied if you have marked the start and finish of your video.
- As soon as the "Making a Transcript" message box appears. It displays details like the file name and duration, and you can choose to copy just one track or the entire audio mix. As of right now, you can also record between the in and out locations, select a language, or opt to segregate when various persons are speaking.

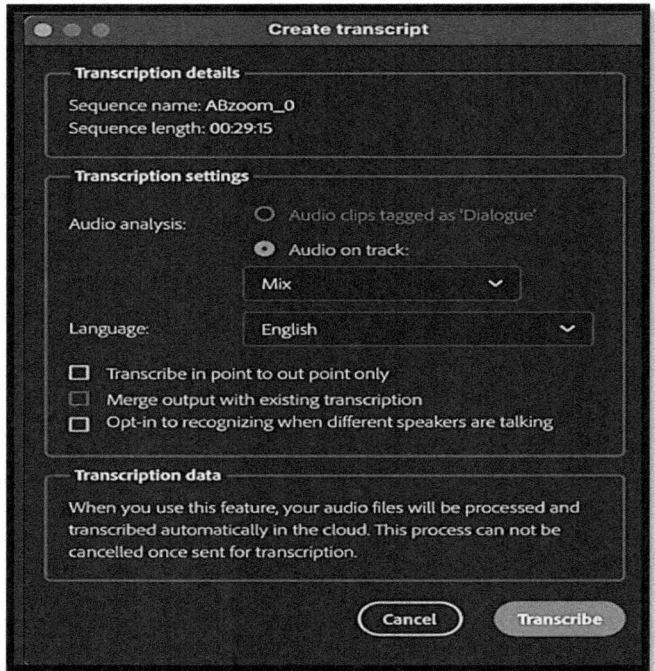

- Select what you want, click OK to proceed, and the procedure will start.
- Your writing will appear in the panel after it is finished. You can click the three dots in the far-right panel to check the spelling or email it as a text file.

Making Captions

Similar to closed captioning on TV, you can add comments to your video after creating the description. It's an easy process. Once your recording is complete, select the Caption link located on the panel's left side.

How to accomplish it:
- The Create Captions text box appears when you click the Create Captions button.
- Select the options that excite you. See the right for details on how to rearrange the Timeline's comments.

+ Click OK once you've finished editing the titles. As seen in the yellow figure below, the captions will be synchronized with the video's speech and put to the Timeline's Captions Track.

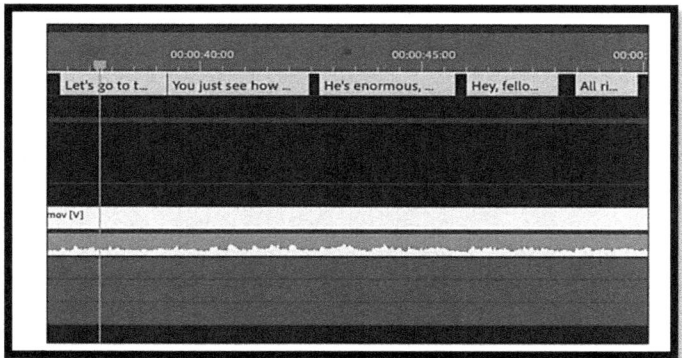

Understanding the Controls for Creating Captions

+ **Create from sequence transcript:** By selecting this option, you can use the transcript you just created to create subtitles.
+ **Create blank track:** This option button allows you to either create a blank space for manually adding comments or load an existing one.srt file.
+ **Caption preset:** The Subtitle Default option is frequently the finest selection from the drop-down menu when it comes to the caption setting.
+ **Format:** When choosing a caption style, the pull-down bar typically indicates that Subtitle is the best option.
+ **Stream:** You can modify the description of certain video formats that stream using this option.
+ **Style:** Any style selections you saved here can be retrieved if you used this tool.

These three options allow you to adjust the length, frequency, and spacing of the comments. You can choose between single and double space for the last option.

Using Text Effects

Text editing

Technologies for transcribing speech to text are almost as accurate as human speech. Nevertheless, misspelled or mispronounced words might lead to errors or improper language. Don't worry; you can easily fix your transcription. Double-click the text box in the transcription to quickly fix these mistakes.

Graphics Editing

After you've chosen the right image, drag it onto the Timeline and position it as you like. Double-click it, and then complete the forms. That's how simple it is.

Finding a graphic is simple

Enter the name of the image or title in the search box to locate it. You can choose between the My Templates button at the top of the panel, which gives you access to templates that are already loaded in Premiere, and Adobe Stock, where you can find more or free graphics in the Creative Cloud. By checking the Libraries and Local Templates Folder checkboxes, you can focus your search. The first shows the templates that have been imported into Premiere, while the second gives access to particular libraries. Swiping over the visual option allows you to see if the impact is what you want. Click the star to make it your favorite if you're still undecided. You can locate exactly what you're looking for later by going through your favorites. Drag your selected effect onto the timeline.

The Browse Section

To find more, look through the local templates that are accessible or use Adobe Stock. Some require money, while others are free. These well-designed templates are simple to modify by just dragging them onto the timeline. For more options, check out the Adobe Stock marketplace, which offers titles, images, and motion graphics.

The Editing Section

After dragging the visual template onto the timeline, you can now add text. On your timeline, click the image. This section offers a place to enter text, attributes, and alignment controls for particular selections in the required fields. This is simpler than entering your data straight into the already-filled graphic.

Dissecting text changes

Here's a brief rundown of the editing tools available to you once you've created your text.
- **Align and Transform:** You can change the text's scale and alignment with this feature set.
- **Text properties:** Provides the entire basic text configuration options, including font type, style, size, and tracking.
- **Appearance:** Four color-selection tools allow you to select the fill, stroke, background, and shadow.

Modifying Fonts

Are you unhappy with the size or font you selected? No issue. You only need to click once to update or replace them in Premiere Pro. For instance, you can use the Replace Fonts command in Projects to change the font on all levels of a design with multiple text layers at once if you decide that the MS Gothic font lacks the pizazz of Century Gothic bold.

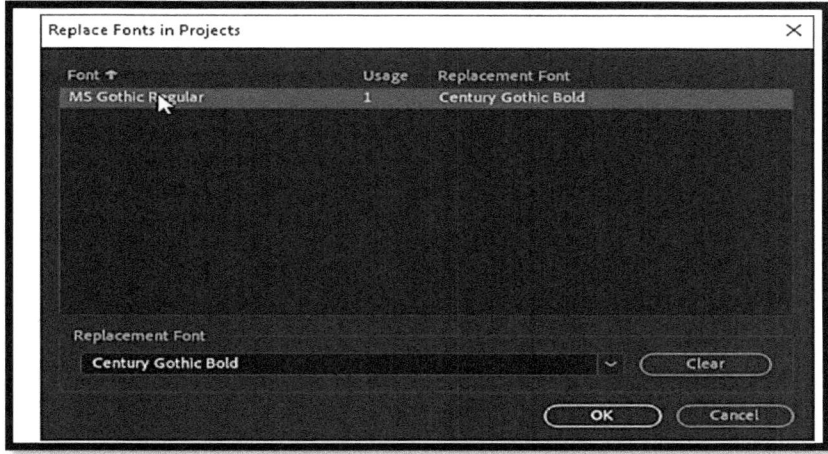

This is how to go about it:
+ Select Graphics and then Fonts to alter the fonts used in a project. The dialog box Replace Fonts in Projects opens. A list of fonts used in the project is shown below.
+ Draw attention to the typeface you want to alter.
+ Utilizing the Replacement Font drop-down option located at the panel's bottom, choose the font you wish to use.
+ Click the OK button.

Exporting Titles

There is a problem with Premiere Pro that prevents titles from being saved. This could be problematic, particularly if you wish to use the same title for multiple projects. By choosing File > Export > Title, you can export the title even though it cannot be stored. Name the title (which appears clear), select a location, and click Save. Then, just like with any other asset, you can import it into a project.

Create Graphics

The graphic settings in Premiere Pro allow you to have a large number of text, shape, and clip layers. Multiple layers can be combined into a single visual track item in your sequence. A graphic clip with a freshly produced layer is added to your timeline.

Exporting graphics from Premiere Pro to a Motion Graphics Template folder, Local Drive, or Creative Cloud Libraries allows you to share or reuse them. As previously noted, most visuals can be adjusted directly on the image; however, others require input through the Edit tab.

Adjusting graphics

Graphics must occupy the layer above the video track, regardless of whether the title is moving or static. You may add transitions, position it exactly where you need it on the timeline and, in most cases, modify the length by clicking and dragging the edges, just like with any other clip.

Creating a layer of text

There are a number of simple ways to include text in your movie in Premiere Pro. Using the Text tool, which is accessible by clicking the T symbol in the Toolbox, is the simplest choice. To start entering text, select the Text tool and click anywhere on the video. After you're done, you can change the style, size, and font. **You may also use a menu command to access it by choosing the Type tool, clicking on the region you want, and then choosing Graphic New Layer Text Commands.**
+ Select Align and Transform to change the placement, opacity, and other settings.
+ Adjust the timeline's headline to the exact spot you desire.
+ To make the title fade in and out, right-click on the end of the clip and select Default Transition from the menu that displays.

Creating titles

Although the titles you use in your movie might aid in telling the plot, how you use them is just as crucial. Whether you're creating title sequences, lower thirds, or motion graphics for your videos, these pointers can help you pick the ideal typeface.
+ **Keep things simple:** Steer clear of gaudy fonts and excessive effects. That can take away from the image and rapidly become outdated.

- **Keep it short:** Be mindful of the attention span of your audience and make sure you get right to the point. Credits for closing are not required.

Including titles that are static

Not all titles must move or do any actions. In a similar vein, specific visual components on the screen convey a message in just a few words. You could put a static courtesy in the upper right corner, for instance, if you're using someone else's video. As an alternative, you might use a locator, such as the one below, to inform your visitors of the location of the scene. Here are a few scenarios where static titles can in handy. **Although there are many more, these are some of the most fundamental justifications for using text graphics in your film.**

- **Headline:** Clearly obvious. This informs the audience of the title of the movie, TV show, or installment.
- **Location:** Indicates to the viewer where the scene is set. A lower third is often used in this kind of artwork.
- **Deference:** Give due acknowledgment to the studio, author, or distributor when using someone else's creations. It is typically found at the top right corner of the screen.
- **Lower third:** The speaker's name and identification are shown on camera in the lower third. Documentaries and news articles are the most popular uses for this. Normally, this image should be shown for five to 10 seconds. Particularly in a news section, a topic rarely resurfaces once it has been established. Showing a documentary occasionally helps viewers' memories to be renewed.
- **Date:** You can specify the day or year of the scenario. It may also refer to a more general term, such as FILE or ARCHIVE.
- **Chapter or title card:** Scenes, times, locations, and other elements can be divided using the chapter or title card. Title cards are common in Quentin Tarantino's films. For instance, Kill Bill: Vol. 1 mentions each killer.
- **Opening credits:** The title and creators of the movie are mentioned in the opening credits. The cast and directors come last, followed by the title and production company.
- **Closing credits:** These provide additional details on actors, artists, crew, locales, and other elements by flipping the opening credits.

Action Safe and Title Safe

Ever wonder what the rectangular rectangles at the border of a video frame mean? They highlight which parts of the movie will be displayed safely and which ones might not. More importantly, it evokes memories of tube TV, when defining a zone where the most pertinent content could be seen was crucial due to rounded edges and different overscans (which magnified the image). They are highly prized today. To prevent cropping of your image (and, in this case, the text and graphics) when viewed on a smartphone, stay within the title-safe zone.

Creating a visual title

Creating a visual title for a chapter or section is easy. Double-click the Titles folder to open it after finding it in the Graphics workspace.
- On the timeline, drag the Film Presents Graphics template onto a video track.
- Adjust the length to suit your requirements and provide a transition to make the emergence seamless.
- Make use of motion graphics precisely as your project calls for. Simply use Option-drag on MacOS or Alt-drag on Windows to replicate the effect in different areas of the edit.

Making your movie smarter

It's rare to consider titles, and you can even turn off the television or exit the theater as the credits start to roll, but it's difficult to picture a movie or TV show with no dialogue. Text is necessary because it is commonly used in social media video. Even though they might not be very attractive to viewers, credits are a well-known fact in movies and television shows.

Giving your film credit

Your movie may become a high-end Hollywood production with the right cast, crew, locations, and etiquette. Additionally, your credits will probably be far shorter than those in larger movies, which can have roll credits that are as long as a short film and up to three whole songs playing in the background. You need adhere to some structural guidelines, though. Although there are several conventional methods for creating titles, there are no predetermined standards.

That's how they work. Here are some tips for organization:
- Double-check spelling: Make sure names are spelled correctly to prevent offense and time-consuming fixes.
- Check the title information: Inaccurate names and titles can come across as strange and unprofessional.

Here are some credit examples:
- **Title:** The name of the movie or TV show.
- The cast list that shows up at the beginning of a movie or TV show is known as the opening credits.

- **End credits:** A list of the actors, crew, and other participants from a television show or movie.
- **Identification titles:** To identify the person speaking on camera, a lower third is used in news programs and documentaries.

Setting up the credits for your opening film

The name of the studio or production company usually appears first in the opening credits, which usually follow a standard format. Next is the title of the film, then the actors and producers, and lastly the director. That is basic; the scope of the project and your obligations to the actors and crew will dictate what more you mention in the credits. In addition to being purely entertaining, movie credits try to acknowledge the cast, actors, and contributions. This does not imply, however, that a little flair is always inappropriate. The fonts you use and how they look on the screen are up to you. The opening credits of the most well-known films follow a particular arrangement. **Let's examine the sequence.**

- Production Company
- A film by...
- Title of film
- Main actors
- Supporting actors
- Music composer
- Costume designer
- Associate producers
- Editors
- Production designer
- Director of cinematography
- Executive producer
- Producer
- Screenwriters
- Director

Credits closing

There is more to the closing credits than simply signaling when it's time to switch channels or leave the theater. Moreover, they are not merely against openness. A list of everyone involved in the project can be included in the end credits. This is why they can continue for so long. Since it's unlikely that hundreds of individuals worked on your movie, your closing credits should be simple. Additionally, they sometimes offer surprising components, such hints about a potential follow-up or extra scenes that the filmmaker or editor omitted from the original movie. Depending on how long your photo is, there is an option, but it is not the subject of this discussion. This could be an illustration of a shortened closing credits sequence. Take a look at the concluding titles to see what a high-budget movie lacks. The credits of the most well-known films are arranged in a particular way. Let's examine the sequence.

- Production Company
- Director
- Writers
- Producer
- Executive producer
- Cast roles
- Director of photography
- Production designer
- Editor
- Associate producers
- Costume designer
- Music composer
- Casting director

Including credits in your film

You can choose templates for your movie credits in Premiere Pro; however they are only one page long. If you want rolling credits, you can purchase them from Adobe Stock or as a plugin. One of the options in your templates folder is Film Credits. By dragging it into the timeline, as demonstrated below, you can make changes immediately.

Creating your rolling credits

Installing a plug-in that was specifically designed to create a rolling title, buying content from Adobe Stock, or using the templates folder's static option were the previous options.

CHAPTER SEVENTEEN
ABOUT VIDEO COMPOSITE CONSTRUCTION

You will recognize that there is a specific order to construction if you have ever played a computer game such as Sim City. You will need to develop a higher, layer-by-layer city since, even if your city grows to encompass suburbs, there won't be enough room for everything. Multiple clips or other materials can be combined to produce a powerful visual for editing or content for creating a movie. You will discover how to incorporate this type of vertical growth, which is frequently referred to as compositing in the business. I would respond, "Yes...video clips stacked atop one another can only reveal the top one," if I could read minds at this point. That proves to be just partially accurate because clip dimensions allow for the simultaneous display of many layers. An excellent example is the picture-in-picture feature, which displays a little portion of the scenes footage, like an over-the-shoulder commentary perspective. Or maybe you'll make a multiple-shot composite that resembles the opening credits of the 1970s version of The Brady Bunch. Maybe a split screen with two shots might work better. This method is frequently used in movies, particularly to depict phone calls. It can be applied in a number of situations, though. Combining two clips is the next stage. An effect akin to a lengthy dissolve or another special effect can be achieved by varying the opacity of the top clip placed on top of another clip. You could want to use a green screen, which can also be blue, to overlay pictures from somewhere else behind the topic. The following sections can assist you in developing your film in a number of ways, regardless of your premise.

Comprehending Compositing

In science class, do you recall the books with the acetate pages that depicted the entire human body, including the skeleton? More layers of exposed organs, muscles, nerves, and other bodily components emerged as you turned each translucent page. The foundation of composition is the same idea. You're adding elements, some of which vary in size and opacity, that can come together to create a complicated single image. A news anchor performing a program as video feeds from another location play over their shoulder is a typical example. But that's not all. From a clever element to a cool special effect, a number of different scenarios add to the visual narrative of the plot. Remember that compositing includes elements like titles, green-screen keys, and picture-in-picture.

Clips that are layered

There are several kinds of bent chips available on the market, and they have a tendency to stack. That is the implication in those TV commercials, at least. You may do the same with your video clips. You can position a clip on a track above an existing one instead of dragging it next to it on the timeline, as shown in the image below. That is the main compositional strategy.

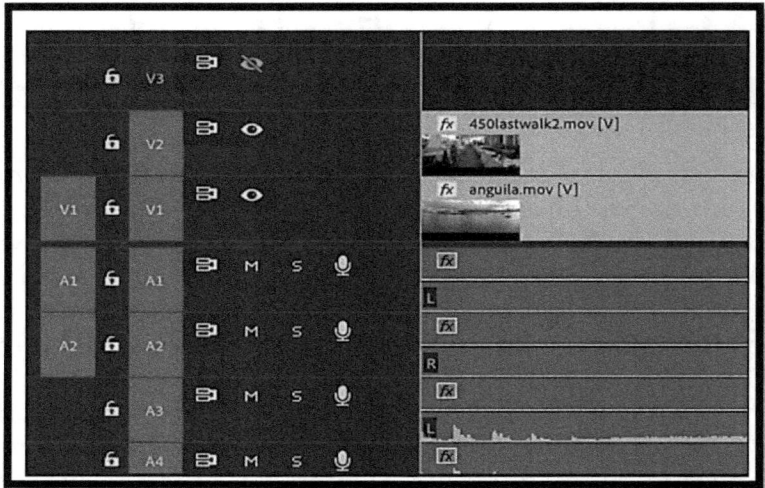

There are several techniques to construct a composite.
  + Project panel clips can be dragged and dropped into specific tracks.
  + **Pasting:** It is possible to paste a copy of an object from another location. As long as the track target is set to the correct track, you can alter it.
  + **Overlay:** Drag a clip from your bin to the Program Monitor to overlay it. Above a recorded track, the clip will show up on the timeline as the subsequent free track.

Changing the opacity to disclose

Layers can be seen through, much like transparent clothing or cell animation. In Premiere Pro, this procedure is called blending. Instead of being arranged side by side and played out in a straight line, the clips are layered on top of each other. By default, only the top clip is shown unless you expand it, use a Blend mode that adjusts to the color and density of the clips, or alter the opacity of the top clip to create a pattern.

Changing the opacity

Despite headlines, a stunning image is not usually created by stacking clips on top of each other and adjusting their blend or opacity. It can produce what looks like an error or a shoddy example of how to accomplish something. You can, however, use this tactic to your advantage and present a positive image in some circumstances. Each image's hue and density, as well as the positioning of the main subject, are taken into consideration while determining these. It's usually better to utilize a simple texture image, such clouds, waves, or abstract landscapes, to create an eye-catching impression.
This is how you go about it:
  + Drag the basic clip into the timeline if it isn't there already.
  + Drag the selected blendable clip over the base clip of the track.

Go to the Effect Controls after selecting the track. Once you've reached that level, as shown in the image below, adjust the Opacity to 25% to view the full clip. You can now view the basic clip, but it will have the texture of the clip over it.

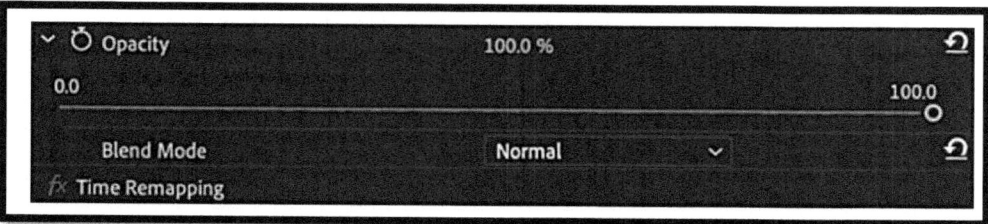

Utilizing the Blend and Opacity Modes

You may quickly add a distinctive effect to your movie that will enhance the cinematography and increase its visual attractiveness by using the Opacity and Blend modes. It's also a great technique to add texture to the text of a title. This calls for two clips: the first is the basic clip, which displays the full action in the first image. It could be a pivotal moment in the action or the main focus of the video. The second clip is at the top and may be seen in the second picture. As seen in the third image, it functions as a blend and can assume more abstract forms like rain, waves, clouds, or any other image that fills the entire frame.

The following are some items to consider:

- Is the clip pristine? Make sure the clip is clean and devoid of any additional features before applying a blend layer to get an overlay effect.
- **Correction:** By stacking the same clip and applying a mix, a clip with problems with density or contrast can be fixed. Simply Option-drag the layer over itself to accomplish this. For instance, placing a copy of the lighter image on top of the lighter one will improve density due to the multiple mix.
- **Add texture:** You can easily achieve a textured or dreamy appearance by overlaying another clip with a simple pattern.
- **Titles:** Compositing can improve simple titles' aesthetic appeal.

Now let's examine the Blend Modes. Blend modes create an effect by comparing the pixel values in each layer's image. They alter the pixel values between the layers to produce a particular effect. For instance, by boosting the darker pixels while leaving the lighter ones alone, the Screen Blend option contrasts two layers and brightens the visuals. As you can see above, consider the various ways that each mix affects the image.

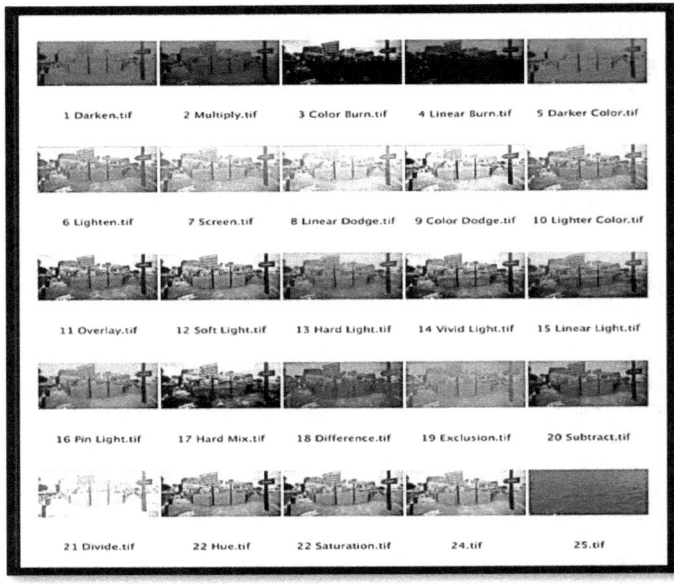

Presenting the Blend modes

In the menu, the Blend modes are divided into six groups, each denoted by a line instead of a name. Let's quickly review each section's discussion of the blending process.

First Group: The most fundamental

The first portion of blend grouping includes blends that contribute to normal density results. How typical is this? The first is thought of as typical.

- **Conventional:** Typical is the default option; until the opacity is decreased, it has no effect on the layer underneath it. The uppermost stratum is now intermingled. When the opacity is decreased, the layer underneath becomes more visible.
- **Dissolve:** This method makes a portion of the source layer's pixels translucent, exposing the bottom layer. Usually, the opacity of this parameter needs to be changed.

Second Group: The subtractive

Since this category contains selections that enhance and darken the final image's density, it is best characterized as subtractive. **The most popular method for altering the shadow levels in two photos is multiply, which is utilized in all of them.**

- **Darken:** Compares each pixel in the image to identify the layer that is the darkest. Lighter pixels are substituted, whereas darker pixels that are not the blend color remain unaltered.
- **Multiply:** This well-liked technique lowers an image's density. To put it another way, this mode darkens the image mathematically by comparing the two layers and calculating the grayscale values from the chosen layer by the lower layer, then dividing the result by 255.
- **Color Burn:** This option will help you achieve a darker tone than usual by reducing highlights while raising contrast and saturation.
- **Linear Burn:** As you can already see, each subset becomes more severe as you proceed down the list. By boosting contrast and lowering brightness in the darker tones, this mode produces a darker image without sacrificing overall color saturation, in contrast to multiply and Color Burn.
- **Darker Color:** Although not as bright as Darken, the color is still discernible. You guessed it: this option compares the two layers and retains the darker one. Pixels are not combined by it.

Third Group: Expanding Density

The subsequent set brightens the last layer, in contrast to the preceding group's emphasis on shifting contrast and density. The highlight values of the image are used by this team. The most often used is the screen.

Many of the selections in this subset alter color via mixing, much like how color may be altered by blending projected light.

+ **Lighten:** Following foundation assessment and layer mixing, this process keeps the lighter version. If every pixel is the same, they are unaffected.
+ **Screen:** To lighten darker regions without hurting brighter ones, this widely used technique involves superimposing numerous photos. This is useful for exposures that are darker. To add brightness to the entire image while maintaining detail, the layer can be copied.
+ **Color Dodge:** This color scheme complements correction effectively. The original color is made lighter and less contrasted by this layer mix.
+ **Linear Dodge (Add):** This feature creates a tone that is softer and less contrasting by combining the Screen and Color Dodge settings.
+ **Lighter Color:** Lighter Color does not apply the blend to individual channels, but it selects the lighter pixel for the source and underlying color value, just like its sister blend mode Lighten.

Fourth Group: Creating a difference

Difference is the next category. By utilizing the variations between the sources and underlying hues, these blend modes alter the blend's color. These effects affect contrast by either brightening or darkening the final colors, depending on the parameters. The two photos' midtone values are changed by this group. **Soft Light is the second most common option, after Overlay.**

+ **Overlay:** This Blend option can add a little pizazz to an image by combining the Screen and multiply modes. This is how dark areas darken and bright parts lighten.
+ **Soft Light:** Colors with lower grayscale percentages will appear lighter, while colors with higher grayscale percentages will appear darker. Textural blending works best in this setting.
+ **Hard Light:** This effect doubles darker pixels to 50% gray and screens brighter pixels, just to Soft Light. This produces a powerful image that almost always needs to be adjusted in terms of opacity in order to look real.
+ **Vivid Light:** The Vivid Light mix's dramatic contrast from fading hues above 50% gray necessitates significant dilution.
+ **Linear Light:** This Blend option modifies brightness rather than contrast, much to Vivid Light. It works well for enhancing the color in photos, but the effect is still intense and will need to be adjusted for opacity.
+ **Pin Light:** This additional Blend mode has a narrow range of applications. With the exception of selecting the top or bottom pixel based on brightness, leaving lighter tones alone, or combining pixels on either layer that are darker than 50% gray, it functions similarly to the Lighten and Darken Blend modes.
+ **Hard Mix:** This is perhaps the most unusual Blend setting. In contrast to the other options, it transforms each hue into one of eight primary hues (red, green, blue, cyan, magenta, yellow, black, and white) to produce an artistic, nearly active

impression. However, it really shines (pardon the pun) when it comes to bringing dull, low-contrast video footage with subdued hues to life. You may achieve a fantastic look by stacking the video on top of the Hard Mix Blend option, as shown in the image below.

Fifth Group: The HSL classification

These mix modes can produce some really strange and fascinating effects.

+ **Difference:** To increase brightness, the Difference feature subtracts base and blend layer pixels. When pixels of the same value are eliminated from every layer, the outcome is black. This is excellent for producing a psychedelic effect or differentiating between identical photos, and it functions best when using a tripod.
+ **Exclusion:** Exclusion is comparable to Difference but less powerful. Additionally, Difference displays, well, distinctions in black, while this one is all about gray.
+ **Subtract:** This technique produces a darker image by moving values from one layer to another. Since the layers' order is crucial, altering the layers' order will provide different outcomes. Black regions will stay the same while white areas will darken.
+ **Divide:** In mathematics, dividing is the opposite of subtracting. This is excellent for situations where there is a lot of white, and it shifts the overall color best when paired with a solid off-white finish.
+ The hue, saturation, color, and brightness of your video clip are included in the final category.
+ **Hue:** Hue modifies the underlying color's saturation and brightness to match the hue of the top layer.
+ **Saturation:** Raises the saturation of the image's top layer while preserving the underlying color's brightness and hue.
+ **Color:** Perfect for bringing color to grayscale images and boosting color photos. It functions by preserving the hue and saturation of the top layer's color as well as the brightness of the underlying color.

- **Brightness:** Rather of mixing the source color, this option preserves its brightness. In contrast, the image often disappears.

Dissection of Blend Mode Elements

- The layer's color while the Blend mode is selected is referred to as the source color.
- The mix applied to the composite determines the result color; the underlying color applies to the track layer in the timeline beneath the source layer. The opacity of each blend can also be changed to affect its effect.

Using an adjustment layer in Blend mode

An adjustment layer can be used to change the Blend mode. Because Premiere Pro works with moving images and can apply a Blend mode or opacity changes to a variety of clips, it is more radical than Photoshop. Just select the Blend mode from the Effect Controls menu under Opacity on the adjustment layer. Comparable to copying a video clip onto an already-existing clip on a video track and then changing the Blend mode is this process. Before changing its size, an adjustment layer might be given an effect, like a tint or color correction effect. This technique can be used to draw attention to a certain region of the screen.

Layers of adjustment and transformation effects

A series of clips (or still photos) can be animated by applying a transform effect, such Rotate or Scale, to an adjustment layer. This method allows you to create motion effects that were previously limited to nested clips. A dynamic effect that animates over two or more clips will appear when you play back the sequence.

Clips merging in a nest

The process of combining disparate footage into one is known as this. You're headed in the correct direction because that seems well-organized. But that's not the point. (In fact, that is the objective.) Another justification is when you wish to produce a powerful scene. For instance, choosing every clip and nesting them together is a productive way to have a portion of your sequence in black and white.

Here's how to build a nest of clips:
- Choose which clips you want to combine.
- Right-click and choose the selected clips to bring up the Nest menu.
- Click OK after giving the nest a name in the window that appears.

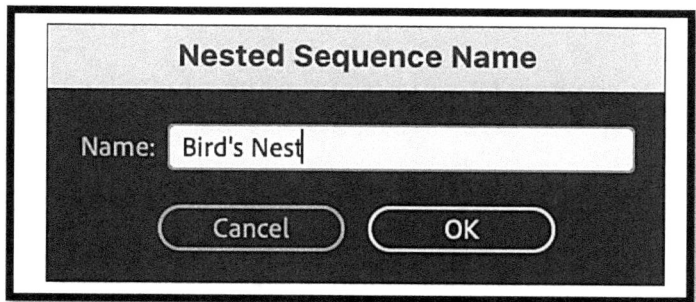

Utilizing the nested clip

It's easier to move a single clip around the timeline when multiple clips are bundled together. It is not the same as having just one clip, though, because you can access all of the components. The primary distinction is that the clips appear on the timeline instead of in your project folder, like when you put them in a bin or other container. However, it is simple to change the color of any one of the three clips in this nest if necessary.

Here's how to do that:

+ Double-click the clip that is nested.
+ The individual clips show up when the timeline opens. Make the necessary changes to every clip.
+ Right-click on the clip and choose Next to restore it to its initial state as a single nested clip.

Investigating Compositing Methods

Alpha Channel: What Is It?

The red, green, and blue portions of the light spectrum are captured independently by cameras. Channels of a single hue are said to as monochromatic. These three monochromatic (single-color) channels are used by Adobe Premiere Pro to generate the required primary color channels. Together with additive color, they form a full RGB image. Your eyes perceive the three channels as a full-color video. The process of combining many monochromatic colors to create a full color spectrum is comparable to combining two mono audio channels to create a stereo mix. The fourth and last monochromatic channel is denoted as alpha. There is no mention of color on the fourth channel. It affects opacity, which is the degree of visibility of each pixel. Visibility, transparency, blending, and opacity are some of the ways that this fourth channel is defined. The name doesn't really matter. Pixels of any hue must have their opacity altered since the alpha channel is different from the color channels. Just as color correction may be used to alter the amount of red in a clip, opacity controls can be used to alter the amount of alpha. The alpha channel or opacity of clips is set to 100% or fully visible by default. This value is equal to 255 on an 8-bit visual scale that goes from 0 to 255. There won't be an alpha channel in every medium. Alpha channels, for instance, are not recorded by video cameras. In practice, most codecs (image and sound data storage techniques) cannot save an alpha channel. Alpha channels are commonly used to indicate whether image components are opaque or transparent in animation clips, titles, and images.

Including compositing in your work

Your post-production work could reach new heights with the use of compositing controls and effects. As you begin to use Premiere Pro's many compositing effects, you'll find new ways to capture and arrange your edit, which will make picture mixing simpler. Combining proper effect layout, filming procedures and preproduction preparation will yield the best compositing results. Combining static photos of places with intricate, captivating patterns can create amazing, complex emotions. As an alternative, you can remove inappropriate portions of an image and swap them out for something else. One of the most creative, flexible, and enjoyable aspects of Premiere Pro's nonlinear editing is compositing.

Using compositing in videography

When the scene is being prepped during pre-production, most of the best compositing work starts. You may experiment immediately with a variety of techniques to help Premiere Pro identify the parts of the image that you want to make translucent. Think about chroma keying, a popular special effect in large-scale film productions that enables action to occur in places that would otherwise be too risky or physically impossible, like the interior of a volcano. A solid green screen serves as the backdrop for the actors. Pixels that ought to be transparent are indicated by the color green. With some visible pixels (the actors) and transparent pixels (the backdrop) (the green background), the actors' video image forms the foreground of the composition. Placing the foreground video footage in front of another backdrop image is the next stage. For an epic action film, it could be a composite made by visual effects experts, a real location, or a pre-built set. A composite composition is the end outcome. Making a plan in advance can greatly enhance the caliber of your compositing. The backdrop needs to be the same color in order for the greenscreen effect to function properly. Additionally, it must be a color that is unique to the subject. For instance, using the chroma key technique might make green jewelry translucent. The final product can be significantly impacted by how you film greenscreen content. When trying to match the lighting of your subject to the intended replacement background, take into account the direction of the shadows.

The Opacity Effect in Action

Keyframes in the Timeline or Effect Controls panels can be used to adjust the overall opacity of a clip.

+ Select the sequence in the Timeline box if it isn't already open.

+ The Video 2 track's height ought to be somewhat increased. This can be done by changing the track header's dividing line between Videos 2 and 3. You can also use the mouse wheel or touchpad to navigate while holding Option (macOS) or Alt (Windows) and dragging the cursor over the Video 2 track header.

+ Select Show Video Keyframes from the Display Settings menu in the Timeline window. Now you may use the rubber band (the thin horizontal black-and-white line on clips) to adjust the parameters and keyframe effects. Because each clip has a single rubber band, only one control can be adjusted at a time.

+ Try moving the elastic band up and down in Video Clip 2 using the Selection tool. Aim for a precise 50% value. More accurate adjustments can be made by holding down Command (macOS) or Ctrl (Windows) while dragging.

+ The rubber band can be changed using the Selection tool in this manner without requiring the installation of extra keyframes.

CHAPTER EIGHTEEN
ABOUT PROJECT EXPORTATION

The Quick Exporting

With just a few clicks, you may export a media file with the right settings for your current sequence or clip using Premiere Pro's rapid export feature. H.264 MP4 files created with this technique are appropriate for streaming services and social networking.

The actions are:

+ Open the folder and select a project.
+ Launch the sequence for the Review Copy.
+ Clicking the Quick Export icon in the Premiere Pro window's top-right corner will bring up the Quick Export dialogue box.
+ The button that opens the Save As dialogue box is the blue text that contains the output name. Text-as-a-button functionality is also supported by Adobe Media Encoder. Click the output name now. Give the file the name Review Copy.mp4 and choose a location.
+ From the Presets menu, select Adaptive High Bitrate as the Match Source. If you export a sequence (or clip), these options are automatically formatted to match it. In order to conform to a specific delivery standard, you can also choose between 4K (Ultra High Definition), HD (High Definition), and SD (Standard Definition) settings.
+ To generate a new media file, choose Export.

Comprehending All of the Media Export Choices

You have a number of export choices, regardless of whether you've finished a project or just want to send in a draft for approval.

+ You can export to the codec, file type, and format that correspond to the distribution media of your choice.
+ You can export a sequence or a single frame.
+ There are three output options: full audio/video, video-only, and audio-only.
+ It is possible to add, integrate, or save captions in a different file.
+ For convenient reuse, exported media can be reimported into the project.
+ When exporting a file, there are a number of additional factors to take into account in addition to selecting an export format (frame size, frame rate, etc.).
+ You can compress them to make them smaller for sharing, or you can output files with the same format, visual quality, and data rate as the original content.
+ Transcode your media using various codecs so that you can share it with other creative people.
+ If a preset doesn't work for you, adjust the frame size, frame rate, data rate, audio and video codec, and setup options.

- To assign a look, color lookup tables (LUTs) can be utilized. Accessible features include audio normalization, HDR to SDR conversion, and a video limiter.
- Timecode, name, and image overlays could be burned in.
- It's easy to share exported files to Adobe Stock, FTP servers, and social media accounts.

Exporting Individual Frames

While working on an edit, you can decide to export a still frame for a teammate or client to approve. Additionally, you have the option to export a picture to be used as the thumbnail for the video when it is posted online. **Premiere Pro produces a still image with the same resolution as the source video file whenever you export a frame from the Source Monitor.**

- Premiere Pro produces a still image with the same resolution as the sequence when a frame is exported from the Program Monitor.
- Proceed with the Review Copy procedure. Align the playhead with the frame you want to export in the Timeline.
- In the lower right corner of the Program Monitor, click the Export Frame button. Try adjusting the Program Monitor's size if the button is not visible.
- You might need to move the panel if the button is not visible. Another possibility is that you have modified the buttons in the Program Monitor. To export a frame, choose the Timeline window or Program Monitor and press Shift+E (macOS) or Shift+Ctrl+E.
- In the Export Frame dialog box, type a filename.
- From the Format option, select a format for still photos. All users have universal access to JPEG, PNG, and BMP files (only on Windows). In web design, JPEG and PNG files are frequently utilized. Print and animation applications can benefit from the use of TIFF, TGA, and PNG file formats. Digital filming and color grading (fine color finishing) both make extensive use of DPX. Wide dynamic range photos are stored using OpenEXR.
- The generated image file will have a different aspect ratio than the original if the pixels in your video format are not square. This has to do with the use of square pixels in still image formats. A photograph can be horizontally extended in Adobe Photoshop while keeping its aspect ratio intact.
- Click the Browse option to choose where the new still image will be stored. Under your folder, create a folder named Exports. Then, pick it and press the Choose button.
- Images in the following formats can be exported from Windows: BMP, DPX, GIF, JPEG, OpenEXR, PNG, TGA, and TIFF. Exporting to DPX, JPEG, OpenEXR, PNG, TGA, or TIFF formats is possible on MacOS.
- Choose Import Into Project and then OK to include the new still image in the current project.

The file extension will be.tif instead of.tiff if you export a TIFF file with Premiere Pro. Both are equally useful and sincere.

172

Making a Master File Export

An unaltered digital version of your upgraded product that can be stored for later use is called a master copy. It is a completely rendered output file of your sequence that is self-contained and of the best quality and resolution. Without opening the original project in Premiere Pro, this kind of file can be utilized as a source media file to create a range of compressed output formats. Although there is a slight quality loss (one digital generation) when additional copies are based on this digital master, many editors find the time and convenience savings make the trade-off worthwhile.

Sequence settings that correspond

The frame size, frame rate, and codec of a master file should ideally match those of the source sequence almost exactly. There can seem to be a ton of options to choose from when making a new exported media file. **Aligning the parameters of your sequence or source material is easy using Premiere Pro.**

- Continue working on the Review Copy Sequence forever.
- Either open the Timeline panel while it is active (blue outline) or pick File > Export > Media using the sequence that was chosen in the Project panel. The Export Settings dialog box opens as a result. You can also use Ctrl+M (Windows) or Command+M (macOS).
- For the time being, choose the Match Sequence Settings option.
- To change the media file's name and save it, click the blue text.

Adobe Media Encoder in use

Adobe Media Encoder is a separate application that can be used without Premiere Pro. The ability to send an encoding task straight from Premiere Pro and go on editing while it's being processed is one benefit of using Media Encoder. Media Encoder will create the file in the background without interfering with your editing if a client requests to view your work before you are done. When a video is played in Premiere Pro, Media Encoder immediately stops encoding to improve playback performance. The Premiere Pro Playback settings can be used to modify this.

Selecting a format for export files

It could be difficult to figure out how to display finished work. Selecting distribution formats is basically a case of planning backwards; if you are aware of the file's intended distribution; it is usually easy to determine which file type is ideal for the job. It is easy to choose the right encoding options because customers will often have a delivery specs document.

Choosing a format

Numerous formats are supported by Adobe Media Encoder. Choosing which settings to utilize could be challenging. Let's examine a few typical scenarios and formats. Although there aren't many absolutes, they should assist you approach the intended outcome. Before creating the full file, it's a good idea to test your result on a small section of your video. **By doing this, you'll avoid wasting time waiting for the full version only to find out there's a better option.**

+ Widescreen, SD, HD, and 4K video settings are available in the H.264 format on well-known websites including Facebook, Twitter, Vimeo, and YouTube.

+ Use the Wraptor DCP format with a frame rate of 24 or 25 for theatrical distribution. Choose 24 frames per second as the DCP output if the frame rate of your sequence is 30 frames per second. There aren't many configuration options to guarantee compatibility with traditional DCI-compliant theatrical projection systems.

+ The majority of Premiere Pro presets is conservative and yield satisfactory results with default settings; the presets have been tested and will work as intended. It's unlikely that changing them will result in higher quality.

Putting Content on Social Media

Publicizing the video is typically the next step after encoding. **You can set up publishing preferences in the Export Settings dialog box to send your encoded video as soon as it's finished.**

+ Share exported films to YouTube, Vimeo, Twitter, Facebook, Adobe Stock, Adobe Behance, and an FTP server (File Transfer Protocol).

+ This function is quite helpful because it saves selected parameters as an export profile. By choosing a preset, you can modify your social media uploads once and then use the same settings for numerous subsequent posts.

+ Activate the Timeline panel, then choose File > Export > Media to open the Export Settings dialog box. As an alternative, hit Ctrl+M (Windows) or Command+M (macOS).

+ Move the Publish tab to the top and go over your selections.

+ When finished, click Cancel to close the Export Settings dialog box.

Although every platform has different distribution needs, you can usually choose a high-quality master file and let the platform create additional, compressed copies. For instance, a large variety of video formats and codecs are supported by Adobe Stock. The server will handle the rest if you create a high-quality UHD file.

Using Other Editing Apps to Exchange Projects

Collaboration is essential in post-production. The great majority of the best editing and color-grading programs on the market are compatible with the project and video files that Premiere Pro can read and produce. Sharing creative work with collaborators is made easy by this, even if you both use different editing software. Edit Decision Lists (EDLs), Open Media Framework (OMF), Advanced Authoring Format (AAF), Avid Log Exchange (ALE), and Extended Markup Language (XML) may all be imported and exported using Premiere Pro. AAF can be used as a bridge to send clip information, updated sequences, and particular effects when working with an Avid Media Composer editor. Similarly, you can utilize XML as a mediator when using an Apple Final Cut Pro editor. To export a sequence from Premiere Pro to an AAF or XML file, simply select it and then File > Export > Final Cut Pro XML or File > Export > AAF.

Exporting to OMF

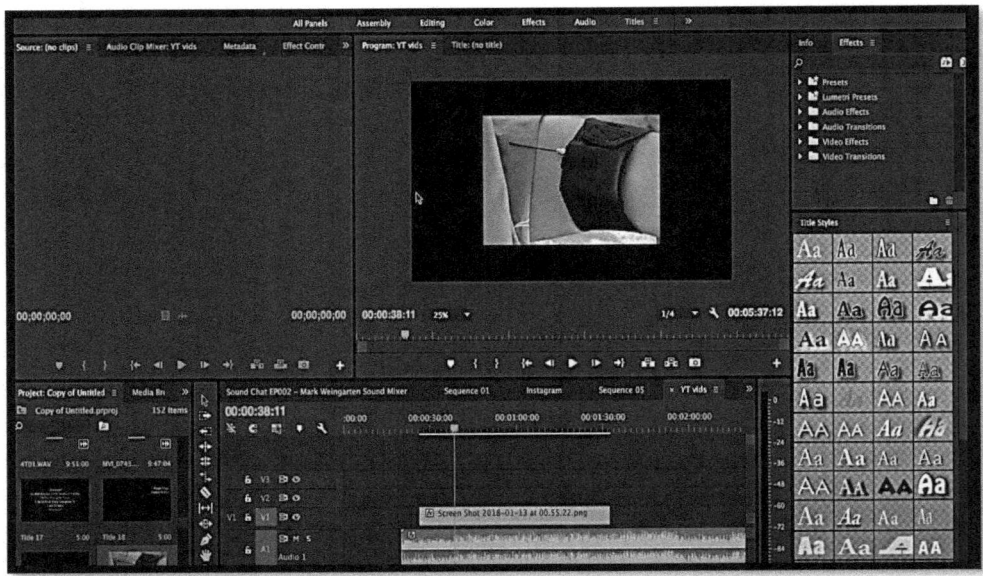

The common audio file format for data transmission between computers (typically for audio mixing) is the Open Media Framework (OMF). An OMF file that has been exported often yields a single file with all of the audio files in a sequence as clips on audio tracks. The clips will show up on tracks and be timed and manipulated similarly to how they do in the Premiere Pro sequence when an OMF file is opened by compatible software. **The steps to create an OMF file are as follows:**

> ✦ After choosing a sequence, select File > Export > OMF. In the OMF Export Settings dialog box, type the file name in the OMF Title area.

✦ Verify that the video and the Sample Rate and Bits per Sample parameters match. The most often used default values are 16 bits and 48000 Hz.

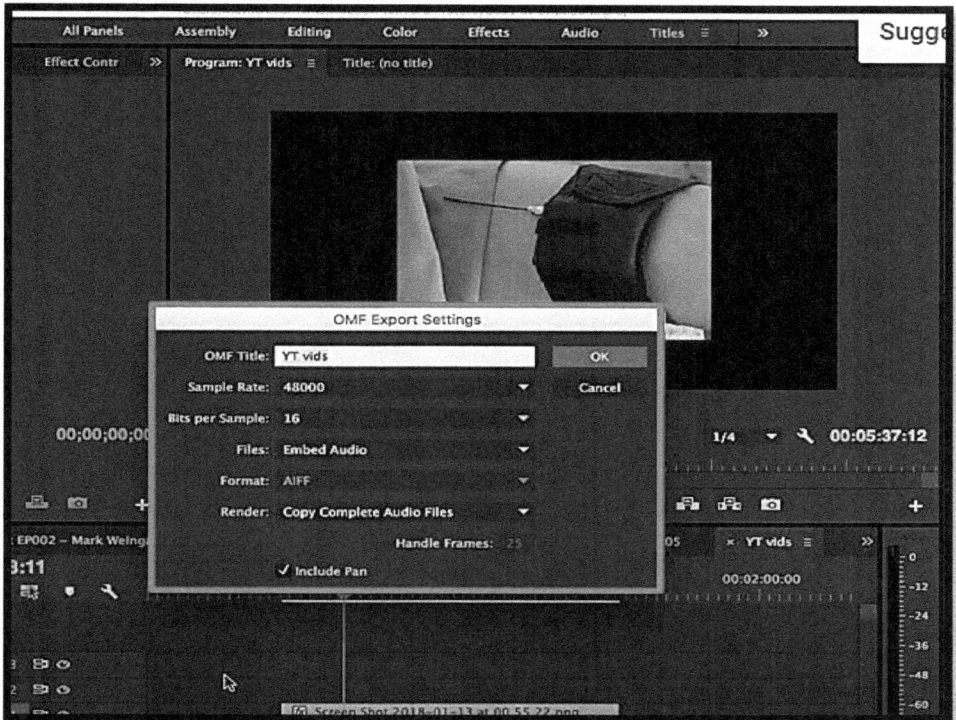

Choose one of the following choices from the Files menu:

+ With this option, an OMF file containing the audio files and project metadata for the specified sequence is created.

+ The option exports audio recordings to the omfiMediaFiles folder after separating them into mono files, even stereo recordings. When using sophisticated audio mixing techniques, audio professionals often adhere to this standard.

+ When utilizing the Separate Audio option, choose between the AIFF and Broadcast Wave formats. Both are excellent, but be sure you have a good strategy in place before switching. The best suitable format is often AIFF files.

+ Use the Render menu's Copy Complete Audio Files and Trim Audio Files choices to reduce the size of your files. When editing and combining clips, you can request that handles (additional seconds) be added to give you more control.

+ To create the OMF file, click OK.

+ Click Save after selecting a location. The Exports folder is available for temporary use. When the export is finished, the OMF Export Information dialog box opens. It provides export details and alerts users to any issues found.

+ Click OK to close the dialog box.

CHAPTER NINETEEN
ABOUT VIRTUAL REALITY (VR) EDITING

Overview of Virtual Reality Editing

Virtual reality video production and editing are made simpler using Adobe Premiere Pro. These movies transport audiences to a 360-degree setting. Videos in virtual reality provide an immersive experience that draws viewers into the story. The smooth import and editing of VR content is made possible by this software's compatibility with a number of common VR video formats. The "auto-aware VR" feature in Premiere Pro automatically recognizes and configures the necessary settings for VR films. Features and tools in Premiere Pro are especially well-suited for editing virtual reality movies. To improve the immersive experience, these consist of titles, images, transitions, and effects created especially for virtual reality. Using a VR headset, Premiere Pro users may instantly preview their VR video, giving editors a more realistic way to experience and evaluate the impact and caliber of their VR films. Generally speaking, Adobe Premiere Pro gives producers all the resources they require to produce visually stunning immersive virtual reality videos.

How to use Adobe Premiere Pro to edit VR videos

First Step: Bring Your Video in

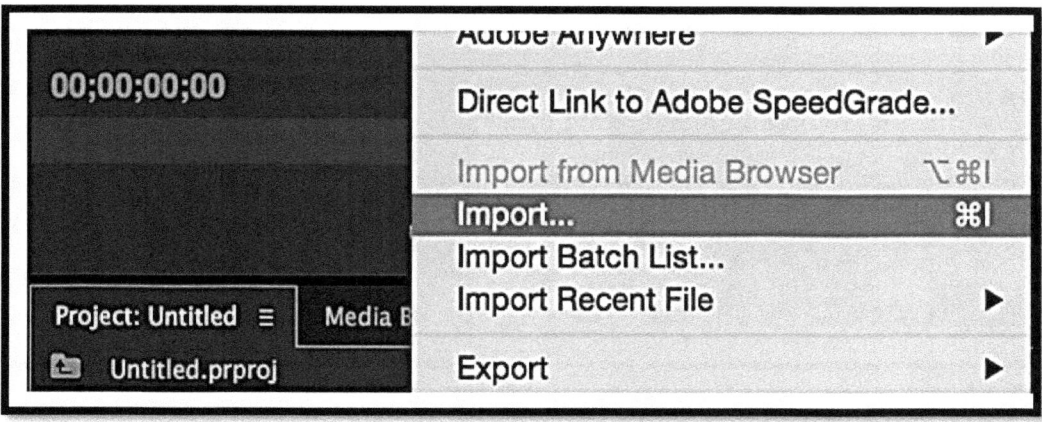

Simply put, equirectangular VR cinema is a 360-degree view created by stitching together video. The only significant distinction between equirectangular and regular video footage is resolution and pixel stretching. It's easy to import VR video into Premiere Pro: double-click in the project window or hit Command+I on your keyboard.

Second 2: Modify Your Preferences

Your equirectangular video clip will appear warped in the preview tab after import; this is typical of VR material. Click the small wrench icon in the preview window's lower right corner to adjust the video's display in the preview panel. From this menu, select VR Video > Settings. Here, you can modify your video clip to suit the particular requirements of your project. For instance, if you used a Theta S to record standard equirectangular footage, your settings will probably be monoscopic, with a 180-degree vertical field of view and 360-degree horizontal field of view.

Third step: Put the VR mode on the preview window

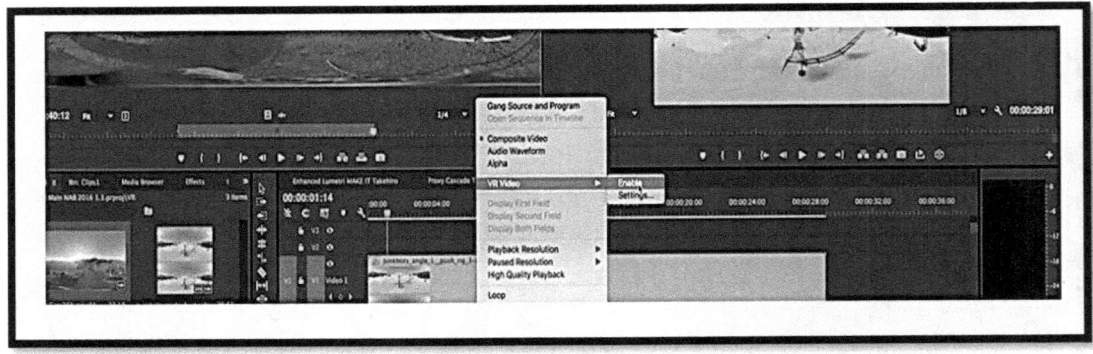

You can preview your video project by turning on the VR mode once you've set up the parameters. There are two ways to do this:

+ **Using the Wrench Icon:** Choose VR Video > VR Mode after clicking the wrench icon. This action puts your project in virtual reality viewing mode.
+ **Choosing the VR Mode Button:** Click the plus icon in the button menu to bring up the VR Mode button. Additionally, this option activates VR mode for your project.

In VR mode, you can use sliders around the edges of the frame or click and drag inside the frame to move around the preview window. The VR previewing in Premiere Pro has similar navigation to YouTube VR, if you are familiar with it.

Footnote: Premiere Pro's Preview and Program Monitor both allow you to view the VR footage.

Fourth Step: Edit your video

Next, the editing process for VR video is similar to that of standard video editing within a timeline. VR editing necessitates treating the content as discrete chunks within a timeline, even if it is a more recent approach of dealing with video. You may perform editing tasks like slicing, trimming, and color correction exactly like you would with regular video footage as long as it is equirectangular. However, some transformational effects, like warp stabilizers, might not work as intended because to the nature of 360-degree video.

Is it possible to edit VR videos with Adobe Premiere Pro?

It is possible to edit virtual reality videos with Adobe Premiere Pro. It comes with a number of tools made especially for creating and modifying virtual reality media. Using a range of specialized tools, such as "auto-aware VR," which recognizes and applies the appropriate settings for the sort of VR film you're working with automatically, users may import and start editing their 360-degree footage. Additionally, Adobe Premiere Pro offers a VR video display feature that lets users see their work in real time through a headset, giving them a preview of how it will appear in the finished product. It is now easier for editors to make accurate edits and produce realistic VR experiences. Because of this, Adobe Premiere Pro offers a number of tools to facilitate the editing process in addition to its ability to edit VR footage.

Exporting and Sharing Virtual Reality Experiences

To guarantee the best quality and cross-platform compatibility, some precautions must be followed while exporting and sharing Virtual Reality (VR) experiences made with Premiere Pro.

- **Thorough Preparation of Your VR Project:** Make sure to thoroughly edit and polish your content before exporting your VR project. To create a captivating and immersive VR experience, make sure that all necessary effects, enhancements, and adjustments are applied. Additionally, make sure that all of your project's parameters—such as resolution, frame rate and other crucial elements—exactly fit the specified VR video requirements.

- **Selecting the Correct Export Settings:** Select Export > Media from the File menu to open the Export Settings box. There will be options for you to modify the export settings for your VR content. Selecting an appropriate codec, such H.264 or H.265, is crucial, depending on the platform specifications for the VR project you intend to deliver.

- **Changing Video Codec:** Set the Video Codec in the Export Settings box to correspond with the format that was previously chosen. Additionally, look over the VR Video settings in the Video tab. To give viewers the most immersive experience possible, select the proper VR video layout (monoscopic or stereoscopic) and then adjust the field of vision parameters.

- **Modifying Audio Settings:** Take care to set up the audio parameters to ensure that they meet the requirements of the VR platform of your choice. To make your VR content more immersive and provide viewers with a more realistic and captivating auditory experience, think about utilizing spatial audio techniques.

- **Saving Customized Export Settings:** Save the export parameters as a preset after you've adjusted them to perfectly match your VR project. This facilitates exporting and ensures quality standards across several projects by allowing for easy implementation and consistency in subsequent projects.

- **Making Use of Adobe Media Encoder and Export Queue:** To move your project to Adobe Media Encoder for background processing, click the Queue button. This makes it possible to handle exporting tasks more quickly and efficiently. You can review and change options in Adobe Media Encoder to further customize or optimize it to your specific requirements.

- **Examining File Exports:** Examine the exported files carefully when the export process is finished. Verify that they meet your quality standards by looking for visual and aural irregularities. Make sure the exported content provides viewers with the necessary immersive experience by confirming compatibility for appropriate playback in VR settings.

Sharing Virtual Reality Content

- **Distribution Platform Selection:** You must first decide where you want to expose your VR content before deciding how to distribute it. This choice involves identifying the platforms that are best suited to hosting virtual reality experiences, including both specialized websites created specifically for VR content consumption and more traditional options like YouTube or Vimeo. Selecting the right platforms for your content and target audience is essential because each one has a different audience and set of features.

+ **Platform-Specific Requirements:** Depending on the platform, different standards and requirements apply for hosting VR content. Examining the characteristics of each platform in detail is essential. Certain file formats, resolutions, or other metadata included in the VR content may be necessary for certain platforms. By adhering to these guidelines, you can be sure that your material satisfies the platform's standards for accessibility and ideal display.

+ **Metadata Integration and Tagging:** It's imperative that your VR video files have all pertinent information. This metadata gives specific details about the video format and any needs for VR playback. By using this information, platforms can better classify and display your content, making it simpler for users to locate and engage with your virtual reality experiences.

+ **Uploading and Testing:** It's time to upload your VR content after it has been produced in accordance with the platform's guidelines. However, thorough testing is necessary prior to going online. This involves making certain that the material functions smoothly on the selected platforms, plays back appropriately, and retains high quality. Testing helps find and fix any potential problems that could affect the user experience.

+ **Promotion and Sharing Strategies:** To boost the visibility and interaction of your VR content, you must develop a comprehensive promotional strategy. Your material can reach a wider audience if you use a variety of marketing strategies, such as social networking sites and targeted virtual reality communities. Advertising campaigns can boost engagement and draw in new viewers by targeting consumers interested in virtual reality experiences.

+ **Tracking User Feedback and Responsiveness:** After the content has been posted online, it is imperative to consistently track user input. You can better understand the preferences and issues of the audience by paying attention to user reviews, comments, and reactions. Resolving any issues or suggestions as soon as feasible demonstrates responsiveness and a commitment to enhance the general client experience. Additionally, you can improve your VR content by considering updates or enhancements depending on audience input.

+ **Ensuring Cross-Platform Compatibility:** Make sure your VR content works with a range of VR platforms and devices to reach a wider audience. Increasing accessibility by optimizing content for cross-device compatibility enables users to interact with your content on any VR platform or device.

CHAPTER TWENTY

TIPS AND TRICKS FOR BEGINNERS AND EXPERTS

Techniques for Keying and Green Screening

Chroma Key processing and its operation are likely to pique the interest of those who are fresh to the editing industry. The technique of changing a video's backdrop color to a different preferred background color in order to improve the video's visual appeal is called chroma key, sometimes referred to as green screen key. The Adobe Premiere Pro platform's Ultra Key tool gives you a variety of editing options and makes it easy to make such changes. We'll walk you through the steps of using Premiere Pro's Chroma Key and offer some advice on how to make it look its best.

Getting Started in Premiere Pro before Compositing Green Screen Video

If you're wondering where to get the green screen backdrop resource, you can either record the green screen video yourself or look for both free and paid background materials online. **A few fundamental requirements must be met in order to capture and create your green screen film, including the following:**

- Because shadows may be hard to perceive, exercise caution when filming performers' feet in green screen footage.
- Performers should maintain a minimum of 10 feet between themselves and the green screen environment. Light will not leak out around their shoulders or other parts of their body as a result.
- To ensure that you can photograph against a smooth background, make sure the backdrop is well-lit. During the play, the actors should also have access to sufficient illumination.
- For a smooth green backdrop, use paint instead of materials to prevent undesired creases and folds.

How to Use Adobe Premiere Pro's Chroma Key

Here are some easy steps to do if you're prepared to use the Chroma Key effect in your videos created using the Adobe Premiere Pro platform:

1. Users must first import green screen footage into the timeline of Premiere Pro. Users then need to get the video they want to put the Chroma Key effect on. Simply choose the Import option from the drop-down menu that shows up after choosing the File menu to finish this process. This program will make it simple for you to select media files that are saved on your computer.

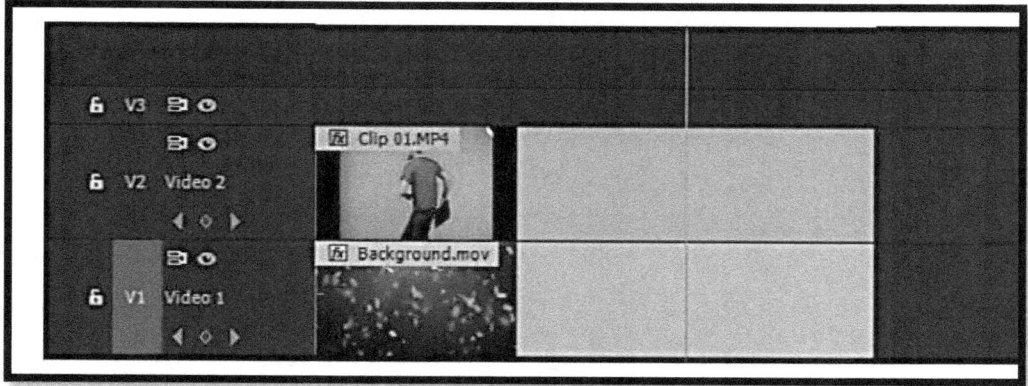

2. At this stage, you only need to add the imported video clip that will take the place of the green screen to the Video 1 track of the Premiere Pro timeline.

3. In this step, put the green screen with the movie to the Video 2 Track in the timeline. The Video 1 track will be covered by the green screen.

4. Navigate to the Effects panel, which houses all of the imported clips and is situated next to the project tab. If the Effects panel is not visible, click on Effects after choosing Window to bring it up. Choose Keying and then Ultra Key from the Video Effects menu. Another option is to enter Ultra Key into the search bar and then drag it to a green screen video clip in the timeline.

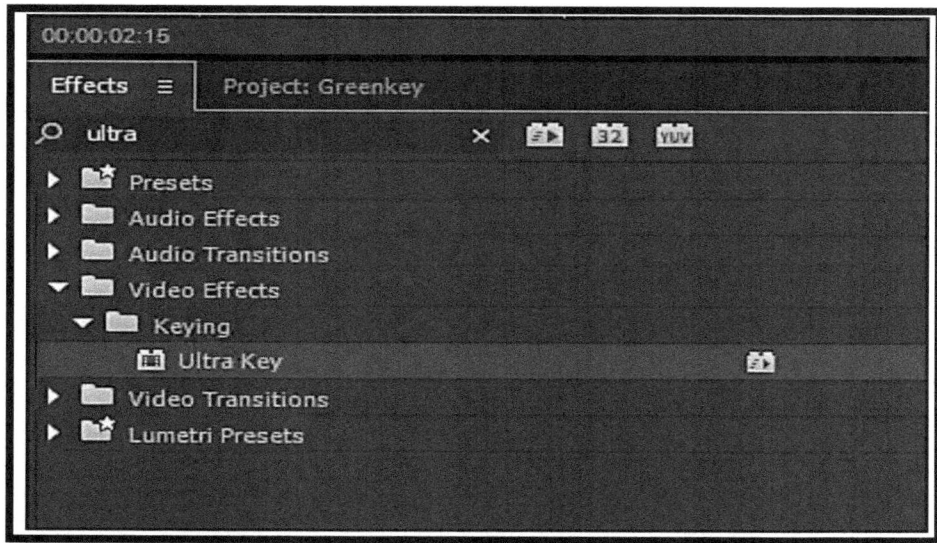

5. Click the arrow next to the Effects option to enlarge the Video Effects settings panel.

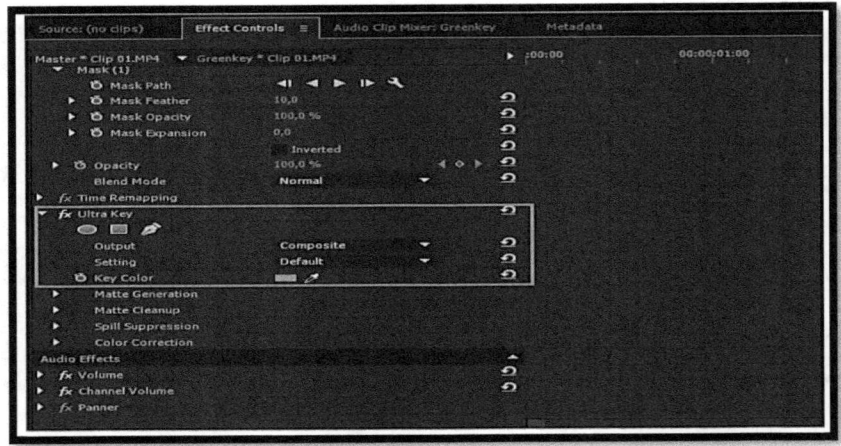

6. Choose the Key Color Picker tool from the menu of options after navigating to the Ultra Key controls. Just select the green screen area from the backdrop in the preview window, and the green screen of the movie in Track 1 will replace the background you selected in a matter of seconds. You must choose a darker or brighter shade of green for the green screen footage you captured in the video clip. This is due to the possibility that there was insufficient illumination. The following procedures may also be necessary to perfect the chroma-keying effects in Premiere Pro.

7. Utilize the Choke, Highlight, and Transparency options in the Matte Generation menu to lessen highlights and shadows. This will assist you in making your green screen look better. Additionally, you can use the options provided in Matte Cleanup to alter the item's borders. The edges will become smaller when the Choke option is chosen, and they will become fuzzy when the Soften option is chosen. To get rid of the spill and alter the edge color, use the Spill Suppression option.

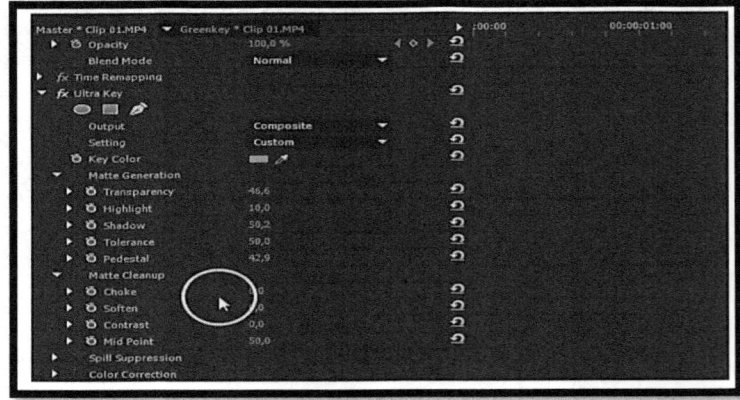

The following advice can help you achieve a better compositing result in most situations. These pointers will help you get the best key effects in Premiere Pro. **The Crop effect is an additional option for removing an unnecessary green screen backdrop.**

8. Simply save your project after making all of these adjustments.
9. Render the project you have saved
10. Save your project once again after rendering it, then export the video as you choose.

Creating Creative Effects Using Masks

Using masks, you can designate a region inside a clip that you wish to color correct, blur, cover, highlight, or apply effects to. You may apply effects with masks as well. There are numerous shaped masks that may be constructed and modified, such as the Ellipse and Rectangle. Additionally, you can create free-form Bezier shapes with the Pen tool.

Use shapes to create masks

A four-sided polygon can be made with the Rectangle shape tool, and a circular or ellipse-shaped mask can be made with the Ellipse form tool.

Before masking   *After masking*

+ In the Timeline box, pick the clip you wish to mask.
+ In the panel, select the desired effect for the clip.
   + Choose Video Effects > Stylize > Mosaic to add the Mosaic effect to your video.
+ Drag the chosen effect from the Effects panel to a clip in the Timeline panel to apply it to that clip. As an alternative, you can double-click the clip in the Effects panel after selecting it to apply an effect.

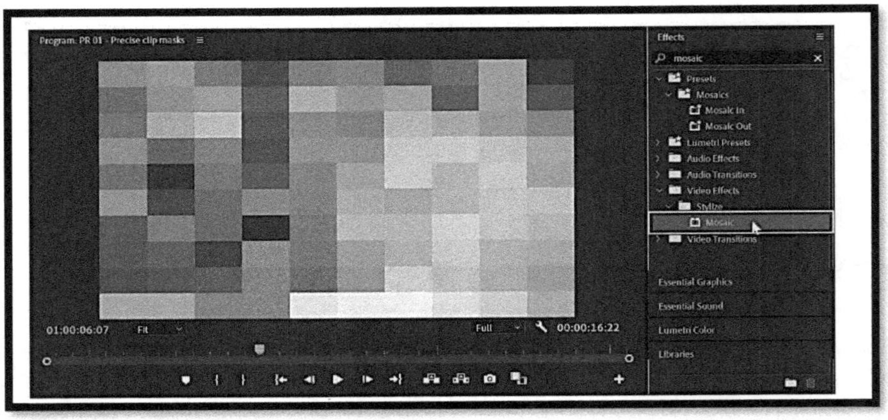

- Go to the Effect Controls panel to see the effect properties. Clicking the drop-down arrow will bring up the controls.

You can draw an ellipse or a rectangle if you'd like. The Pen tool can be used to create freeform forms. When making changes to a mask, you can specify values that alter the mask using the Effect Controls panel. The controls will adjust in accordance with the selection you make.

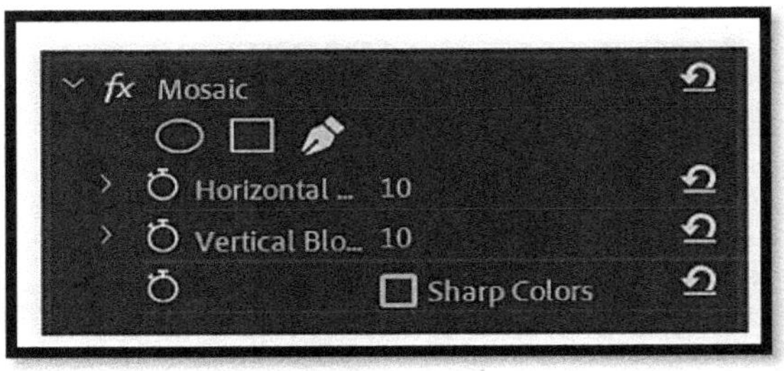

- The Rectangle shape tool can be used to create a rectangle mask, while the Ellipse form tool can be used to create an ellipse mask.

The effect is limited to the masked area inside the layer of the clip that is displayed in the Program Monitor.

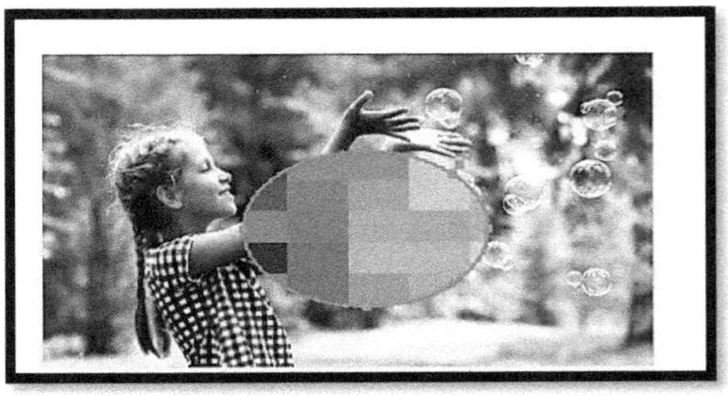

+ The Effect Controls tab allows you to change the mask's forms and sizes.

Several Camera Editing

Videos of the same scene or subject shot from many cameras and viewpoints can be edited. We call this multi-camera editing. By showing the same scene or subject from multiple angles, you may make the video more engaging to watch. Presenting the same image from multiple angles is another usage for this method. Numerous cameras are used in commercial commercials, soap operas, reality TV, live performances, music videos, and weddings.

Easy Steps for Editing Multiple Cameras

First Step: Make a Multi-Camera Source Sequence

Put all of your video clips from different angles in a bin called Multi-Cam, which is Premiere Pro's word for a box that you create in your Project Panel. I have given each of my three camera perspectives a name:

- Cam 1 (this one contains the high-quality audio track)
- Cam 2
- Cam 3

Audio Tip: I suggest recording the sound from each camera and placing the high-quality audio track on one if you're editing with many cameras. You'll need at least one camera viewpoint with high-quality audio in order to edit a multi-camera source sequence. Sound and any images captured on camera may not be of high quality. From the context menu, choose Create Multi-Camera Source Sequence after performing a right-click on the bin. The Multi-Camera Source Sequence dialogue box will then open.

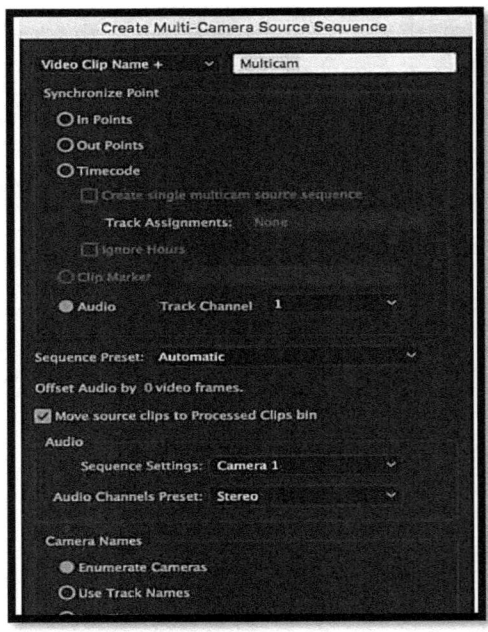

You can decide how to merge video snippets from different cameras here. Clips can be joined by matching timecodes, audio waves, or in-and-out points. I'm going to merge the clips now using Premiere Pro's robust audio-sync waveform feature. You must choose the Audio Sequence Settings after clicking Audio. **The following three alternatives are yours to choose from:**

+ **Camera 1:** All video clips will be synced to the audio track from camera 1 when this option is chosen. The remaining cameras' audio will be silenced. As a result, camera 1's audio will be prominent and steady throughout your multi-camera source sequence.

  All cameras: In video clips, this option will combine audio tracks from every camera.

+ **Switch Audio:** This option enables the use of the source audio for each camera viewpoint. You will hear audio from Camera Viewpoint 2 if you choose it in Step 4 of the revision process. You will hear sounds from Camera Viewpoint 3 if you select it, and so on.

In this case, the high-quality audio track I need for my finished video is only accessible in Camera Angle 1, thus I don't want to use the Switch Audio option. Additionally, since I don't want to hear audio tracks from various rooms, I don't want to choose All Cameras. In order for all camera angles to sync with the audio from Camera Angle 1, I have chosen the Camera 1 option.

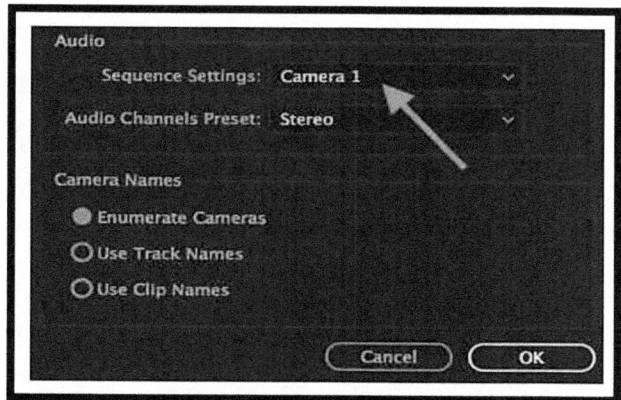

Second Step: Establish a Target Sequence for Multiple Cameras

The target sequence allows you to change and switch between camera perspectives. Right-click on the new multi-camera source sequence in the Project Panel, then select New Sequence from Clip from the context menu to create a target sequence. To open this sequence and start editing, just double-click on it.

Third Step: Turn on the Program Monitor's multi-camera editing feature

Drag the Toggle Multi-Camera View icon onto your toolbar after selecting the Plus button in the Program Monitor to start customizing. Multi-camera editing mode will be enabled as a result. Click on it to activate it.

Quick Tip: The keyboard shortcut Shift+0 can also be used to activate multi-camera editing mode.

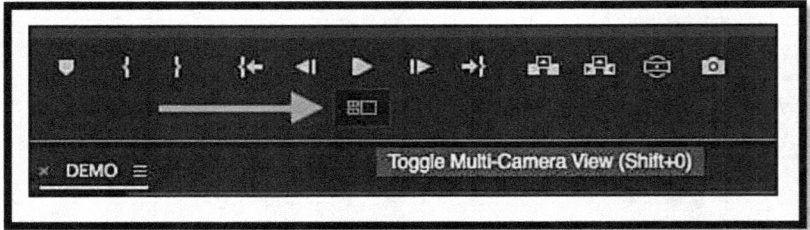

Two windows will appear in the Program Monitor when you switch to multi-camera editing mode. The left pane displays every camera view in the multi-camera source sequence. Currently, three camera viewpoints ought to be accessible. By choosing Edit Cameras from the pop-up menu in the Source Monitor, you may also change the sequence order or disable the camera views. When the video is finished, it will look like the combined goal sequence in the right window.

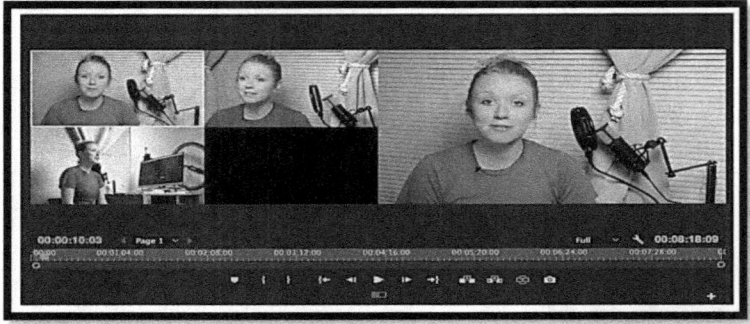

We haven't told it to switch to a different perspective yet, so if you skip through the sequence now, you'll only see Camera Perspective 1.

Fourth Step: Changing Camera Angles and Editing

Start the sequence by using the space bar. Next, click on the camera point you want to see in real time using the time code you chose.
Editing Tip: Use the numeric keys on your computer to change the direction.

1. Camera Angle 1.
2. Camera Angle 2.
3. Camera Angle 3.
4. Finally, Camera Angle 4.

Until you obtain the desired sequence, switch between the perspectives frequently. Use the space bar to end the session when you're done. You can see that Premiere Pro has copied

191

and pasted the new angle for each timecode you choose if you zoom in on the sequence. Magic with several cameras!

Fifth Step: Modifying and Improving Your Sequence of Multi-Camera Targets

The Rolling Edit tool can be used to edit and improve clips. Pressing N will launch the rolling edit tool, or you can choose it from the menu. Next, choose the cut and roll it to the sequence's preferred timecode.

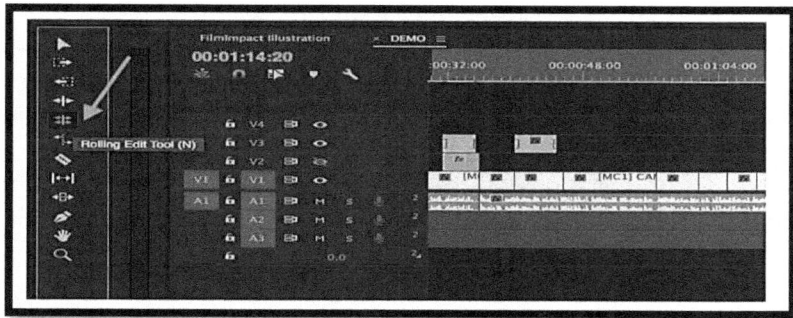

Additionally, let's say you want to switch from Camera Angle 2 to Camera Angle 3. By clicking on the clip in the sequence and then tapping the desired angle number, you can change the angle. It really is that easy! Lastly, apply any required effects, such color correction, music, or transitions, just like you would with any other Premiere Pro sequence.

Moving Between Camera Angles and Syncing

As you play, you can change the movie in real time by using the number keys on your computer. Pressing number one will display view camera 1, pressing number two will display view camera 2, and so on. It's quite easy. Easy, isn't it?

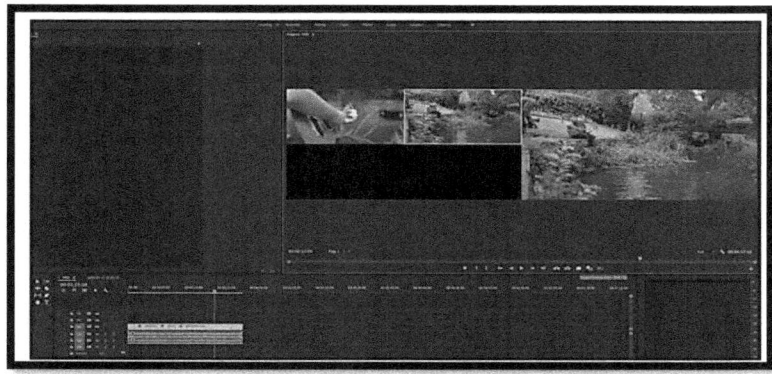

Until you have the desired effect, switch between camera angles as often as needed. Press the space bar to end. The new camera views for each timecode you chose have been copied and pasted by Premiere Pro, as you can see if you closely examine the timeline. This is how several cameras work!

Final Thoughts

Well done for finishing this guide to Adobe Premiere Pro 2025! Now that you know the tools and methods, you can confidently produce video edits of expert quality. You possess the skills necessary to realize your imaginative concept, from grasping fundamental timetable functions to utilizing sophisticated features. Keep in mind that video editing requires both practice and creativity. Continue to experiment with effects, learn new tools, and improve your process. Premiere Pro 2025 has everything you need to produce amazing results, whether you're editing a personal project, a social media video, or a motion picture masterpiece. Continue to be creative and inspired, and allow your edits to convey the narratives you envision. With this book, you're prepared to take full advantage of the endless possibilities of the video editing world. Have fun with your edits!

INDEX

M

200